Modern Techniques
in the Wing-T

Ronald Carbone

ISBN: 978-1-58518-062-2
Library of Congress Control Number: 2007936242

Book layout: Bean Creek Studio
Cover design: Bean Creek Studio
Front cover photo: Brian Baer

Coaches Choice
P.O. Box 1828
Monterey, CA 93942
www.coacheschoice.com

Dedication

This book is dedicated to my wife, Rosemarie, and to my five children: Mary, Ron Jr., Gary, Nancy, and Paul. They always have and always will give meaning to my life.

Acknowledgments

I owe a debt of gratitude to many persons who have assisted me in my quest to complete this book. First, I want to thank George DeLeone, the offensive coordinator at Temple University, for convincing me that of the need for an innovative book on the wing-T, and for encouraging me to start the project. I've known George for 40 years, and during that time we spent countless hours together talking football into the early morning hours. George moved on to the college and pro levels, but he never forgot his friends. If I—or any other coach—needed his advice on a football-related issue, he always made time to respond to our phone calls. He's one in a million, and I consider myself greatly blessed to have him for a friend.

I'm indebted to my co-worker, Karen Dempsey, for introducing me to the wonderful world of computers and all the marvelous things they can do. She taught me how to make documents, spell check, cut and paste, use a thumb drive, and numerous other details that I've already forgotten. Only Mother Teresa could have demonstrated greater patience.

Dr. Jim Rhodes, professor of English at Southern Connecticut State University, and a longtime friend, made helpful suggestions in Chapter 1, preface, and conclusion sections of this book. An author himself, he was a valuable resource.

The person who tackled the laborious job of recreating all my hand-drawn diagrams on the computer was my son, Paul. I was totally incapable of doing this task, and I would never have attempted it on my own. Paul spent time after work and on the weekends to get it done. Without his help, this book would never have been completed.

I would be remiss not to acknowledge all the valiant young men who played for me and contributed so much to programs that I've headed. Also, I have been blessed with associate coaches who were not only excellent technicians, but more importantly they were good family men, and true and loyal friends. The coach who was with me the longest, and on whom I relied the most, was my high school teammate and lifetime friend Gennaro Germe. I owe Gennaro, my associate coaches, and my former players a debt I will never be able to repay.

Finally, I'm grateful to my wife and five children for allowing me to remain in a game that demanded so much of my time. Marriage is supposed to be a 50/50 proposition, but women who are married to coaches know that it doesn't always work that way. During the season, my wife took care of the needs of our children so that I could have the time that coaching football demands. She made that sacrifice for over 25 years, and now I'll try to find some way to reciprocate.

Foreword

I have been blessed to have the opportunity to coach football at the college and NFL levels for 37 years. In that time, I have recruited in high schools all over the United States as part of my duties for the six different colleges for whom I've coached. I've seen many great high school teams, tried to recruit many great players, and met many great high school coaches. At every stop, I've tried to study and learn from the great coaches I've met. I would always ask what style of offense they were running to see if I could steal a play or two. Over the years, it was always amazing to me how many high school football programs successfully employed the wing-T offense. The wing-T offense is everywhere. I've seen some of the most successful high schools teams in California, Texas, Georgia, New Jersey, Pennsylvania, and New York all run versions of the wing-T. This offense knows no regional boundaries.

The reasons why this offense is so successful for so many teams are numerous. First of all, you run an offense—not a bunch of plays. Each play is part of a series that sets up and builds upon other plays that all look the same to the defense. Secondly, this offense can utilize and feature weapons personnel-wise that are available to the high school coach. For example, if a good fullback is available, he can be highlighted with the series that feature its fullback. If you have a strong quarterback, the play-action passes can be employed to take advantage of his talents. This theory of versatility applies to all skill positions, and it is a huge feature of the offense as the high school coach can use the best players available in any given year within the same wing-T offense. Thirdly, the angle and down-block schemes allow for less-than-dominant offense lineman and tight ends to have success. Most importantly, this offense is based on misdirection, which can nullify the defense's natural instinct to run to the football. What an advantage that is.

High school coaches who have tried to research this offense have been limited in their search to learn more about the wing-T because of the lack of new information about this offense. With the University of Delaware no longer in this offense, one of the last sources of wing-T information has dried up. Coach Ron Carbone, a Connecticut Hall of Fame high school coach, has stepped in the breach and delivered an answer to the prayers of a high school coach who has interest in learning about wing-T football. Few have the experience in the wing-T scheme that Ron possesses. As a player at Kansas State, he played in the offense. As a successful coach at three difficult high schools, he employed this offense in championship seasons. He has researched the details of the offense for many years. What a resource.

What Coach Carbone has done in this book is present a historical perspective on the offense that gives the coach a great sense of how this offense can apply to the present day. In meticulous fashion, Coach Carbone explains each series in the wing-T and develops them for the high school coach to install easily in his program. Most importantly, Coach Carbone presents the defensive problems that will arise to stop the wing-T and gives the high school coach the solutions to those problems. Ron Carbone has given to the game of football his whole life in so many ways. This book has become his ultimate gift.

George DeLeone
Offensive Coordinator
Temple University

Contents

Introduction

My first introduction to wing-T football occurred in the late 1950s, when I entered Kansas State University in Manhattan, Kansas. I was a fullback at Wilbur Cross High School in New Haven, Connecticut, and I was recruited by Kansas State. I started on the freshman football team at fullback, but I was moved to left guard in the spring of my freshman year. That move was a traumatic experience because I had never played in the offensive line before. However, I worked hard and became proficient enough to start at left guard in my junior and senior years. Therefore, it was my good fortune to have experienced the wing-T offense as a running back and as a lineman, and I learned first-hand the various techniques that were pertinent to both positions. Since my ambition was to become a high school football coach, this experience was invaluable for me.

Other teams in the Big 8 (now called the Big 12 Conference) besides Kansas State were running the wing-T offense. Nebraska (under head coach Bob Devaney) and Missouri (under head coach Dan Devine) are two examples of national powers that featured the wing-T. Colonel Earl "Red" Blaik at West Point in the 1940s, Ara Parseghian at Notre Dame two decades later, and Joe Paterno at Penn State also ran the wing-T. Many high schools and some small colleges still run it today. Harold "Tubby" Raymond ran the wing-T at Delaware from 1966 (when he was named head coach) to 2001 (when he retired). Many offensive trends have come and gone over a 50-year period, but the wing-T has stood the test of time. Elements of the wing-T can still be seen in nearly all offensives that are popular today. Bootlegs, men in motion, reverses, counters, shifts, and play-action passes are all integral to—and parameters of—the wing-T.

The most interesting team in the Big 8 Conference was Iowa State University. In the late 1950s and early 1960s, Iowa State was still running single-wing football. It may have been the only major college football team in the country that was doing so. What made Iowa State so unique was that it was running wing-T plays from a single-wing backfield and a balanced offensive line. Watching Iowa State on film was an exhilarating experience. The graceful movement of backs and the fluid pulling of linemen was evocative of a perfectly orchestrated ballet. Dwight Nichols was the tailback at Iowa State, and he was among the nation's leading rushers. He excelled in both running and passing the ball, and was an extremely durable player. The Iowa State coaching staff wanted all their plays to begin with the football in his hands. In an earlier era, the famed Fritz Crisler, head coach at the University of Michigan, did the same thing with two-time All-American Tommy Harmon. The advantages of having your best back handling the ball on every play are obvious; however, this strategy has disadvantages too. The most salient one is not being able to replace the starting tailback with an athlete of equal ability. This limitation was a major factor in the decision to abandon the single wing in favor of a formation that featured three running backs, a mirrored offense, and a passer at quarterback—the wing-T.

This book is addressed mainly to high school football coaches running the wing-T offense. One of the great advantages of the wing-T is that superior personnel are not a requirement for success. Deception, double-team blocks, trap blocks, multiple formations, and use of motion are a few of its features that have a neutralizing effect on opponents with better personnel. Of course, a steady stream of talented players will add to the productivity of the wing-T. However, a high school coach does not have the luxury of recruiting talented players; he has to play the hand he is dealt. The talent level varies from year to year, and an offensive system is needed that can be adapted to personnel on any given year. College coaches can recruit talented players who have the skills to fit into a particular offensive system. Today, great passers and speedy receivers are a high priority for the wide-open offenses featured in college football. Without a constant supply of such talented players, these offenses would lose their effectiveness. The wing-T, on the other hand, will be successful with average players, and it will be highly successful with talented players. It's a win/win situation.

The wing-T was a popular high school and college offense from the late 1940s to the late 1960s. Over the years, it has lost some of its allure, and some coaches feel it's no longer a viable offense. The goal of this book is to stimulate thought on innovative ideas that will keep the wing-T offense just as effective today as it was in its heyday, which I believe is possible by making minor adjustments and adding subtle nuances to traditional wing-T plays. Recalling the old Navy admonition, "That which is not inspected is neglected," we are reminded that change is inevitable, and the need to adapt is necessary for survival. The pioneers of the wing-T made it the most prolific offense of the latter half of the 20th century. This book was written to build on their work and to keep the wing-T just as productive in the 21st century. Many innovations will be suggested in this book, and coaches may not be interested in all of them. However, if a coach sees merit in a few ideas—or becomes self-motivated to seek new ways of running traditional plays—the purpose for writing this book will be realized.

You will find times in a game when a team has to revert to a passing game to come from behind, or to conserve time at the end of a half or the game. Therefore, this book will offer the wing-T coach a complete offensive package: one that will meet every contingency that may occur in a football game—including a dropback pass game and a two-minute drill. No mention will be made of drills to develop wing-T techniques, and no suggestions will be offered on how to organize practice sessions. Many excellent books are already in print dealing with wing-T drills, and all coaches realize the importance of making the most of what little time is afforded for practice. However, the book will emphasize some important coaching points associated with each illustrated play. Again, the thrust of this book is to take basic wing-T plays and to explore innovative ideas that will revitalize them and make them effective in the 21st century.

Five basic series that have been part of wing-T football for over 50 years will be examined in this book. They are: the teen series (featuring power plays from a straight-T formation), the 20 series (the buck-sweep plays), the 30 series (featuring the belly plays), the 40 series (a sweep and power attack), the 50 series (a toss to the fullback), and the 60 series, which features play-action passes off the buck sweep action. A dropback pass series, the 80 series, will be added to this group of traditional wing-T series.

The 60 series passes will be categorized into passes attacking two-deep, three-deep, and four-deep zones. It will also address man-to-man coverage. The running plays will be diagrammed against the basic 52 and 44 fronts. Most run and pass plays will be diagrammed to the right side of the formation. Blocking rules and coaching points will correspond to these plays. The plays and blocking rules will have to be reversed to simulate them going to the left. Other fronts that have been nettlesome to wing-T teams, such as the 53 stack, the 62 stack, and the 44 stack, will be discussed in Chapter 8. The 65 goal line will also be featured in this chapter. Throughout the remainder of this book, these defensives will be referred to as "heavy fronts."

Reasons for having a straight-T formation as an adjunct to the wing-T will be discussed. These reasons should not surprise anyone familiar with the wing-T because when a wingback comes in motion, the backfield usually ends up in a T formation. Many of the wing-T plays can be executed with a straight-T. It plays an important role in short-yardage and goal-line situations and when you are operating close to your own goal line. Therefore, consideration will be given to its role as a complement to the wing-T.

This book also deals with multiple formations, various types of motion, and backfield and formation shifts. The reason for all of these strategies is to simply enhance the running and play-action pass game. Open formations will be used mostly in definite passing situations or to gain an advantage in the running game. Most formations illustrated in this book will be closed formations. No attempt will be made to use open formations simply to spread the defense. If spreading the defense is a coach's major concern, the wing-T is not an offense to be considered. Open formations compromise much of the character of the traditional wing-T plays. You need a tight end to run off-tackle power plays, you need a tight end and a wingback to run power plays off the edge, you need a tight end to run an effective counter crisscross, you need two tight ends to run a truly mirrored attack, and you need three backs in position to receive the ball to maintain the integrity of the wing-T. All of these characteristics of a wing-T offense are compromised by open formations.

1

Introduction to the Wing-T

The Evolution of the Wing-T

In the discourse to follow, concerning the evolution of the wing-T, its inception, and its history, this book has relied on Forrest Evashevski's *Scoring Power with the Winged-T* as a guide. Evashevski was especially instructive in regards to some of the examples of drawings he used to illustrate the relationship between the single wing and the wing-T, as well as in the gradual addition of plays that sustained the offense in the early days, and which eventually became the core plays of the wing-T offense.

In the late 1940s, most college football teams were making the transition from the single wing to the T formation. The reasons for making the change will be discussed later in this chapter. Bud Wilkinson was experimenting with a split-T at the University of Oklahoma, and Bobby Dodd was running a belly series from a straight-T formation at Georgia Tech. Other coaches were trying to incorporate elements of the single wing into the new T formation. Coaches experimented with balanced and unbalanced lines, and single- and double-wingback formations. While no single person can be credited for developing the wing-T, several were pioneers—men such as Delaware's Dave

Nelson and Harold "Tubby" Raymond are two coaches always mentioned in any discussion of the wing-T. Both men are highly regarded for their contributions to the offense. In 1908, Glenn "Pop" Warner introduced some innovative strategies to the burgeoning game of football: pulling linemen, single- and double-wing formations, inside and outside reverses, all of which were eventually incorporated into the wing-T. Since that time, the wing-T has captured the interest of numerous coaches, who have added to its development. The origin of the basic buck-sweep series featured in the wing-T is easily traced back to single-wing football. In their book *Scoring Power with the Winged-T Offense*, coaches Forest Evashevski and Dave Nelson demonstrate that the fullback spinner series—an attribute of the single wing—was the prototype for the wing-T buck-sweep series. Figures 1-1 through 1-6 are based on the illustrations in their book, and leave no doubt about the accuracy of that statement.

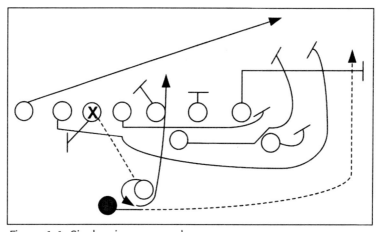

Figure 1-1. Single-wing sweep play

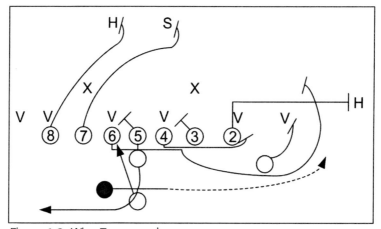

Figure 1-2. Wing-T sweep play

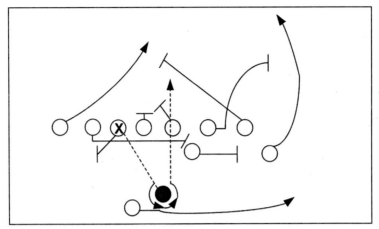

Figure 1-3. Single-wing trap play

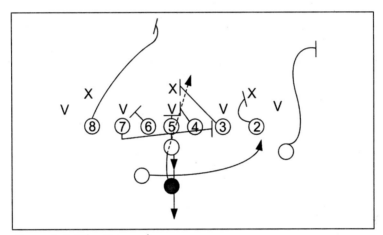

Figure 1-4. Wing-T trap play

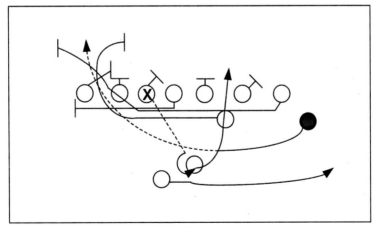

Figure 1-5. Single-wing counter play

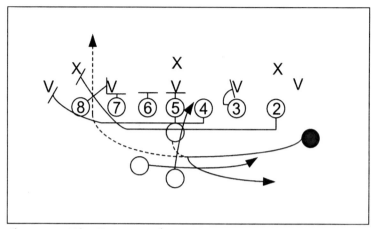
Figure 1-6. Wing-T counter play

The development of the wing-T began in the early forties. Herbert O. "Fritz" Crisler at the University of Michigan started the trend of using a multiple offensive system. It consisted of a combination of single-wing plays, and T-formation plays; both types of plays were executed from an unbalanced line. Other coaches in the Big 10 Conference and throughout the country began to use the same system. Michigan beat Southern California in a 49-0 victory over Southern California in the 1948 Rose Bowl. Michigan returned to the Rose Bowl in 1951, and Michigan State—using the same offense—went to the Rose Bowl in 1953 and 1955. Under Head Coach Duffy Daugherty, Michigan State's multiple offense had one unit run its plays from a balanced line, while the other unit ran a completely different series of plays from an unbalanced line. For their opponents, it was like playing against two different teams on the same Saturday afternoon. At that time, no limits were placed on football scholarships, and some teams had enough personnel to run two completely different offensive attacks.

The End of the Multiple Offense System

During the decade of the late forties, Forrest Evashevski at Iowa and Dave Nelson at Maine also used the multiple-offense system. In spite of the success both coaches had with it, they decided to switch to the wing-T. They made the change for the very same reasons that single-wing coaches switched to the T formation. The reasons are as follows.

Neither team had the number of players needed to field an unbalanced line with the back-ups necessary to replace injured starting players. An unbalanced line does not allow a coach the flexibility to replace a weakside lineman with a reserve strongside lineman. Weakside players and strongside players have different blocking rules, and this approach precludes players from switching sides without learning a new set of rules. Consequently, a coach is not able to replace an injured player with his third-best guard, tackle, or end. If a team used a balanced line, the linemen can operate on the "pair and a spare" paradigm: using your third-best guard, tackle, or end to replace an injured player. And, if you run a balanced offense, you can build a team around the best 18 players available—11 starters and seven replacements: one at center, guard, tackle, and end, and one at the quarterback, fullback, and halfback positions. These reasons were part of what precipitated the change from an unbalanced line to a balanced line, and the incorporation of a balanced offensive attack.

Neither team had the talent and depth at the center position to stay with the direct snap featured in the single-wing attack. Without claiming expertise on single-wing football, the task of looking through your legs, making a perfect pass to the tail or fullback, and then blocking an opponent is a major athletic challenge for any player. Two outstanding athletes were needed to fill the center position. It doesn't take much imagination to understand what would happen if the regular center were injured and an inadequate replacement entered the game. The tailback would spend the remainder of the afternoon chasing bad snaps, and close games would be turned into routs. This scenario happened often enough in the late '40s to convince coaches that placing the quarterback under the center to receive a direct snap was the most secure method of putting the ball in play.

Neither team wanted to put the responsibility of passing and running on one man, and neither team had an athlete good enough to warrant that responsibility. Coaches who have experienced the split back veer or the wishbone offense know what can happen to a team that loses its quarterback to an injury, and which does not have an adequate replacement. The offense will virtually shut down. The same point can be made regarding I-back teams that do not have a suitable replacement at tailback. Not having such a player, and realizing that two were needed, coaches Evashevski and Nelson made the decision to reject the multiple offense in favor of the wing-T.

With no reason to eliminate the numbering system of the multiple offensive, it was retained. The post-lead principles for blocking the interior plays (and the blocking schemes for running outside) were compatible with the old numbering system—and they were also retained. The challenge now was to install a series that would complement the new changes. Both Iowa and Maine were impressed with the cross-buck series run by Colonel Earl "Red" Blaik at West Point. This era was that of Felix Anthony "Doc" Blanchard (Mr. Inside) and Glen Davis (Mr. Outside). Both men were All-America at Army, and both men won the Heisman Trophy. Blanchard was featured in the fullback trap up the middle, and Davis ran off-tackle and outside. The Army cross-buck series was an adaptation of the single-wing fullback spinner series, and it was the first series installed by Evashevski and Nelson in the new wing-T. Illustrated in Figures 1-7 through 1-9 is the Army cross-buck series.

Coaches Nelson and Evashevski were also impressed with the bootleg that Dartmouth College ran, and it too was added to the offense. The pitch to the fullback—used in the multiple system—fit in nicely with the wing-T. The halfback hand-back trap that accompanied that play was also added. Both plays are illustrated in Figures 1-10 and 1-11.

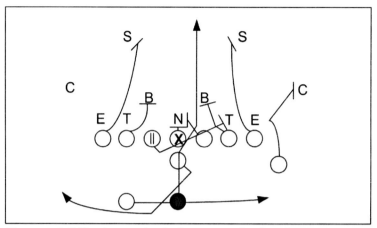

Figure 1-7. Fullback trap play in Army cross-buck series

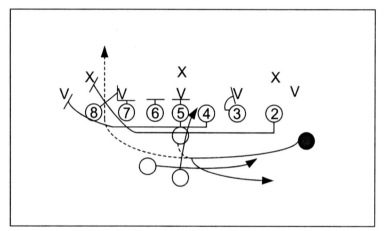

Figure 1-8. Half-back off-tackle play in Army cross-buck series

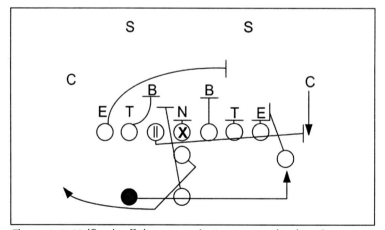

Figure 1-9. Halfback off the corner in Army cross-buck series

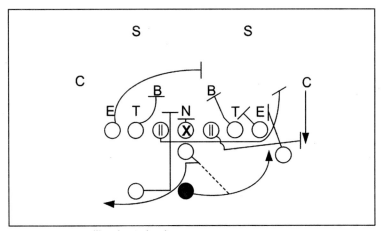

Figure 1-10. Fullback pitch play

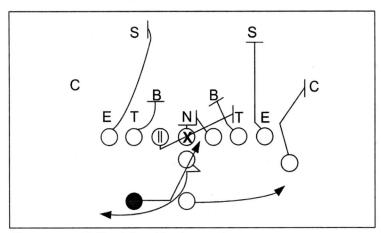

Figure 1-11. Halfback hand-back trap play

The single-wing power play off-tackle and the power sweep were also added to the new wing-T. These original three series were the ones installed by Dave Nelson at the University of Maine in 1950. Later, a counter off the cross-buck series and a bootleg off the counter were added to the offense. Both plays are illustrated in Figures 1-12 and 1-13.

Very little passing was done at this time. In 1950, Maine only threw 32 passes the entire year, and 10 of those were screen passes. Later, the play-action pass would become the most prolific (and most feared) aspect of the wing-T. In 1951, Dave Nelson was named the head coach at the University of Delaware. He established the wing-T at Delaware, and it lasted for 50 years. Since its inception, new adjustments were made each year to keep up with defensive attempts to countermand the wing-T. The addition of the play that Evashevski called "124 pass" was added to the offense to exploit the keying of linebackers on pulling guards. The play appears in Figure 1-14 as it is illustrated in Evashevski's book.

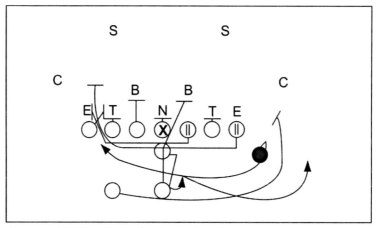

Figure 1-12. Wing-T wingback counter play

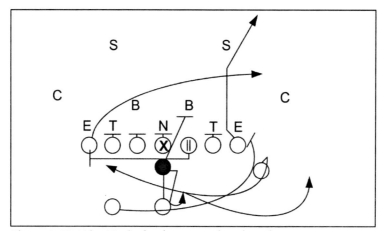

Figure 1-13. Wing-T wingback counter bootleg play

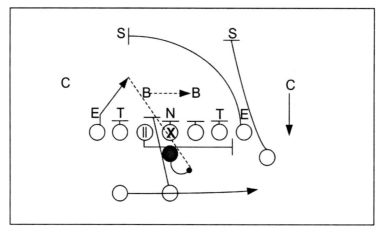

Figure 1-14. 124 pass

Another important change was making the 128 counter an inside handoff, an adjustment suggested by Harold Westerman of the University of Maine. The bootleg off 128 counter was also an important innovation. Both plays have been illustrated. The 138 counter crisscross was added to discourage defensive ends from charging upfield and tackling the quarterback on bootlegs. It is diagrammed in Figure 1-15.

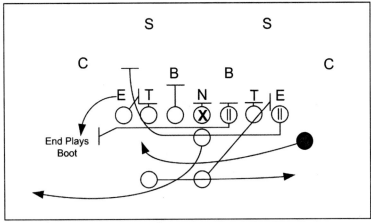

Figure 1-15. 138 counter crisscross

In 1954, Iowa and Delaware added a belly series to the offense, and in 1956, both teams ran all of their plays from just two formations: wing left or wing right, with a balanced line and two tight ends.

Scope and Parameters

Every offense has a set of rubrics that governs its play selection relative to field position. The field is divided into three zones (the critical zone, the go zone, and the score zone) that determine the type of plays suitable to that particular area of the field. The field chart is diagrammed in Figure 1-16.

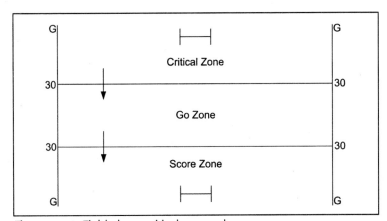

Figure 1-16. Field chart: critical, go, and score zones

Obviously, the critical zone is an area that dictates a cautious offensive approach because an error committed in this zone—such as a turnover—will result in an excellent scoring opportunity for your opponent. When operating close to your goal line, give the ball to a back who is not likely to fumble it, and don't hand the ball to a back when he is in his end zone. Run plays that hit quickly and straight ahead until you have room to run your complete offense. Select pass plays that will get the quarterback on the perimeter with a pass/run option. Of course, the time remaining in a game (and the score) will affect rules dictating your style of play—regardless of where you are on the field. Although caution should be emphasized in this zone, a wing-T team should never be reluctant to use play-action passes in any zone of the field.

The go zone is an area where you are free to execute every phase of your offensive repertoire. In this area, you can take a chance with reverses or other types of plays that have a higher risk of losing yardage than your bread-and-butter plays do. This area is excellent for counter plays of all kinds. Play-action passes are high-consideration plays in the go zone.

The score zone is four-down territory, and although you like to score from anywhere on the field, it's paramount for your team to put some points on the scoreboard in this zone. The offense should expect a more aggressive defense in this area. Short-yardage and goal-line-type defenses should be anticipated. Again, this zone is good for play-action passes and for getting the quarterback on the corner with pass/run options. Get the ball to your best back and run him over your best blocker.

Finally, the necessity of multiple formations, combined with the flexing and splitting of tight ends, are other considerations that are integral to the purpose of this book. Subtle blocking adjustments to the basic plays, and taking advantage of certain defensive keys, are needed to keep the wing-T effective. Hopefully, these subtleties will be illustrated throughout this book, and, more importantly, it is hoped that the reader will like some ideas enough to make them a part of his offensive repertoire.

Nomenclature and Offensive System

In the early days of the wing-T, the basic formations were simply wing right and wing left, and they featured two tight ends. As the wing-T developed, wing-T teams began to expand their offensive formations by splitting ends and aligning backs in a variety of positions. The purpose for these changes was not solely to enhance the passing game; they were employed because of advantages they presented in the running game. Consequently, the multiple formations created still retained the integrity of a three-back offense. The wing-T always was and will continue to be predicated upon a sound running game that is complemented by a play-action pass game. The formations presented in this chapter are consistent with that principle.

Formations

Any discussion of formations must include the spacing of offensive linemen. Although line splits will and should vary from play to play (and from front to front), a general starting point is needed. Against an odd front, the guards take a one-foot split from the center, the tackles take a two-foot split from the guards, and the ends split two feet from the tackles. Against an even front, the guards can stretch their split to two feet, the tackles close to a foot split, and the tight end can increase his split to one yard. Against goal-line, short-yardage, "stacked" fronts, and other penetrating defenses, the linemen close their splits to one foot. The wingback is placed one yard outside and one yard behind the tight end. In a slot formation, he is one yard behind, and two-and-a-half yards outside the tackle. The first formation to be defined is the wing right and wing left formations. A wing left is called a Liz formation, and a wing right is a Rip formation. Both formations are illustrated in Figures 1-17 and 1-18.

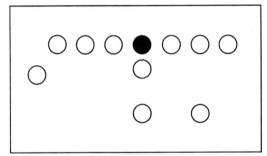 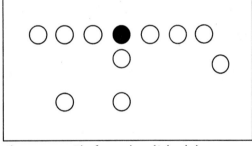

Figure 1-17. Liz formation (A backs)   Figure 1-18. Rip formation (A backs)

Unless a word follows Liz or Rip, it is understood that both ends are tight, and the backfield is aligned with a fullback and halfback in their normal positions. This backfield set is referred to as A backs. Split backs are called B backs, and a strong backfield is C backs. The quarterback can change the backfield set to Rip B or Liz C. Liz or Rip double would be a double wing. These formations are diagrammed in Figures 1-19 through 1-21.

Words are needed to affect the position of the end opposite the wingback. Three different positions are available for that end: he can be flexed three to four yards from the tackle, he can be split five to seven yards, or he can be spread eight to 12 yards from the tackle. Three examples of formations with open ends are: Liz flex (Figure 1-22), Rip split (Figure 1-23), and Liz spread (Figure 1-24). Examples of formations with an open end and a different backfield set are Liz B flex (Figure 1-25) and Rip C split (Figure 1-26).

The second formation to be defined is the slot formation. The word Len is used for a slot left (Figure 1-27), and Rob for slot right (Figure 1-28). The position of the open end will vary from seven to 12 yards, depending on his assignment. As with Liz and Rip, unless a word precedes Len or Rob, it is understood that the end opposite the slot

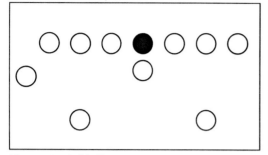

Figure 1-19. Liz B

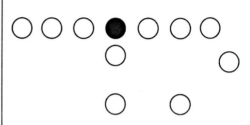

Figure 1-20. Rip C

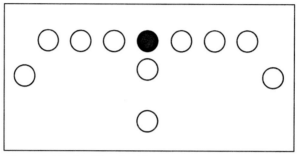

Figure 1-21. Liz/Rip double

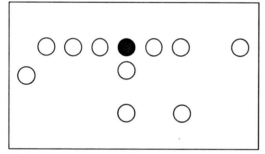

Figure 1-22. Liz flex three - to four-yard split from tackle

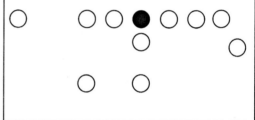

Figure 1-23. Rip split five- to seven-yard split from tackle

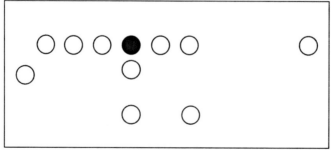

Figure 1-24. Liz spread eight- to 12-yard split from the tackle

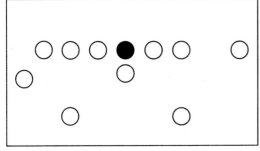

Figure 1-25. Liz B flex

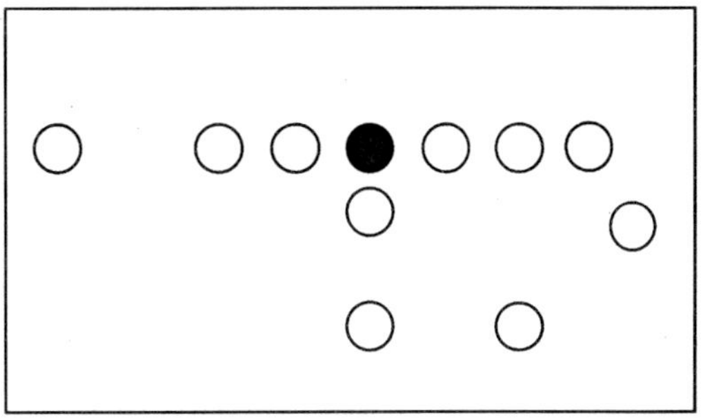

Figure 1-26. Rip C split

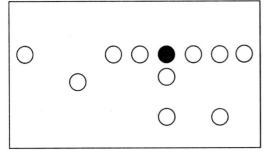

Figure 1-27. Len formation

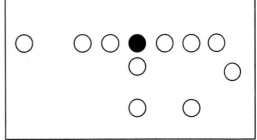

Figure 1-28. Rob formation

is tight and the backs are aligned in A backs. The end to the slotside is in a spread alignment. If variations are desired, they can be achieved using the same method as in Liz and Rip formations. Backs can align in B or C sets, and the end opposite the slot can be flexed, split, or spread. If a double wing is needed, the call is simply Len double (Figure 1-29) or Rob double (Figure 1-30). This formation affords the offense a slot to one side and a wingback to the other side of the formation. To get into a mirrored formation (a double slot to both sides of the formation), the word ace would be invoked, and the call would be Len ace or Rob ace (Figure 1-31).

The third formation is a tight slot alignment. The formation-side end will open four to five yards from the tackle, and the slot will align as he does in Rob or Len formations. This formation to the right side is Army (Figure 1-32), and to the left side is Navy (Figure 1-33).

As in Liz and Rip, and Len and Rob, if the Army/Navy call is not followed by a letter, the backs align in A backs, and the end opposite the formation is tight. To alter the Army/Navy formations, the same system used for Liz/Rip and Len/Rob formations is applied. For example, Navy B split (Figure 1-34) or Army C flex (Figure 1-35) will alter the regular Army/Navy formation.

You can get a tight wing away from Army or Navy formations by adding the word "double" to the formation call (Figures 1-36 and 1-37). To get the same look to both sides of the formation, the word ace must be used, as in Army ace or Navy ace (Figure 1-38).

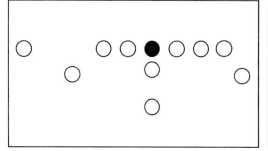
Figure 1-29. Len double

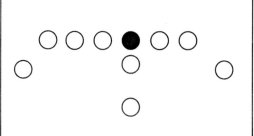
Figure 1-30. Rob double

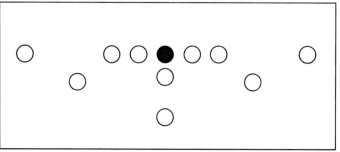
Figure 1-31. Len/Rob ace

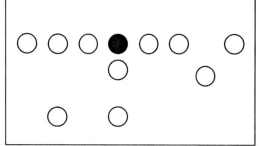
Figure 1-32. Army formation

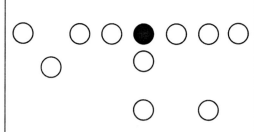
Figure 1-33. Navy formation

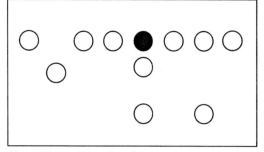
Figure 1-34. Navy B split

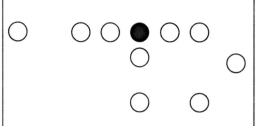
Figure 1-35. Army C flex

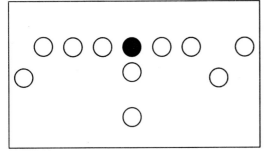

Figure 1-36. Army double

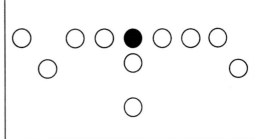

Figure 1-37. Navy double

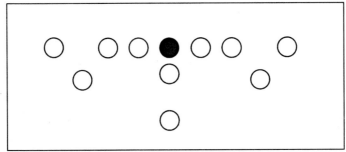

Figure 1-38. Army/Navy ace

The fourth formation is the T formation. Usually the T is used in conjunction with two tight ends. However, by saying T split left (Figure 1-39) or T flex right (Figure 1-40), you can get into the formation that will give you the best chance to be successful against a particular defensive front. The next formation is an end-over formation called east and west. East is an end over to the right and a wing left (Figure 1-41), and the west formation is an end over to the left and a wing right (Figure 1-42).

In the east formation, the right end will flex three to four yards from his tackle, and the left end will line up five yards outside of the right end. West formation would be just the opposite alignment. The method for variations in backfield alignments, double wings, and ace formations is the same as described in the previous sections.

The last formations are called pro (to the right) and con (to the left). Pro (Figure 1-43) and con (Figure 1-44) consist of a split end, a tight end, and a flanker. They can be combined with A, B, or C backfield. Again, if not designated by adding a letter after calling pro or con, the backfield alignment will be A backs. These formations are used primarily in passing situations. This system of calling formations gives the wing-T coach a variety of sets for use in exploiting defensive fronts.

Motion

The use of motion is integral to the wing-T. Some types of motion do not have to be added to the play called. For example, if you are in a Len formation and you are running

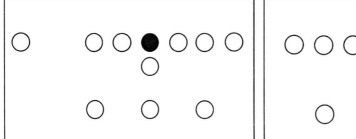

Figure 1-39. T split left

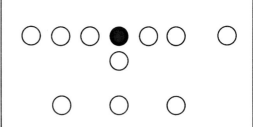

Figure 1-40. T flex right

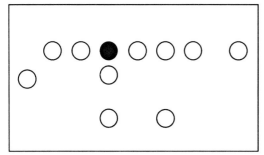

Figure 1-41. East formation

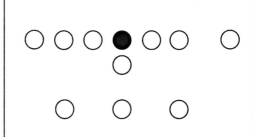

Figure 1-42. West formation

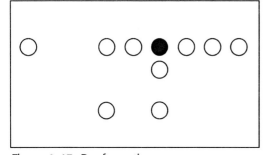

Figure 1-43. Pro formation

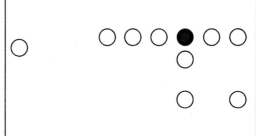

Figure 1-44. Con formation

a sweep to the tight-end side, it is necessary for the left halfback—aligned in the slot—to come in motion and be in his regular left-half position when the ball is snapped.

Knowing when to go in motion is the back's responsibility. The rhythmic cadence used in the wing-T enables backs to start their motion on different cues, and to be in the optimal position to execute the play called in the huddle. This method is superior to the quarterback starting backs by elevating his heel. The former allows the quarterback to concentrate on other things, such as his mechanics, the defensive alignment, and secondary coverage. On occasions when you would like to run a play (that normally requires motion) without the back going in motion, the quarterback will call a formation and play and add "no mo," which tells the back who is supposed to go in motion not to do so. Following are four types of motion than can be added to the play called:

Run-To

Run-to is a wingback motion toward the center of the formation. The wing comes in control motion, facing the opposite sideline, and deep enough to clear the quarterback. This motion is used when the wingback is asked to trap a defensive lineman. The word "smash" is used to describe the wingback's block. The quarterback will tell the wingback where he should be at the snap of the ball by saying, for example, "run to 4," where the back should be behind the 4-man when the ball is snapped. Two examples of run-to motion are Liz flex, run-to-7, 26 smash (Figure 1-45) and Liz double, run-to-3, 33 smash (Figure 1-46). It is the wing's responsibility to control his speed so he is exactly where he should be when the ball is snapped. The motion gives a new look to a standard play.

Slide-To

Slide-to is a wingback motion toward the center of the formation. The wing comes in control motion, facing the line of scrimmage, and deep enough to clear the quarterback. This motion is used when the wingback is asked to lead up the hole to block on a linebacker. Two examples are: Rip B, slide-to-7, 42 counter crisscross, wingback lead (Figure 1-47) and Liz, slide-to-6, 26 wingback lead (Figure 1-48). Again, the motion gives a basic play a new look, and the use of the word "lead" distinguishes slide-to motion from run-to motion.

Out-To

Out-to is a wingback motion away from the center of the formation. This motion will put the wingback in a flanker position at the snap of the ball, and it will change the force at the corner. It is a combination of run-to for the first five yards and slide-to motion for the last five yards. An example is Rip, out-to-1, 31 keep switch (Figure 1-49).

If the secondary rotates to the motion, run the fullback toss away from formation, or get into B backs and run 40 series plays away from the rotation. You be the judge of how you can best exploit a rotation to out-to motion with formations and plays away from the motion.

Cross-To

Cross-to is a wingback motion across the center of the formation to the opposite flank. It starts with run-to motion and ends with slide-to motion, and the ball is snapped with the wing in the flanker position. This motion is good to get an extra blocker at the point of attack. Again, if the secondary rotates to the motion, get into a formation that will give you the best chance of attacking away from the motion with a run or pass. An example of cross-to motion would be Liz B flex, cross-to-1, 41 wham (Figure 1-50).

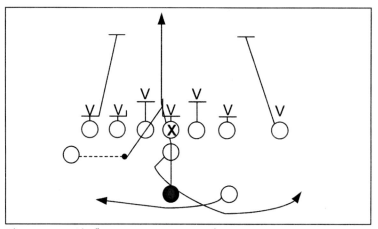

Figure 1-45. Liz flex, run-to-7, 26 smash

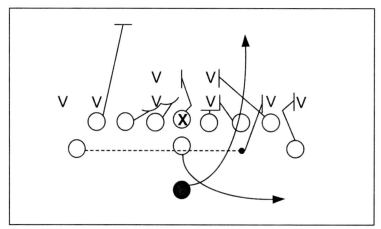

Figure 1-46. Liz double, run-to-3, 33 smash

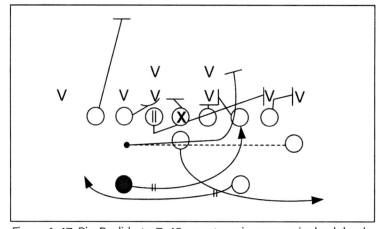

Figure 1-47. Rip B, slide-to-7, 42 counter crisscross, wingback lead

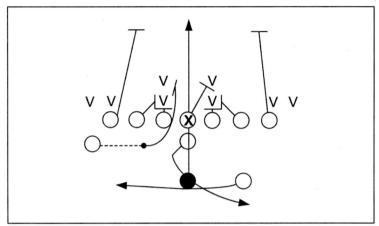

Figure 1-48. Liz, slide-to-6, wingback lead

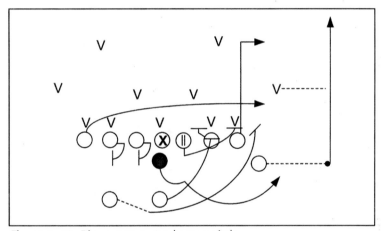

Figure 1-49. Rip, out-to-1, 31 keep switch

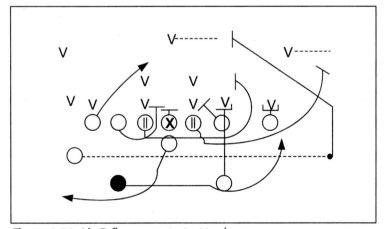

Figure 1-50. Liz B flex, cross-to-1, 41 wham

Shifts

Changing formations just prior to the snap of the ball can be an effective strategy—and disconcerting to the defense. It requires the opponent to line up against your initial formation, and then realign to the formation you shift to. Such a shift in alignment is not only difficult to do, but it takes up valuable practice time to prepare a team to realign correctly. It is particularly troublesome to teams that play a strong-safety-type of defense, that flop their defensive personnel. The shift is called in the huddle. As an example, the quarterback says Rip to Len (Figure 1-51), or Rob to Liz, and then he would call a play.

The shift is executed on the "now" call by the quarterback. If the huddle call was Rip to Len 26 trap, the quarterback would say "319, 319" at the line of scrimmage. After the second 319, he would say, "Now," and the shift would occur. The quarterback would then continue his cadence. (Note: All plays illustrated in this book can be executed after a formation shift.)

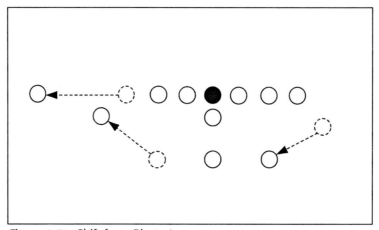

Figure 1-51. Shift from Rip to Len

Hole Numbers

As mentioned in the introduction of this chapter, when the change was made from the single wing to the multiple offense, and from the multiple offense to the wing-T, it was agreed that the single-wing numbering system did not need to change. Therefore, many wing-T teams use it to this day. It's a perfect match for coordinating post-lead-blocking plays directed at the internal holes, and it facilitates the calling of plays that are designed to attack the defensive perimeter. It's a simple system that starts at the right flank; the system numbers that area number 1 and the opposite flank number 9. All other numbers are assigned to players rather than areas because the post-lead principle is designed for plays to hit over offensive linemen. Therefore, the right end, right tackle, and right guard are the number-2, -3, and -4 men. The center is the number-5 man. The left guard, left tackle, and left end are the number-6, -7, and -8 men. Those numbers throughout the remainder of this book refer to linemen, and plays will be called using the numbering system just described (Figure 1-52). The 1 hole will be the right-flank area, and the 9 hole will be the left-flank area.

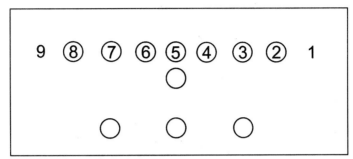

Figure 1-52. Hole-numbering system

Huddle and Play Calling

The open huddle—with the center facing the line of scrimmage about seven yards from the ball—is an efficient configuration for communicating plays and getting to the line of scrimmage (Figure 1-53). The left guard and left tackle line up to the left of the center, and the right guard and tackle to the center's right. All have their hands on their thigh pads and are bent at the waist with their heads up. The left end, left halfback, fullback, right halfback, and right end line up in that order behind the linemen. All stand erect and clasp their hands behind their backs .

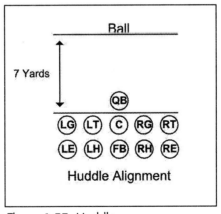

Figure 1-53. Huddle

The quarterback stands in front of the center and calls the play. He will call the formation, the play, and the snap number in that order. An example is "Rob 26, counter-on-2." He will repeat the call twice and then say, "Center out." The center will run to the ball and get set. As he sets over the ball, the quarterback will say to the remaining players, "Break." They will respond by simultaneously clapping their hands, shouting "Hard," and hustling to the line of scrimmage. When they arrive at the line of scrimmage, they will take their spacing and align in a two-point stance with their forearms on their thigh pads.

Cadence

Knowing when the ball is going to be snapped is a definite advantage for the offensive team. To maintain that advantage, the offense must alternate its snap count. A sound cadence allows the quarterback to change the play at the line of scrimmage, go on a quick count, and (on dropback passes) snap the ball when the offensive linemen are in a two-point stance. This procedure is as follows:

- After calling a play in the huddle (Rip flex 29, wham-on-1), the first thing the quarterback does at the line of scrimmage is to confirm or change the huddle call by making a three-digit call, like 1-33-H.

- If the first digit of the three-digit call (1-33) is a repeat of the snap number, the play is changed from 29 wham to 33-H. If it is a different number, the huddle call (29 wham) stands, and the ball is snapped on one. For simplicity and consistency, all audible calls are snapped on the second go.

- The next word out of the quarterback is "Now." On the "now" command, all shifts are executed, then the quarterback calls "Set," and the linemen assume three-point stances.

- The best cadence to accommodate motion and alternate the snap count is the old Delaware system of a rhythmic series of "red-readyyy-go." Wingbacks can go in motion on "red" or "readyyy," depending on where they want to be when the ball is snapped. The preparatory word "red" is omitted after the first "go." If the snap count is on three, the quarterback's cadence is: "1-44, 1-44, set, red-readyyy-go, readyyy-go, readyyy-go." The ball is snapped on the third "go."

- If a dropback pass is called in the huddle, it is advantageous to have linemen in a two-point, rather than a three-point, stance. In this situation, the ball is snapped on "now." Doing so accomplishes two objectives: it allows the quarterback to change the pass route if the coverage is not what was expected, and it allows the linemen to remain in a two-point stance when the ball is snapped.

Play Selection

A legitimate criticism of the wing-T is that it has too many series and too many plays. A football game would have to last for several hours to set up the big plays in each series. Big plays refers to play-action passes that will average 12 to 15 yards per completion, and runs that will average eight to 10 yards per carry. The pass plays will come from play-action, and the runs will generally be misdirection plays. Therefore, it is advisable to concentrate on a couple of series, and spend most of your practice time perfecting them.

The two series a coach chooses is mainly contingent on personnel. For example, if you have a quarterback who can run as well as pass, choose plays that will get the quarterback on the perimeter with a pass/run option—plays like the belly-keep pass, the waggle pass, and bootleg pass/run option. If your fullback blocks well, the 40 series is a good choice. Talented halfbacks can be showcased in all series.

Although every series cannot be run in a single game, each series has its particular time and place. For example, short-yardage situations always occur, and the teen series is an excellent short-yardage and goal-line series. So, in addition to the two series you emphasize, the teen series is needed when the tactical situation calls for it. Assume you have chosen the 20 and 40 series—two traditional wing-T series. Then, assume that neither series is going well in a particular game. You can try to jump start the offense by going to the 30 series or the 50 series, or you may rely more heavily on the play-action passes of the 60 series. The point is: although you should not try to run all series in a single game, each series must be maintained so you can use it when it is needed.

Another important issue in play calling is to make sure the plays with "big-play" potential are called often in a game. You don't want to be entering the third or fourth quarter without having called the plays that have big play potential. The best way to avoid this situation is to script your plays so those with big-gain potential are called often. George DeLeone, the former offensive coordinator at Syracuse (and currently serving in that capacity at Temple University), is a master at scripting plays. Coach DeLeone shared some information that is germane to the importance of using a script to call your plays. He cited a study done in the NFL that stated if a team completes more passes of 16 yards or better than its opponent, has more runs of 12 yards or more, and wins the turnover battle, that team will win 95 percent of the time. This study speaks volumes for the benefit of scripting your plays to make sure those that have the best potential for big gains are called often.

2

The Teen Series

The teen series is a secure power series that hits quickly, and will gain positive yardage. It is executed from a straight-T formation and usually with two tight ends. It is a good change-of-pace offense, and is often used when the wing-T attack is bogging down. It is also an excellent short-yardage and goal-line offense. It is perfect when operating close to the goal line and need a secure power play to gain some operating room. Of course, a wing can motion to the halfback position and be in a T formation when the ball is snapped. Doing so allows all plays in the teen series to be run with motion. And, most of the counter runs and pass plays from other series can also be run from a straight-T formation.

A unique aspect of the teen series is that linemen do not pull to trap or pull to lead up a hole as they do in all other series. Those assignments are given to halfbacks and the fullback. The halfbacks in the teen series are the kickout blockers, and the fullback is the lead blocker. This approach minimizes the threat of defensive penetration and the loss of yardage that could result from it, which is why the teen series is so valuable in the critical zone. The teen series is comprised of four running and four passing plays. The running plays will be presented first and the pass plays will follow.

RUNNING PLAYS IN THE TEEN SERIES

T 13 J

T 13 J (Figures 2-1 and 2-2) is a power play featuring a double-team at the point of attack, a kickout block by a halfback, and a lead block by the fullback. To the left, the play is T 17 J.

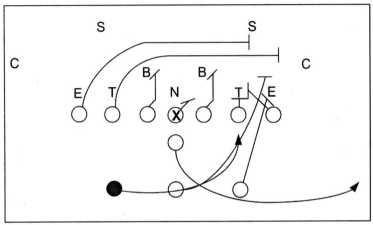

Figure 2-1. T 13 J against 52 defense

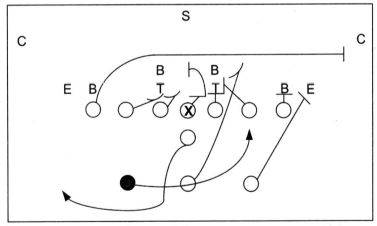

Figure 2-2. T 13 J against 44 defense

BLOCKING RULES, TECHNIQUE, AND COACHING POINTS FOR T 13 J

2-Man

Rule: If #3 is covered by a hard man, leads to his post; if not, blocks the first backer on or inside of him.

Coaching Points: As he leads to #3's post, he should be ready to read-up if the man on #3 slants to the inside. If blocking a backer, he steps through the C gap and uses a high-pressure control block. He must get his head to the backer's downfield side. Against a 44 stack, he uses a gap read-up rule.

3-Man

Rule: If covered by a hard-man, posts him; if not, leads to #4's post.
Coaching Points: As he leads to #4's post, he should be ready to read-up if the defender slants to the inside. Against a 44 stack, he uses a gap read-up rule.

4-Man

Rule: Blocks the man on or over him: posts the man on him if #3 is open.
Coaching Points: Against 53 and 62 stack defenses, he is responsible for the frontside B gap. Against the 53 stack, he eyeballs the stacked backer on #3 as he steps to the frontside B gap; if the backer comes, he blocks him, if not, he looks to the inside and walls off the middle backer. Against the 62 stack, he eyeballs the frontside backer as he begins a co-op block with #5. If the backer comes, he blocks him: if not, he stays with his block on the hard man. Against a 44 stack, he uses a gap read-up rule.

5-Man

Rule: Blocks the man on or over him. If open, blocks the backside backer through frontside A gap.
Coaching Points: Against 53 and 62 stack defenses, he is responsible for the frontside A gap. Against the 53, he eyeballs the middle backer as he begins the co-op block with #6. If the backer threatens the frontside A gap, he blocks him; if not, he comes off the block late and blocks the backside backer. Against the 62 stack, he starts the co-op block with #4. If the 2i defender slants to him, he takes over the block; if not, he gets off the block and walls off the backside backer.

6-Man

Rule: Blocks the man on or over him.
Coaching Points: Against 44 and 53 stacked fronts, he is responsible for the backside A gap. Against the 44, he eyeballs the backside backer as he begins a co-op block with #7. If the backer threatens the backside A gap, he blocks him. If not, he stays with his block on the 3 technique. Against a 53 stack, he eyeballs the middle backer as he begins a co-op block with #5 on the nose man. If the backer threatens the backside A gap, he blocks him; if not, he takes over the block on the nose man as soon as he can, and #5 will go up on the middle or backside backer. If the nose man slants away from him, he makes a vertical release and looks for the middle backer. If the backer rushes

the backside A gap, he blocks him; if the backer runs to the ball, he turns back and walls off the backside backer.

7-Man

Rule: If covered by a hard man, releases inside and blocks across the hole. If open, secures the backside B gap with #6.
Coaching Points: Against a 44 front, he eyeballs the backside backer as he begins a co-op block with #6. If the backer threatens the backside B gap, he blocks him: if not, he takes over the block on the 3 technique as soon as he can. Against a 53 or 62 stack, he makes a vertical release and walls off the backside backer.

8-Man

Rule: Crosses the field, inside releases, and blocks across the hole.
Coaching Points: He should not be any deeper than five yards from the line of scrimmage as he blocks across the hole.

Quarterback

Technique: Reverse pivots with his back to the hole. The first step with the left foot is on the midline. The second step with the right foot is slightly across the midline. Hands the ball to left halfback on his second step. Allows the left halfback to pass him and fake a keep at one.
Coaching Points: He checks the defensive spacing to determine who will be the post man. If #3 is the post man, he fakes a keep; if #4 is the post man, he fakes a bootleg. He is sure not to force the left halfback too wide on his second step. That step should just slightly cross over the midline. He is bent at the waist as he hands the ball to the left halfback. The handoff is with the left hand, and is followed by the third step with his left foot. That step starts him on the keep path. After the handoff, he brings both hands to his right hip, bends at he waist, drops his left shoulder, and starts the keep course. It will take him five to six yards off the line of scrimmage moving toward the perimeter. This entire action is one fluid and continuous movement. If the double-team is with the 3- and 4-men, he fakes a bootleg rather than a keep. The hole is much tighter when the double-team is with the 4- and 3-men. With the quarterback out of the way, the bootleg action allows the ballcarrier to bend his course and run over the outside leg of #4.

Left Halfback

Technique: Comes across the backfield through fullback position. Receives the ball and heads for the tail of #3.

Coaching Points: He starts a parallel course across the backfield with controlled speed. As he receives the handoff, he bends his course to the tail of #3 and runs off the double-team block. If the double-team is with the 3- and 4-men, the hole will be a little tighter. Again, he uses controlled speed so he can hit over the double-team block.

Fullback

Rule: Aims for the tail of #3, and leads through the hole.
Coaching Points: He is the lead blocker and is responsible for the frontside backer. He knows where the double-team is, and runs tight to it. He stays on his feet as he blocks the backer. He hits on the rise and keeps his feet moving. He does not stop and congest the hole. If he has no one to block, he sprints downfield to block.

Right Halfback

Rule: Kicks out last man on the line of scrimmage.
Coaching Points: If the last man on the line of scrimmage is lined up on or outside the 2-man, he runs a straight line for the inside leg of #2. As he gets to the line, he assumes the hitting position, and explodes into the defender with his outside shoulder. He does not try to turn the defender out immediately; he just keeps his body between the defender and the ballcarrier, and drives him back. What is important is to hit in a good, fundamental position, and to keep his feet moving. After contact, he can attempt to turn the defender to the outside. If he faces an overhang defender, his reference point is the outside leg of #2. He uses the same blocking technique on the overhang player as he does when blocking a man lined up on or outside of #2.

T 13 Bounce

T 13 bounce is designed to look exactly the same as T 13 J (Figures 2-3 and 2-4). It is used when the defender responsible for the off-tackle hole closes down hard to squeeze the power play. Instead of kicking out the first man past #2, the right halfback logs that defender to the inside. The fullback runs for the same reference point as on T 13 J. When he is about two yards from the line of scrimmage, he swings around the right halfback's block and leads the left halfback to the outside. The left halfback runs as he would on T 13 J and fakes7 the off-tackle play by dipping into the hole and quickly swinging back outside following the fullback. To the left, the play is T 17 bounce.

BLOCKING RULES, TECHNIQUE, AND COACHING POINTS FOR T 13 BOUNCE

2-Man

Rule: Blocks the first backer on or inside of him.

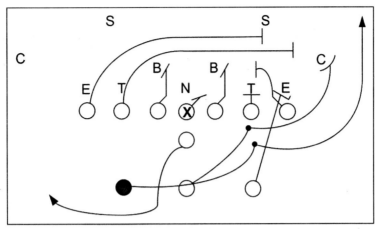

Figure 2-3. T-13 bounce against 52 defense

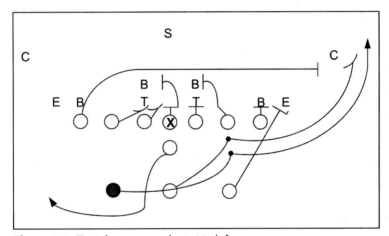

Figure 2-4. T-13 bounce against 44 defense

Coaching Points: He uses a high-pressure control block to seal the frontside backer. He puts his head to the downfield side of the defender. Against a 44 stack, he uses a gap read-up rule.

3-Man

Rule: Blocks a hard man on him. If open, blocks the first backer inside.
Coaching Points: Against a 53 stack, he uses a zone technique to block the hard man on him. If blocking a backer, he uses a high-pressure control block. Against a 44 stack, he uses a gap read-up rule.

4-Man

Rule: Blocks the man on or over him.
Coaching Points: Against a 53 stack, he is responsible for the frontside B gap. As he

steps to the B gap, he eyeballs the stacked backer on #3. Ff the backer comes in the B gap, he blocks him; if not, he turns back on the middle backer. Against a 62 front, he co-op blocks the 2 or 2i technique with #5. If a backer threatens the B gap, he blocks him. Otherwise, he stays with his block on the 2 or 2i technique. Against a 44 stack, he uses a gap read-up rule.

5-Man

Rule: Same as T 13 J.
Coaching Points: Same as T 13 J.

6-Man

Rule: Same as T 13 J.
Coaching Points: Same as T 13 J.

7-Man

Rule: Same as T 13 J.
Coaching Points: Same as T 13 J.

8-Man

Rule: Same as T 13 J.
Coaching Points: Same as T 13 J.

Quarterback

Technique: Opens with his back to the hole. His first step is with the left foot slightly under the midline and it points toward the left halfback. His second and third steps are toward the left halfback and the handoff is made between the second and third steps. Hands the ball to the left halfback with his left hand and makes a bootleg fake at the 9 hole.
Coaching Points: He always makes a bootleg fake when running 13 bounce. After the handoff, he brings both hands to his left hip, bends at the waist, drops his right shoulder, and sprints on his bootleg course. The bootleg is an arc course about five to six yards from the line of scrimmage. It is run at full speed. He always checks the reaction of the contain man on the side of the bootleg.

Left Halfback

Technique: Same footwork as T 13 J. Aims for tail of #3 and bows course around load block by the right halfback.

Coaching Points: He runs this play at controlled speed. As he bends his course, he should be about one-and-a-half to two yards from the line of scrimmage before he bounces to the outside.

Fullback

Technique: Same technique as T 13 J. Bows around the load block by the right halfback and blocks the first perimeter defender he encounters.
Coaching Points: Same coaching points as left halfback regarding proximity to the line of scrimmage before he swings to the outside.

Right Halfback

Technique: Same approach as T 13 J, except logs the defender to the inside.
Coaching Points: He approaches the defender on the same angle used when he J-blocks. A change in his angle would tip off his intentions, so he waits until the last moment to get his head outside the defender to log him. He does not try to turn the defender on contact. He blocks with his left shoulder and drives the defender back a few yards before he wheels him to the inside.

T 13 Lead

T 13 lead is a power play that gives linemen a chance to come off the ball and drive block defenders (Figures 2-5 and 2-6). The fullback will lead through the A or B gap and the right halfback will lead through the C gap. In defensive fronts, when the 4-man is covered by a hard man and the 3-man is not, the 3-man will double the hard man on #4. To the left, the play is T 17 lead.

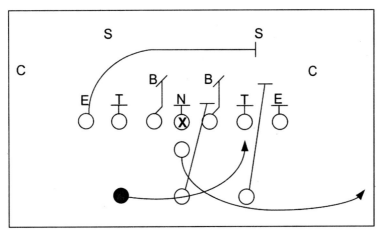

Figure 2-5. T-13 lead against 52 defense

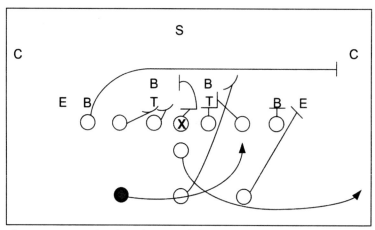

Figure 2-6. T-13 lead against 44 defense

BLOCKING RULES, TECHNIQUES, AND COACHING POINTS FOR T 13 LEAD

2-Man

Rule: Blocks the man on or over him.
Coaching Points: He takes a short, controlled step with his inside foot and blocks the inside number of the defender on him. He stays on his feet and positions his body between the defender and the ballcarrier. If the defender slants inside, he fronts him and takes him in the direction he chooses to go. Against a 44 stack, he uses a gap read-up rule.

3-Man

Rule: Blocks a hard-man on him. If open, doubles man on #4.
Coaching Points: He takes a short, controlled step with his inside foot and blocks the defender's inside number. He takes him in any direction he can and maintains contact until the whistle blows. If he is open, or has a backer over him, he double-teams the defender on #4. Against a 44 stack, he uses a gap read-up rule.

4-Man

Rule: Blocks the man on or over him. If #3 is open, posts the hard man on him.
Coaching Points: Against a 53 stack, he blocks the stacked backer on #3. Against a 44 stack, he uses a gap read-up rule.

5-Man

Rule: Blocks the man on or over him. If uncovered, blocks the backside A gap.
Coaching Points: Against a 44 front, he steps to the frontside A gap and protects it. If no threat appears, he turns back on the backside backer.

6-Man

Rule: Blocks the man on or over him.
Coaching Points: Against a 44 front, he co-op blocks with #7. Against a stacked 53, he co-op blocks with #5. He uses the same techniques against a 53 and a 62 stack, as described for T 13 J.

7-Man

Rule: Blocks man on or over him.
Coaching Points: Against a 44 front, he co-op blocks with #6. Against a 53 stack or 62 stack, he vertical releases through the backside B gap and walls off the backside backer. Against a 44 stack, he uses a gap read-up rule.

8-Man

Rule: Makes an inside release, and blocks across the hole.
Coaching Points: Same as T 13 J.

Quarterback

Technique: Same footwork and technique as T 13 J.
Coaching Points: Same as T 13 bounce.

Left Halfback

Technique: Same as T 13 J. Aims for the tail of #3 and runs to daylight.
Coaching Points: He comes across the backfield with controlled speed. He accepts the handoff from the quarterback, and heads for the tail of #3. He gets his shoulders square to the line of scrimmage and runs to daylight.

Fullback

Technique: Aims for the tail of #4 and leads through the hole.
Coaching Points: If #4 is covered by a hard man, his path should be through the frontside B gap. If #4 is open, or covered by a backer, he leads through the frontside A gap. In either case, he blocks the first man to cross his face.

Right Halfback

Technique: Aims for the inside leg of #2, leads through the hole, and blocks any defender in the area. (Note: Against an overhang look, blocks the last man on the line of scrimmage.)

Coaching Points: He checks the defensive spacing on #2. If no overhang player is present, he leads through the C gap and blocks the first defender to threaten the play. If an overhang player is present, he blocks him.

T 13 QB @ 1

T 13 QB @ 1, the run by the quarterback, is primarily a goal-line or short-yardage play (Figures 2-7 and 2-8). It looks just like T 13 J, except the quarterback keeps the ball and takes it outside with the frontside guard leading him. To the left, the play is T 17 QB @ 9.

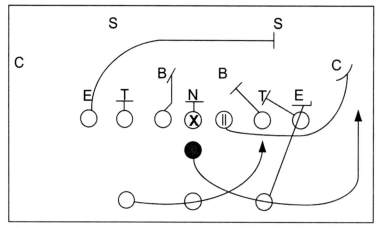

Figure 2-7. T 13 QB @ 1 against 52 defense

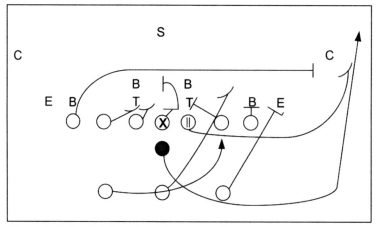

Figure 2-8. T 13 QB @ 1 against 44 defense

BLOCKING RULES, TECHNIQUE, AND COACHING POINTS FOR T 13 QB @ 1

2-Man

Rule: Blocks down on the first man inside, on or off the line of scrimmage.
Coaching Points: As he blocks down, he locks on any defender who may cross his face. Against a 44 defense, he blocks the man on him whether he aligns in a 6 or 7 technique. Against a 44 stack, he uses a gap read-up rule.

3-Man

Rule: Blocks down on the first man inside, on or off the line of scrimmage.
Coaching Points: As he blocks down, he locks on any defender who may cross his face. Against a 44 stack, he uses a gap read-up rule.

4-Man

Rule: Pulls around the log block by the right halfback and leads the quarterback on the perimeter.
Coaching Points: He pulls flat down the line of scrimmage on his first two steps. As he passes #5, he begins to bow his course to get around the log block by the right halfback. He turns upfield and gets outside leverage on the first defender he encounters.

5-Man

Rule: Blocks the man on or over him.
Coaching Points: If he is uncovered, he steps to the frontside A gap and secures it. If it is not threatened, he continues up to the second level and turns back to block the backside backer. Against a 53 stack, he uses the same techniques described for T 13 J.

6-Man

Rule: Blocks the man on or over him.
Coaching Points: Against a 44 defense, he and #7 co-op block the 3 technique. He and #7 are responsible for the 3 technique and the backside backer. He uses the same techniques as described for T 13 J.

7-Man

Rule: Blocks the man on or over him.
Coaching Points: Against a 44 defense, he and #6 co-op block the 3 technique and the backside backer. He uses the same techniques as described for T 13 J. Against a

53 stack, he vertical releases inside the hard man to the second level and blocks the backside backer.

8-Man

Rule: Makes an inside release, and blocks across the hole.
Coaching Points: He should not be any deeper than four to five yards as he releases across the field. He blocks the first defender to cross his face.

Quarterback

Technique: Fakes T 13 J, and keeps the ball on the perimeter.
Coaching Points: He uses the same footwork as he does on T 13 keep. He seats the ball as he reverse pivots. As he crosses the midline on his second step, he moves the ball with his right hand to the front of his right hip. He bends at the waist and gives the left halfback a fake with his left hand. He continues to the perimeter as he would on the keep. He turns upfield and picks up the block of the 4-man.

Left Halfback

Technique: Fakes T 13 J.
Coaching Points: He makes a great fake, and runs through the same hole as he does on T 13 J. If he is not tackled, he becomes a blocker, and blocks the first defender who crosses his face.

Fullback

Technique: Same as T 13 J.
Coaching Points: He leads as he would on T 13 J, and blocks the first defender to cross his face.

Right Halfback

Technique: Same as T 13 J.
Coaching Points: He runs for the same reference point as he does on T 13 J. As the defender responsible for the off-tackle hole reacts to the down block, he logs him to the inside.

PLAY-ACTION PASSES IN THE TEEN SERIES

T 13 Keep Pass

The T 13 keep play (Figures 2-9 and 2-10) is a play-action pass that starts out looking exactly like T 13 J. It gets the quarterback on the perimeter with a pass/run option, and threatens the defense in the off-tackle hole and in the flank area. It is a great short-yardage and goal-line play. (Note: All interior linemen block to the pass against all heavy fronts.)

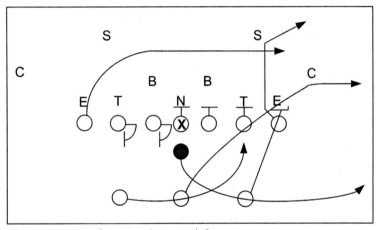

Figure 2-9. T 13 keep against 52 defense

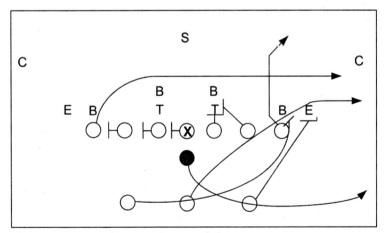

Figure 2-10. T 13 keep against 44 defense

BLOCKING RULES, TECHNIQUE, AND COACHING POINTS FOR T 13 KEEP PASS

2-Man

Rule: Inside releases, and runs a deep flag route.
Coaching Points: His goal is to run past the corner man, and run a flag route. He looks over the outside shoulder for the ball. He reads the safety for an adjustment in his route. Against a three-deep rotation with the corner man in the flat and the safety in the frontside third, he converts his route to a bench. He also converts to a bench against two-deep coverage. Against man coverage, he makes an inside move before breaking to the flag. If the ball is inside the opponent's 10-yard line, he should be one yard inside the end line on his route.

3-Man

Rule: Same as T 13 J. He must not cross the line of scrimmage.
Coaching Points: He must not cross the line of scrimmage. Against all heavy fronts, he blocks to the pass.

4-Man

Rule: Same as T 13 J. He must not cross the line of scrimmage.
Coaching Points: He must not cross the line of scrimmage. Against all heavy fronts, he blocks to the pass.

5-Man

Rule: If he is covered by a hard man, he blocks him. He gets his body between the defender and the quarterback. If he is open, he uses a hinge technique.
Coaching Points: As he hinges, if no threat is present in the backside A gap, he uses the "back door" technique, gets some depth, and blocks backside rushers. Against all heavy fronts, he blocks to the pass.

6-Man

Rule: Hinge technique
Coaching Points: He must not cross the line of scrimmage. Against all heavy fronts, he blocks to the pass.

7-Man

Rule: Hinge technique
Coaching Points: He must not cross the line of scrimmage. Against all heavy fronts, he blocks to the pass.

8-Man

Rule: Crossing route. He should be equidistant between the fullback and #2.
Coaching Points: On his crossing route, he positions himself halfway between #2 and the fullback in the flat. Against man cover, he makes a "hump" move before completing his crossing route. A hump move is made in the middle of the field by driving upfield for three or four yards to force the defensive back to get depth. Then, he breaks into his crossing route, working slightly back to the line of scrimmage. He tries to get as much separation from the defender as possible.

Quarterback

Technique: Same technique as T 13 J. Keeps the ball, and executes a pass/run option.
Coaching Points: He uses the same technique on the keep as he does in executing T 13 QB @ 1. Remember: this play is a pass/run option. He looks deep for the touchdown, then for #8 crossing, and then for the fullback. If no one is open, he shouts, "Go," and runs with the ball.

Left Halfback

Technique: Same as T 13 J. After his fake, he blocks the area over #3.
Coaching Points: As he fakes into the C gap, he blocks any defender in the area. Against a 44 front, he will be responsible for blocking the defender who aligns on #2.

Fullback

Technique: Same as T 13 J, except he goes under or over (preferably under) the load block and continues into the flat area.
Coaching Points: As he runs to his reference point, he eyeballs the load block and decides if his best course is in front or in back of it. He runs a four- to five-yard flat route, throttles down in the flat, and makes himself an easy target for the quarterback. If the ball is inside the opponent's 10-yard line, he runs his route one yard deep across the goal line.

Right Halfback

Technique: Same as T 13 bounce. Loads the last defender on the line of scrimmage.
Coaching Points: He uses the same load technique of aiming his inside shoulder pad for the defender's outside thigh pad and runs through him. He gets him on the ground.

T 13 Throwback

The throwback route is designed to exploit a defensive secondary that reacts quickly to the flow of a play (Figures 2-11 and 2-12). Although the crossing end is usually open, the quarterback looks to the deep pattern first just in case an easy touchdown is available.

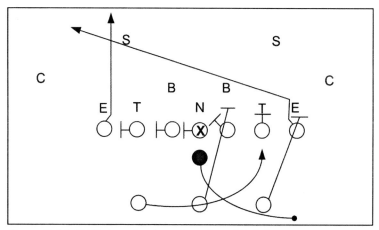

Figure 2-11. T-13 throwback to 8 against 52 defense

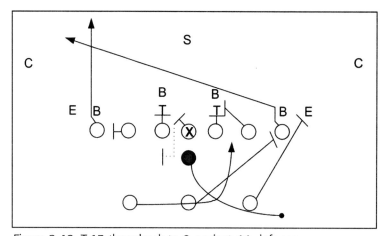

Figure 2-12. T-13 throwback to 8 against 44 defense

BLOCKING RULES, TECHNIQUE, AND COACHING POINTS FOR T 13 THROWBACK

(Note: Against heavy fronts, everyone blocks towards the pass.)

2-Man

Rule: Crossing route about 12 to 15 yards deep.
Coaching Points: Against a zone coverage, he settles in the open area and offers the quarterback an easy target. Against man coverage, he makes a "hump" move before completing the crossing route, and stays on the move.

3-Man

Rule: Same as T 13 keep.
Coaching Points: Same as T 13 keep.

4-Man

Rule: Same as T 13 keep.
Coaching Points: Same as T 13 keep.

5-Man

Rule: Same as T 13 keep.
Coaching Points: Same as T 13 keep.

6-Man

Rule: Same as T 13 keep.
Coaching Points: Same as T 13 keep.

7-Man

Rule: Same as T 13 keep.
Coaching Points: Same as T 13 keep.

8-Man

Rule: Inside releases, and runs a deep vertical route.
Coaching Points: He runs a deep vertical route past the secondary defenders and looks for the ball over his inside shoulder. He allows himself a five-yard cushion from the sideline. If he gets man coverage, he makes a double move to the post.

Quarterback

Technique: Same as T 13 keep, except gains an extra yard or two of depth and pulls up behind #2.
Coaching Points: After giving the left halfback an open-hand fake, he gains a depth of six or seven yards and sets up behind the 2-man's initial alignment. He looks deep immediately. If #8 is open, he throws him the ball. The ball is thrown on a trajectory that will allow the receiver to run under it. He keeps the ball inside the receiver. It should be thrown down the field, not across the field. He should never under throw the deep ball. It is either caught by #8, or it goes over his head and is incomplete. If #8 is not open, he comes down to his second choice: #2 on a crossing route. If #2 is covered, he runs and gets as much yardage as he can.

Left Halfback

Technique: Same as T 13 keep.
Coaching Points: Same as T 13 keep.

Fullback

Technique: Aims for the C gap, and blocks any defender in the area.
Coaching Points: Same as T 13 keep.

Right Halfback

Technique: Same as T 13 keep.
Coaching Points: Same as T 13 keep.

T 13 Bootleg: Quick or Slow

The bootleg—quick or slow—is a misdirection run/pass option play off T 13 J. On a quick call (Figures 2-13 and 2-14), #8 makes a quick inside release and runs a shallow sideline route three or four yards deep, and #2 runs a crossing route at 15 to 17 yards deep. On a slow call (Figures 2-15 and 2-16), #8 blocks his man for two counts, and then runs his shallow route. On both the quick and the slow call, #2 runs the same route. (Note: All interior linemen block to the pass against all heavy fronts.)

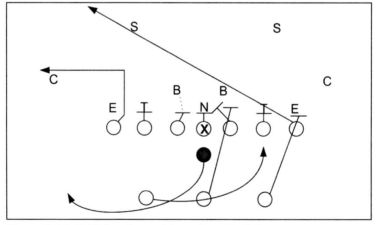

Figure 2-13. T 13 bootleg quick against 52 defense

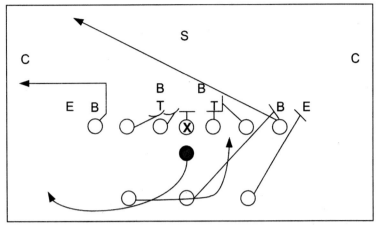

Figure 2-14. T 13 bootleg quick against 44 defense

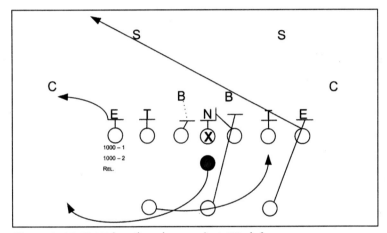

Figure 2-15. T 13 bootleg slow against 52 defense

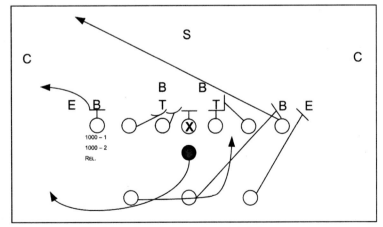

Figure 2-16. T 13 bootleg slow against 44 defense

BLOCKING RULES, TECHNIQUE, AND COACHING POINTS
FOR T 13 BOOTLEG: QUICK OR SLOW

(Note: Against heavy fronts, everyone blocks toward the pass.)

2-Man

Rule: Inside releases, and runs a 15- to 17-yard crossing route.
Coaching Points: Same assignment on both quick and slow bootlegs. Against a zone cover, he reads the reaction of the deep defender to the side of the bootleg. If the defender is fooled by the flow of the play, he tries to get behind him for the touchdown. If he cannot get behind him, he gains a depth of 15 to 17 yards and throttles down in an open area. Against man, he makes the "hump" move before completing his crossing route. He should be ready to block for the quarterback if he shouts, "Go!"

3-Man

Rule: Same as T 13 J. He should not cross the line of scrimmage.
Coaching Points: Same as T 13 J.

4-Man

Rule: Same as T 13 J. He should not cross the line of scrimmage.
Coaching Points: Same as T 13 J.

5-Man

Rule: Same as T 13 J. He should not cross the line of scrimmage.
Coaching Points: Same as T 13 J.

6-Man

Rule: Same as T 13 J. He should not cross the line of scrimmage.
Coaching Points: Same as T 13 J.

7-Man

Rule: Same as T 13 J. He should not cross the line of scrimmage.
Coaching Points: Same as T 13 J.

8-Man

Rule: On bootleg quick, he makes a quick inside release and angles back into the flat area, gaining a depth of three to four yards. On bootleg slow, he blocks the man on him for two full counts, and then releases inside or outside of the defender and runs his three- to four-yard flat route.

Coaching Points: On bootleg quick, he takes the easiest release the defender gives him. An inside release is preferred. If the defender does not allow him to release inside, he releases outside. He gets his head around fast because the quarterback will get to the perimeter quickly and may have to unload the ball in a hurry. On bootleg slow, he uses a high-pressure control block and should not be in a great hurry to come off the block. He holds his block for a full two counts, and then takes the easiest release to get into the flat area. His block will ensure the quarterback getting outside on the perimeter. He should be ready to block for him if he shouts "Go!"

Quarterback

Technique: Fakes T 13 J and starts his bootleg course. On bootleg quick, #8 will come open fast, and he must be ready to unload the ball to him right away. On bootleg slow, #8 will block for two counts, which will allow him to get outside and have more time to look for the deeper receiver.

Coaching Points: On bootleg quick, #8 is the primary receiver. The bootleg in the teen and 40 series gets the quarterback to the perimeter quicker than any other bootleg in the wing-T system. If he can, the quarterback should square his shoulders to the line of scrimmage and be moving toward #8 when he throws him the ball. If under duress, the quarterback continues to move parallel to the line of scrimmage and gets his right shoulder back to make a sidearm throw to the receiver. On the bootleg slow, #2 is the primary receiver. If no overhang defender is to the side of the bootleg, the quarterback will definitely get outside contain and have plenty of time to locate #2 on his crossing route. If open, he throws the ball to #2. If #2 is covered, he comes down to his second choice: #8 on the delay. If #8 is covered, he shouts, "Go," and runs the ball.

Left Halfback

Technique: Same as T 13 J.
Coaching Points: Same as T 13 J.

Fullback

Technique: Same as T 13 J.
Coaching Points: Same as T 13 J.

Right Halfback

Technique: Same as T 13 J.
Coaching Points: Same as T 13 J.

T 13 Y Delay Across

The Y delay across is used as a goal-line or two-point-conversion play (Figures 2-17 and 2-18). It is most effective when run against goal-line or short-yardage defensive fronts. (Note: All interior linemen block to the pass against all heavy fronts.)

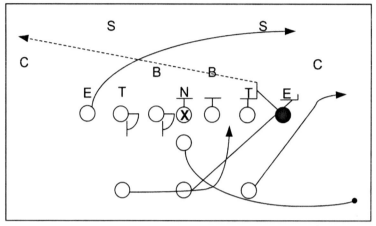

Figure 2-17. T 13 Y delay against 52 defense

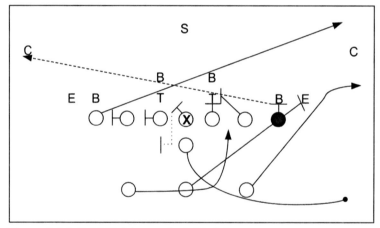

Figure 2-18. T 13 Y delay against 44 defense

BLOCKING RULES, TECHNIQUE, AND COACHING POINTS
FOR T 13 Y DELAY ACROSS

(Note: Against heavy fronts, everyone blocks toward the pass.)

2-Man

Rule: Fakes a down block, and runs a crossing route.
Coaching Points: He steps to his inside gap and makes contact with the defender over

#3. After making contact, he grounds his hands and knees, giving the impression that he lost his block. He scrambles inside, regains his footing, and runs a four- to five-yard drag route across the formation. If he is not covered, he turns to face the quarterback and backpedals toward the sideline—gaining width and depth.

3-Man

Rule: Blocks the man on him.
Coaching Points: Against a traditional 6-5 goal line, he begins a double-team with #2. As #2 leaves the block, he must take it over. Against a tight-tackle-6 look, he starts the double-team with #2, but he should remain aware of the backer in the frontside B gap. If the backer attacks the B gap, he blocks him. If not, he takes over the double-team block.

4-Man

Rule: Blocks the man on him or in the inside gap.
Coaching Points: Short-yardage and goal-line fronts will place a defender on the inside shoulder of the 4-man. He uses a drive block, and keeps his body between the defender and the quarterback.

5-Man

Rule: Hinge technique.
Coaching Points: He steps to the backside gap and hinges. He will most likely end up blocking the 2i technique on #6. If he has a hard-man on him, he blocks him.

6-Man

Rule: Hinge technique.
Coaching Points: He punches the 2i technique with his inside hand and hinge. If no one is threatening the backside B gap, he comes out the back door and blocks the widest rusher from the backside.

7-Man

Rule: Hinge technique.
Coaching Points: He steps to the frontside gap and hinges. He will most likely block the 5 technique on him.

8-Man

Rule: Makes an inside release and runs a crossing route.
Coaching Points: He inside releases and crosses the formation. He gets into the end

zone about two yards inside the end line, finds a soft spot against zone coverage, and stays on the move against man coverage.

Quarterback

Technique: Fakes T 13 J, and throws back to Y on the delay across route.
Coaching Points: After faking T 13 J, he gains depth and ends up rolling toward the sideline about seven to eight yards from the line of scrimmage. He looks for the right halfback in the flat, and the X on the crossing route. If either player is open for a touchdown, he throws the ball to him. If not, he holds the ball until the Y end has had a chance to fake a block and sneak across the formation. He should not overthrow this route; he should throw the ball right at him.

Left Halfback

Technique: Fakes T 13 J.
Coaching Points: After faking T 13 J, he turns into the line of scrimmage and aims for the first backer inside or outside of #3. Against a tight-tackle 6, the backer will be inside #3; against a 6-5 goal line, he will be outside of #3.

Fullback

Technique: Blocks the defender on or outside of Y.
Coaching Points: He sprints for the inside leg of #2, and blocks the defender on or outside of him. He aims his inside shoulder pad for his outside thigh pad. He drives into the defender and runs through him with enough force to knock him down.

Right Halfback

Technique: Runs a fan route.
Coaching Points: He sprints for a spot one yard outside of #2. He continues toward the sideline, gaining width and depth. He should be one yard deep across the goal line and find a soft spot in a zone defense. Against man coverage, he stays on the move and tries to beat his defender.

3

The 20 Series

The 20 series is the most recognizable set of plays in wing-T football. It features the fullback trap play, and its companion play, the buck-sweep—both of which have been standard plays of the wing-T for 50 years. The traditional wing-T sweep is effective against all defenses that are conventionally used against a wingback/tight-end formation. However, it is difficult to mirror the play to the tight-end side against overhang fronts. In the traditional wing-T sweep away from formation, the halfback, from his set position in the backfield, blocks the defender playing on or outside the tight end. This scheme is reasonable against seven-man fronts, but it is difficult against overhang players in eight-man fronts. If an effective sweep cannot be run away from the formation, defenses will begin to overplay the tight-end/wingback side, which will hurt the offense. An innovative idea is to put a flexed end away from the formation and run a pro-type sweep to the flexed end. The flexed end forces the overhang player to align on—and not outside—the tight end. Figures 3-1 and 3-2 illustrate the advantage of a flexed end in neutralizing an overhang player. The split of the end is as wide as necessary to force this adjustment—usually three to four yards.

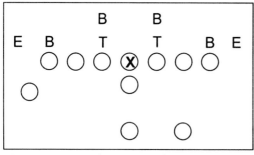

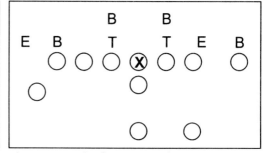

Figure 3-1. Liz tight end overhang against 44 defense

Figure 3-2. Liz flex no overhang against 44 defense

Liz Flex 21 Wham

The sweep to the flexed-end side is called a wham sweep (Figures 3-3 and 3-4). The wham sweep looks very much like the old Green Bay sweep that was run from a pro set and split backs. The difference between the pro-type sweep and the wham sweep is that in the pro sweep, no interior fake will slow down pursuit—it is a fast flow play. Consequently, defenders are quick to pursue it. The wham sweep, with the fullback threatening up the middle, will hold backers and slow down their pursuit. This little nuance gives the wham sweep an advantage not found in the pro-type sweep.

On the wham sweep, the flex end uses an option block on the defender over him, and simply takes the defender in any direction he decides to go. This technique gives the sweep a two-way go, which is an advantage over the traditional sweep. Another advantage is that a bigger, stronger blocker, the flex end, has the key block on the sweep—instead of the halfback. On the wham sweep, the halfback dives for the outside leg of the tackle and blocks any defender in that area. Both guards pull. The frontside guard swings upfield outside the flex end's block, and the backside guard turns up inside the flex end's block. The ballcarrier will read the block of the flex end and run inside or outside of his block. The wham sweep is an innovation that enables the sweep to be run away from formation against any defensive front. Thus, a Rip/Liz flex formation allows the sweep to be run to or away from formation with equal facility and effectiveness.

By going to an end-over formation, or east/west formations (Figures 3-5 and 3-6), the wham sweep can be run with an eligible receiver releasing downfield. If the defense overshifts its front to the end-over side, the quarterback should be prepared to direct the wing-T attack away from the overshift.

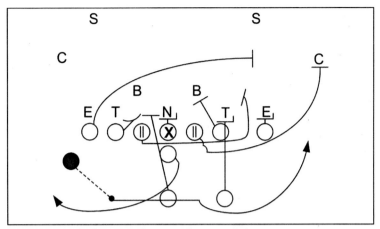

Figure 3-3. Liz flex 21 wham against 52 defense

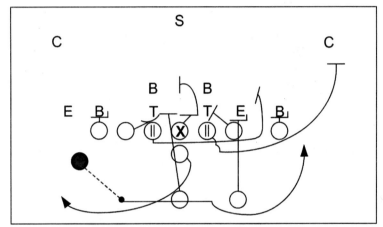

Figure 3-4. Liz flex 21 wham against 44 defense

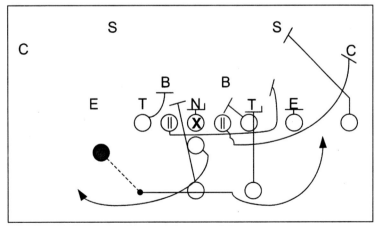

Figure 3-5, East 21 wham against 52 defense

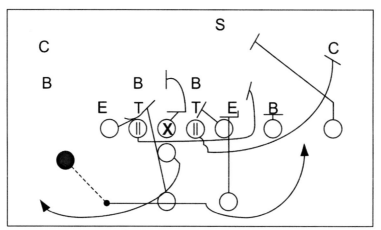
Figure 3-6. East 21 wham against 44 defense

BLOCKING RULES, TECHNIQUES, AND COACHING POINTS
FOR LIZ FLEX 21 WHAM

These rules and techniques are for Liz flex 21 wham. To the left, the play is Rip flex 29 wham and the blocking assignments are reversed.

2-Man

Rule: Flexes three to four yards from #3 and forces the last man on the line of scrimmage to align on him. Uses a high-pressure control block to block the last man in any direction he wishes to go.
Coaching Points: His flex position is an upright stance with his hands on his thigh pads and outside foot slightly forwards. He steps with his inside foot and shoots the palms of his hands for the numbers of the defender. He does not allow the defender to beat him to the inside, and does not get knocked back off the line of scrimmage. He keeps contact and allows the defender to pick a side. Once the defender does, the 2-man takes him in that direction. His block is similar to a pass-protection block. He keeps his hands inside the framework.

3-Man

Rule: Blocks the first defender inside, on or off the line of scrimmage.
Coaching Points: He uses his shoulder when blocking down on a hard man. He uses his hands when blocking backers. Against a 50 look, if the frontside backer escapes his block, he lets him go and walls off on the backside backer. Against a 53 look, he uses a vertical release and blocks the first backer to threaten the frontside B gap.

4-Man

Rule: Pulls deep enough to get around the wham block, and blocks the first defender outside #2.

Coaching Points: He loses ground on his first two steps. He levels off on his third step, gets around #2's block, and blocks the first secondary defender he encounters. If he can log the defender, he should do so; if not, he should kick him out. If #2 is locked up with his man and running toward the sideline, the 4-man turns up inside his block and blocks downfield. If he cannot circle #2 within five or six yards from his original position, he turns up inside #2's block.

5-Man

Rule: Blocks a hard man on him. If uncovered, seals the frontside A gap and blocks back on the backside backer.

Coaching Points: When blocking a middle linebacker, he anticipates him moving in the direction of the play, and aims for a spot where he can cut him off. When uncovered (against a 44 defense), he steps to the frontside A gap and prevents penetration in that gap. If it is not threatened, he goes to the second level and turns back on the backside backer.

6-Man

Rule: Pulls flat past #5, bows enough to get around the wham block, and seals the frontside or middle linebacker.

Coaching Points: He pulls flat across #5, and then bows just enough to get around the wham block by the right halfback. He turns up as soon as he clear the wham block, and squares his shoulders to the line of scrimmage as he turns up the hole. He is responsible for the first inside-out defender to threaten the sweep. He uses his hands to wall off the backer. He keeps contact and runs with him until the whistle blows.

7-Man

Rule: Fills. He, the fullback, and #5 are responsible for sealing both A gaps.

Coaching Points: If #6 is covered by a hard man, both he and the fullback are responsible for the man. He steps with his inside foot, and punches into his near number. He gets a big enough piece of the defender so that the fullback can block him. If #6 is covered by a backer (50 front), he makes a flat release, aiming for a point between the nose man and the backer, and walls off the backer. Against a 53, he makes a vertical release and blocks anyone threatening the backside B gap. If no threat exists, he goes to the next level and walls off the backside backer.

8-Man

Rule: Releases or retains.

Coaching Points: If a backer is on him or #7, he blocks him with a wall-off technique. If not, he releases across the formation. He should not be deeper than five yards from the line of scrimmage when he release across the formation.

Quarterback

Technique: Opens back to the hole and gives the fullback the midline. He makes an open hand fake to the fullback and hands the ball to the left halfback on his third step. Fakes bootleg at the 9 hole.

Coaching Points: After seating the ball, his first step is with his left foot over the midline. He moves his left hand to the back tip of the ball as he steps with his right foot—also over the midline. Then, with his right hand, he fakes a handoff to the fullback. His third step is with his left foot back on the midline as he hands the ball with his left hand to the left halfback. His third step over the midline will put his shoulders at a 45-degree angle to the line of scrimmage. This position will facilitate his bootleg course and get him to the flank as quickly as possible.

Left Halfback

Technique: Comes parallel across the backfield to receive ball from the quarterback. Makes a slight bow that will allow him to square his shoulders to the line of scrimmage. Runs off the tight end's block.

Coaching Points: His eyes should be on #2's block from the moment he starts his sweep course. After receiving the ball, he makes a slight bow in his path so his momentum is moving toward the line of scrimmage. His aim point should be about two or three yards outside the original position of #2, and his shoulders should be square to the goal line as he approaches the line of scrimmage. His intent is to get to the outside. However, if #2 is hooked up with the defender and skating to the sideline, he cuts up inside the block and then tries to get back outside after crossing the line of scrimmage.

Fullback

Technique: Aims for the left leg of #5 as he makes his fake. Seals the backside A gap.

Coaching Points: He dives for the left leg of #5 as he accepts a hand fake from the quarterback. He is responsible for sealing the backside A gap. If a hard man is covering #6, he will get help from #7 in cutting him off from the play. Against a 44 or 53 stack defense, he is responsible for any defender who attempts to penetrate the backside A gap.

Right Halfback

Technique: Sprints for the outside leg of #3 and load blocks the first defender to show in the 5-technique area.

Coaching Points: He runs a direct course for the outside leg of #3 and uses a load block to block any defender in the area. He drives his inside shoulder pad into the defender's outside thigh pad and run through the defender. His intent is to get a 5-technique player on the ground. If #3 is open, he blocks the backer over him. If a hard man disappears inside, he continues up for the frontside backer.

Liz Flex 24 Wham Trap

The second play in the 20 series is a finesse play called Liz flex 24 wham trap (Figures 3-7 and 3-8). To the left, the play is Rip flex 26 wham trap, and the blocking assignments are reversed. The finesse plays in this book are primarily designed against a 52 and 44 defensive scheme.

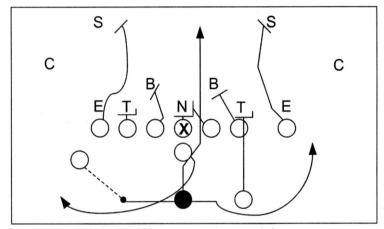

Figure 3-7. Liz flex 24 wham trap against 52 defense

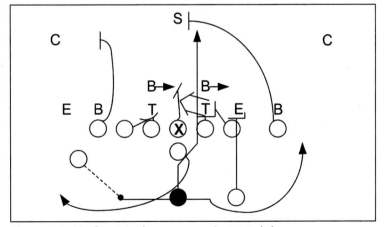

Figure 3-8. Liz flex 24 wham trap against 44 defense

This finesse play is designed to take advantage of and to discourage a 5-technique player from "jumping" outside the halfback's load block. The 5 technique sees the same picture on the sweep and the trap: the tackle blocks to the inside, and the halfback dives straight ahead. He is faced with the dilemma of closing on the tackles down block, or working to get outside the halfback's load block. If he closes, he is vulnerable to the load block, which is good for the sweep. If he attacks the load block, he is vulnerable to the inside play, which is good for the trap.

The wham trap is a great play against a 50 defense because of the pressure it puts on the frontside 5 technique, and also because the backside backer, who is blocked by the tackle in the traditional play—a difficult block—is now blocked by the backside guard. The backside guard has a much better chance of making the cutoff block than the backside tackle does. The frontside backer is not blocked in a 44 defense. He should be moving with the flow of the play. The fullback hugs the double-team block and runs under the frontside backer.

BLOCKING RULES, TECHNIQUES, AND COACHING POINTS FOR LIZ FLEX 24 WHAM TRAP

2-Man

Rule: Against a 50, releases and blocks the middle-third defender. Against a 44, releases and blocks the middle-third defender.
Coaching Points: He uses a stalk technique downfield.

3-Man

Rule: Against a 50, vertical releases for the backer. Against a 44, doubles the 3 technique.
Coaching Points: Against a 44 defense, his double-team block should drive the 3technique parallel to and as far down the line of scrimmage as possible. Good lateral movement is needed for the fullback to make a tight chair move and run underneath the frontside backer.

4-Man

Rule: Against a 50, leads to the 5-man's post. Against a 44, posts the 3 technique and doubles him with the 3-man.
Coaching Points: Against a 44 defense, his double-team block should drive the 3 technique parallel to and as far down the line of scrimmage as possible. Good lateral movement is needed for the fullback to make a tight chair move and run underneath the frontside backer.

5-Man

Rule: Against a 50, posts.
Coaching Points: Against a 44 defense, he steps to the frontside A gap before he turns back for the backside backer. If the frontside backer threatens the frontside A gap, he blocks him.

6-Man

Rule: Against a 50, blocks the backer over him. Keeps contact with the backer until the whistle blows. Against a 44, doubles the 3 technique with #7.
Coaching Points: He uses a co-op block against a 44 defense. He is responsible for the backside A gap and the backside backer if he threatens that gap. The 7-man takes over the block on the 3 technique if the backside A gap is threatened. If no threat is present, both blockers stay on the 3 technique and wall him off from the play.

7-Man

Rule: Against a 50, blocks the 5 technique. Against a 44, doubles the 3 technique with #6.
Coaching Points: He uses a co-op block against a 44 defense. If the backside backer threatens the A gap, the 7-man takes over the block on the 3 technique while the 6-man (who is responsible for the backside A gap) blocks the backside backer. If no threat is present in the backside A gap, both blockers should stay on the 3 technique and wall him off from the play.

8-Man

Rule: Against a 50, inside releases and blocks the backside deep secondary defender. Against a 44, same rule as a 50 defense.
Coaching Points: He uses a stalk block on the deep defender on his side of the field.

Quarterback

Technique: Same as 21 wham, except hands the ball off to the fullback.
Coaching Points: Against a 44 defense, he gives the fullback as much of the midline as possible, and gets him the ball as deep in the backfield as possible. Doing so will enable him to cut outside the post of the 4-man. He carries out his fake to the left halfback and bootleg at the 9 hole.

Left Halfback

Technique: Fakes 21 wham.
Coaching Points: He fakes 21 wham by bending at the waist as the quarterback fakes

the ball to him. He dips his left shoulder, puts both hands to his right hip, and carries out his fake.

Fullback

Technique: Acts as the ballcarrier. Receives the ball and runs to daylight.
Coaching Points: Against a 52 defense, his course is straight ahead. With a good double-team block, he should not need much of a chair move to split the backers. Against a 44 defense, he starts his chair move as soon as he receives the ball and runs as close to the double-team block as possible. He keys the frontside backer. He will not be blocked on 24 wham unless he runs through the frontside A gap. In that case, the center will block him and he should run outside the double-team block, running north and south upfield. If the backer moves with the flow of the play, he stays tight to the double-team and runs under him. The backer will have to reach back to tackle him. He runs with enough power to break an arm tackle.

Right Halfback

Technique: Same as 21 wham.
Coaching Points: He fakes 21 wham. He does not try to kick out the 5 technique. He attacks the 5 technique on the same angle as he does on 21 wham. He puts his inside shoulder pad on the outside thigh pad of the 5 technique and puts him on the ground.

Liz Flex 26 Counter Trap

The third play off wham action is Liz flex 26 counter trap (Figures 3-9 and 3-10). To the left, the play is Rip flex 24 counter trap, and the blocking assignments are reversed. It is another play meant to keep backers from pursuing quickly by countering the fullback away from sweep action: a major change in the traditional 20 series. Counter tells the backs to run opposite the call. So 26 counter tells all the backs—except for the ballcarrier—to run opposite of 26 (which is 24). The ballcarrier—the fullback—runs 26 counter trap; the line blocks 26 counter trap. The right halfback's wham block on the 5 technique in a 50 front is an excellent method of checking him when #3 releases inside to cut off the backside backer. This feature makes the wham scheme superior to the traditional scheme that calls for the tight end to cut off the 5 technique on the trap play.

BLOCKING RULES, TECHNIQUES, AND COACHING POINTS
FOR LIZ FLEX 26 WHAM COUNTER TRAP

2-Man

Rule: Releases crossfield.

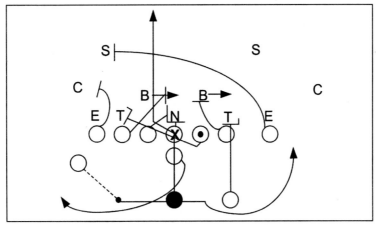

Figure 3-9. Liz flex 26 counter trap against 52 defense

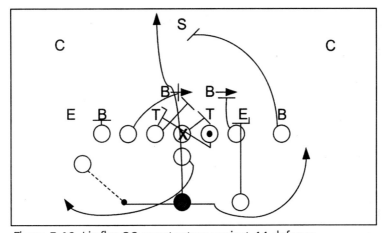

Figure 3-10. Liz flex 26 counter trap against 44 defense

Coaching Points: He releases crossfield and blocks the deep-middle or deep-half secondary defender to the frontside.

3-Man

Rule: Vertical releases and walls off the backside backer.
Coaching Points: Against an Eagle front, he scoops the 3 technique on #4.

4-Man

Rule: Pulls and traps the first man past #5.
Coaching Points: He bears in on his pull and traps the first defender to show past #5.

5-Man

Rule: Posts or blocks back.

Coaching Points: Against a hard man, he posts. If open, he blocks back.

6-Man

Rule: Leads, cracks back, influences, and blocks out.
Coaching Points: He influences and blocks out against a 2i defender. Against a 44 defense, he should be prepared to block the backside backer if he rushes over #5. If the backside backer moves with the flow of the play, he turns back and helps #7 with the playside backer. He prevents him from penetrating the line of scrimmage.

7-Man

Rule: Walls off the backside backer.
Coaching Points: He anticipates blocking the playside backer across the hole because the flow of the play will start him in that direction.

8-Man

Rule: Retains or releases.
Coaching Points: He retains a backer on him. If no backer is on or over him, he walls off the frontside corner.

Quarterback

Technique: Same footwork as 24 trap.
Coaching Points: He carries out his bootleg fake. He must occupy the last man on the line of scrimmage with the bootleg fake. (No one is blocking the last man on the line of scrimmage because he is responsible for taking the quarterback on the bootleg.)

Left Halfback

Technique: Fakes 21 wham.
Coaching Points: He makes the same type of fake as described in 24 trap. He carries out the fake until the whistle blows.

Fullback

Technique: Heads for the tail of #5. Receives the handoff, breaks left, and runs to daylight.
Coaching Points: Against a hard man over #5, he makes a chair move left and expects to get outside the frontside backer. Against a backer over #5, he runs straight ahead and breaks off the block on the backer. The ball should be in his left arm. Against a 44 defense, he breaks behind the block of #7.

Right Halfback

Technique: Fake 21 wham.
Coaching Points: Against an Eagle front, he blocks the backer over #3. Against a 53-stack defense, he blocks the defender who enters the C gap.

Liz Flex 24 Sting

Good defensive coaches teach backers and linemen to read and react to blocking schemes. Backers in 50 and 44 defenses will frequently read guards, and follow them when they pull. Tackles in 44 fronts will read the guard-and-tackle combination, and are well-schooled in reacting to a down block by the tackle and a pull-away by the guard. When they see this scheme, tackles will try to roll out of, or fight through, the down block and chase the guard down the line of scrimmage.

Therefore, some finesse schemes are needed to keep defenses "honest" and slow down their pursuit. The word "sting" is used to describe a false blocking scheme that features guards pulling away from the point of attack. Two examples of sting schemes will be discussed and illustrated against a 50 and a 44 defense. The first one is Liz flex 24 sting (Figures 3-11 and 3-12). To the left, the play is Rip flex 26 sting, and the blocking assignments are reversed.

BLOCKING RULES, TECHNIQUES, AND COACHING POINTS
FOR LIZ FLEX 24 STING

2-Man

Rule: Releases crossfield. Blocks across the hole.
Coaching Points: He should not be deeper than five yards from the line of scrimmage as he blocks across the hole.

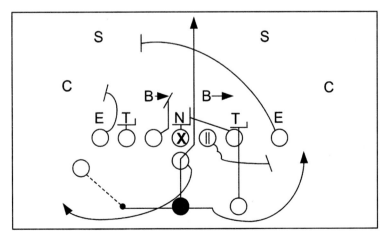

Figure 3-11. Liz flex 24 sting against 52 defense

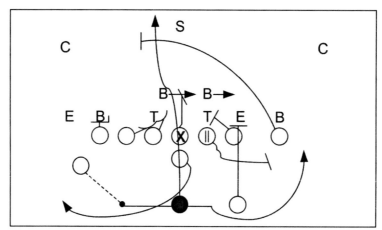

Figure 3-12. Liz flex 24 sting against 44 defense

3-Man

Rule: Against 50, doubles the nose. Against 44, influences the 3 technique.
Coaching Points: Against a 44 front, he blocks the 3 technique high on the shoulder pads so it is easy for him to roll out of his block. He does not drive the defender; he strains into him and allows him to fight his pressure. He does not attempt to take his ground. Against a 50, he comes flat down the line of scrimmage aiming for the near hip of the nose man. He attempts to drive the nose laterally down the line of scrimmage. If the playside backer crosses his face, he blocks him. If the nose disappears, he goes to the second level and blocks the backside backer.

4-Man

Rule: Against 50, pulls around the wham block and blocks the first free defender. Against 44, same as 50.
Coaching Points: None.

5-Man

Rule: Against 50, posts. Against 44, steps to the playside gap and turns back on the backside backer.
Coaching Points: Against 44, he is responsible for the frontside A gap. He blocks any defender who threatens that gap. If the frontside A gap is not threatened, he turns back and blocks the backside backer.

6-Man

Rule: Against 50, walls off the backside backer. Against 44, doubles the 3 technique with #7.

Coaching Points: Against a 44 front, he serves as a lead blocker, and #7 is a post blocker. The 3 technique is to be driven off the line on a 45-degree angle toward the 8-man.

7-Man

Rule: Against 50, blocks the man on him. Against a 44 defense, doubles the 3 technique with #6.
Coaching Points: He has a key block against a 50 front. He aims for the inside number of the 5 technique to wall him off. He works his body between the 5 technique and the ballcarrier. Against 44, he acts as a post blocker and helps drive the 3 technique out and off the line of scrimmage.

8-Man

Rule: Against 50, walls off the corner to his side. Against 44, retains the backer on him.
Coaching Points: None.

Quarterback

Technique: Same as 24 trap.
Coaching Points: He gives the fullback the midline and gets him the ball as deep as possible. He makes a great bootleg fake to occupy the backside contain player.

Left Halfback

Technique: Same as 24 trap.
Coaching Points: After the quarterback fakes the ball to him, he places both hands to his outside hip, bends at the waist, and carries out his fake until the whistle blows.

Fullback

Technique: Acts as the ballcarrier. Same course as 24 trap. Reads the nose in a 50 defense.
Coaching Points: He should be prepared to run under the 50 playside backer. He will not be blocked. He aims for the tail of #5, but anticipates #3 blocking the nose man. He cuts as tight as possible off that block and executes his chair move by running under the playside backer. He is expected to run through an arm tackle if the backer reaches back for him. If the nose slants to the playside A gap, he runs straight ahead and splits the backers.

Right Halfback

Technique: Same as 21 wham.

Coaching Points: He runs his wham course and loads the 5 technique just as he would on 21 wham.

Liz Flex 26 Counter Sting

The second finesse play is Liz flex 26 counter sting (Figures 3-13 and 3-14). Going to the left, the play is Rip flex 24 counter sting, and the blocking assignments are reversed. Like 24 sting, the frontside blocking pattern is designed to looks like wham-sweep blocking, and the ball is given to the fullback who hits over the 6-man. The blocking scheme to the flexed-end side is exactly the same as 24 sting.

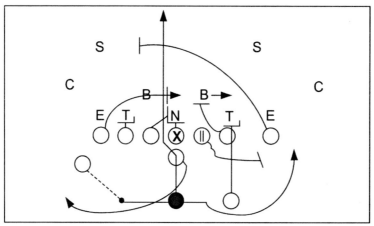

Figure 3-13. Liz flex 26 counter sting against 52 defense

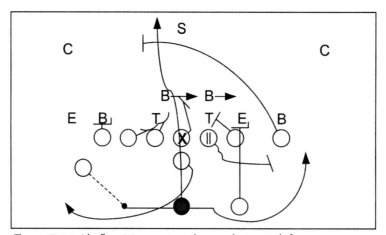

Figure 3-14. Liz flex 26 counter sting against 44 defense

BLOCKING RULES, TECHNIQUES, AND COACHING POINTS FOR LIZ FLEX 26 COUNTER STING

2-Man

Rule: Against 50, releases crossfield and blocks across the hole. Against 44, releases crossfield and blocks across the hole.
Coaching Points: None.

3-Man

Rule: Against 50, vertical releases for the backside backer. Against 44, influences the 3 technique.
Coaching Points: Against a 50 front, the backer should read sweep, and should be moving away from the 6 hole. The 3-man should be able to position himself between the backer and the ballcarrier and wall him off. Against 44 front, he blocks the 3 technique around the shoulder-pad level, but does not try to drive him to the inside. He strains into the defender and gives him a chance to roll out of, or fight through, his block.

4-Man

Rule: Against 50, pulls around the wham block and blocks the first free defender. Against a 44, same as 50.
Coaching Points: None.

5-Man

Rule: Against 50, posts. Against 44, steps to and protects the backside A gap. If gap is not threatened, blocks the frontside backer by the hole.
Coaching Points: Against a 44 defense, the frontside backer should read sweep, and the backside backer will either attack him or move to the flank. In either case, he will be moving away from the 6 hole. He should position himself between the backer and the fullback, and wall him off.

6-Man

Rule: Against 50, leads to the 5-man's post. Against 44 defense, doubles the 3 technique with the 7-man.
Coaching Points: Against a 44 front, he and #7 will double-team the 3 technique. His double-team block should wall off the 3 technique from the frontside A gap. If he gets a 2i alignment, he will post and #7 will lead, and the 2i technique will be driven down toward the 5-man. The fullback will make his chair move outside of the block by the 6-man.

7-Man

Rule: Against 50, retains the 5 technique (key block). Against 44, doubles the 3 technique with the 6-man.
Coaching Points: Against a 44 front and a 3 technique, he joins #6 in double-teaming the 3 technique. He will act as the post blocker, and the 6-man will be the drive blocker. The idea is to keep the 3 technique away from the frontside A gap. If the man on #6 is in a 2i alignment, #6 will post that man, and the 7-man will lead to the post. Now, the idea is to drive the 2i as far inside as possible. Against a 50 front, he has the key block and must position himself between the 5 technique and the fullback. He gets inside and walls him off.

8-Man

Rule: Against 50, cracks the frontside backer. Against 44, retains the 6 technique (key block).
Coaching Points: Against a 44 front, he has a key block—especially if the defender on him lines up in a 6i technique. He gets inside and walls him off.

Quarterback

Technique: Same as 26 counter.
Coaching Points: Same as 26 counter.

Left Halfback

Technique: Same as 26 counter.
Coaching Points: Same as 26 counter.

Fullback

Technique: Acts as the ballcarrier. Same as 26 counter.
Coaching Points: Against a 50 front, he runs deep into the double-team block before making his chair move, which will give the 8-man time to crack the frontside backer. Against a 44 front with a 3-technique player on #6, he looks to run inside the double-team block and outside the block on the frontside backer. If the defender on #6 is in a 2i alignment, he looks to make a chair move outside the double-team.

Right Halfback

Technique: Same as 26 counter.
Coaching Points: Same as 26 counter.

Liz Flex 29 Waggle

The waggle pass is the most popular play in wing-T football. Liz flex 21 waggle (Figure 3-15) is an example of the traditional waggle pass. When running the play to the left, it is Liz flex 29 waggle (Figure 3-16), and the blocking assignments are reversed. The word "waggle" describes a play with the flow of backs in one direction, and the quarterback and the pulling guards going in the opposite direction. A bootleg has the quarterback going "naked," opposite the flow of the backs and the guards. Naked would be a more accurate description of the quarterback bootleg action. Some teams do pull a guard when they move the quarterback opposite the flow, and use the term roll-away to describe this action. That term will be used later in the book.

Volumes have been written on the waggle pass, and all kinds of route adjustments have been explored from all formations. Screens, shuffle passes, and designed

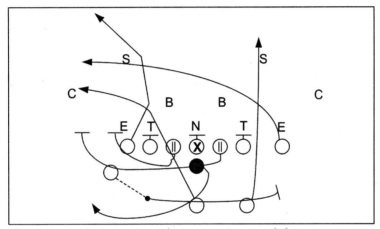

Figure 3-15. Liz flex 21 waggle pass against 52 defense

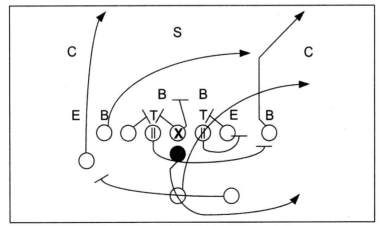

Figure 3-16. Liz flex 29 waggle pass against 44 defense

quarterback runs have been developed to complement this great play. Because so much has been written and is known about the waggle pass, assignments and techniques for it will not be discussed. Instead, an innovation (switching the routes of the frontside and backside ends) to the traditional waggle will be illustrated. The adjustment is Liz flex 29 waggle switch (Figures 3-17 and 3-18). To the left, the play is Rip flex 21 waggle switch, and the blocking assignments are reversed.

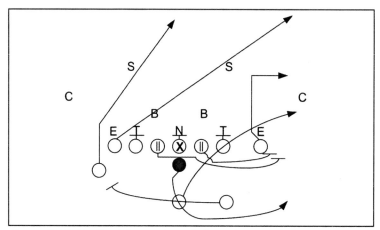

Figure 3-17. Liz flex 29 waggle switch against 52 defense

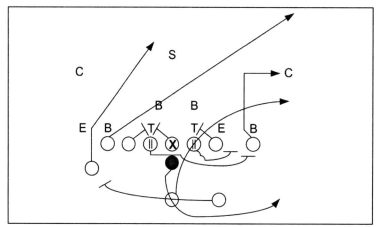

Figure 3-18. Liz flex 29 waggle switch against 44 defense

In the basic waggle, the frontside end runs a flag, and the backside end drags across the formation. Seeing the play so often, backside backers have done a good job of taking away the backside end by running underneath his route. The frontside backer runs with the fullback in the flat, and the frontside defensive back takes the frontside end on his flag route. With the backside end on a deep crossing route, the backside backer no longer has a drag route to run under. The frontside defensive back will have to cover the deep crossing route. The frontside backer can still run with the fullback in the flat, but against all zone defensives the frontside end will be open on his 12- to

15-yard out route. It is obvious that the switch route will cause defenses to find new ways to defend the waggle.

Since a bootleg off the wham sweep is integral to the plays previously mentioned, the next play in the wham sequence is Liz flex 21 wham bootleg (Figures 3-19 and 3-20). To the left, the play is Rip flex 29 wham bootleg, and the blocking assignments are reversed. The bootleg presents the contain man with the following predicament: if he chases a play away from him, he is vulnerable to the bootleg; if he comes upfield to play the quarterback bootleg, he is susceptible to counter plays back to his inside; and, if he "sits" and looks for the counter plays, he loses contain on the bootleg. In plays like Liz flex 26 counter and 26 counter sting, the contain man to the side of the counter is not blocked. Thus, it is necessary to have a bootleg off the sweep to occupy the contain man. The key to a bootleg play is to know when to call it. Every time the quarterback fakes a bootleg, his technique must be perfect, and he must check the play of the contain man. If the contain man does anything other than come upfield to contain the quarterback, the bootleg should be called.

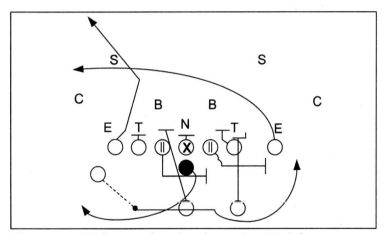

Figure 3-19. Liz flex 21 wham bootleg against 52 defense

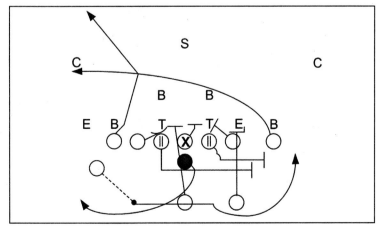

Figure 3-20. Liz flex 21 wham bootleg against 44 defense

BLOCKING RULES, TECHNIQUES, AND ASSIGNMENTS
FOR LIZ FLEX 21 WHAM BOOTLEG

(Note: All interior linemen block to the pass against all heavy fronts.)

2-Man

Rule: Inside releases and runs a 12- to 15-yard crossing route.
Coaching Points: He sprints across the formation, gaining a depth of 12 to 15 yards. Once into the receiving area, he throttles down and becomes an easy target for the quarterback. Against man coverage, he makes a hump move and stays on the move. He should be prepared to block for the quarterback if he hollers, "Go!"

3-Man

Rule: Blocks the first hard man to his inside.
Coaching Points: If #4 is open, he blocks down through the backside A gap all the way to the nose man. He should not cross the line of scrimmage.

4-Man

Rule: Pulls right and traps the first man past #3.
Coaching Points: He bows around the right halfback as he moves to the right flank. He should not cross the line of scrimmage.

5-Man

Rule: Blocks the hard man on him. If open, blocks left.
Coaching Points: He does not cross the line of scrimmage.

6-Man

Rule: Pulls right and traps the first free man past #5.
Coaching Points: He pulls flat and traps the first defender to show past #5. He should not cross the line of scrimmage.

7-Man

Rule: Blocks the hard man on him. If open, protects inside gap.
Coaching Points: If open, he steps to and helps secure the playside B gap. He keeps his eyes on the backer over him. If the backer blitzes, he must block him.

8-Man

Rule: Inside releases and runs a deep flag route.

Coaching Points: Against a three-deep, he runs his deep flag route. If the safety levels, he converts to a bench route. Against a two-deep secondary, he converts to a bench route. Against man coverage, he makes a double move to the flag.

Quarterback

Technique: Opens same as on 21 wham. Fakes to the left halfback and executes bootleg.
Coaching Points: As he seats the ball, he gets off the middle linebacker so the fullback has room to run up the tail of #5. His first two steps—with his left and right foot—are over the middle linebacker, and his back is to the line of scrimmage. No fake is made to the fullback; his proximity to the fullback as he passes is sufficient to get the attention of the defense. Both hands are to the back tip of the ball as it is seated. He steps under the middle linebacker on his third step, and gets his shoulders turned about 45 degrees to the line of scrimmage. Using both hands, he jabs the ball to the inside hip of the left halfback. He pulls the ball back to his belt with both hands. Then, he moves the ball to his left hip with his left hand and allows his right hand to dangle at his side. He bends at the waist and sprints for the perimeter. He should now be about five to six yards from the line of scrimmage with his shoulders facing the sideline. He looks back toward the left halfback, but with his peripheral vision he should see the reaction of the contain man. If the contain man allows him to get outside, he should do so, and redirect his path toward the line of scrimmage so he is running at his receivers. If he can throw for a touchdown, he should do so. If the crossing receiver is open, he hits him. If nothing looks good, he hollers, "Go," and runs with the ball. If he guessed wrong and the contain man plays him, he should not panic and do something foolish with the ball. He should try to elude the contain man and run for as much yardage as he can get. He should not retreat and take a big loss. Losing five yards on the bootleg is understandable; losing 15 yards is unacceptable.

Left Halfback

Technique: Fakes 21 wham.
Coaching Points: As the quarterback makes a fake to him, he puts both hands on his outside hip, dips his inside shoulder, bends at the waist, and carries out his fake until the whistle blows.

Fullback

Technique: Same technique as 21 wham.
Coaching Points: He checks to see if #5 is covered or open. If #5 is open, he aims for the tail of #5 and blocks the area immediately over his position. If #5 is covered, he aims for his left leg and fills in the frontside A gap.

Right Halfback

Technique: Dives for the C gap and continues across the line of scrimmage. Runs a skinny post route.

Coaching Points: He stays at an equal distance between the two deep defenders to the backside of the play. He works for depth, and looks for the ball over his left shoulder.

An adjustment off the regular bootleg is the bootleg slow. The play is called Liz flex 21 wham bootleg slow (Figures 3-21 and 3-22). To the right, the play is Rip flex 29 wham bootleg slow. The bootleg slow adds security to the bootleg by having the frontside end block the last man on the line before releasing into the pattern. When the play of the contain man to the bootleg side is erratic (sometimes disregarding the bootleg and sometimes playing it), blocking him for a count of two enables the quarterback to get to the perimeter to execute the bootleg.

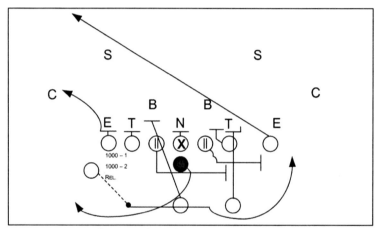

Figure 3-21. Liz flex 21 wham bootleg slow against 52 defense

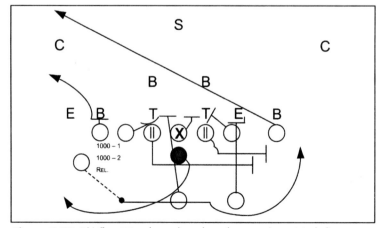

Figure 3-22. Liz flex 21 wham bootleg slow against 44 defense

All assignments are the same as on the regular bootleg, with the exception of the two ends. The frontside end (#8) blocks the man on him for three counts before releasing and running a four- to five-yard flat route. The backside end (#2) runs a deep crossing route, gaining 15 to 18 yards of depth as he approaches the frontside third of the field.

Rip Flex 22 Cut-Sweep

Rip flex 22 cut-sweep (Figures 3-23 and 3-24) features the traditional gap, read-up blocking scheme to the tight-end/wingback side of the formation. Going to the left, the play is Liz flex 28 cut, and the blocking assignments are reversed. This play has been a basic wing-T play for 50 years.

Rip flex 22 cut is so called because a 90-degree cut is required by the ballcarrier to run inside the kickout block by the frontside guard, and to run outside the

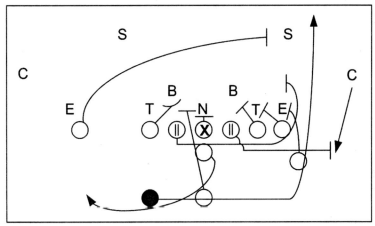

Figure 3-23. Rip flex 22 cut against 52 defense

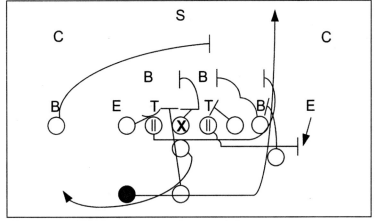

Figure 3-24. Rip flex 22 cut against 44 defense

wingback/halfback's down block. The play attacks off the edge, not out on the perimeter, and calling it 22 cut is more precise than calling it 21 cut. It is a great football play, and it is as effective today as it was in the past. The assignments for this play are well-known to wing-T coaches, and it needs no explanation; it may not need any adjustments, either. However, the following ideas may be of some value to coaches who feature this play.

When running to the flank, one of the toughest things to accomplish is to seal the frontside backer. Against eight-man fronts, this task is not a problem, because the tight end is in an excellent position to block down on him. However, the traditional scheme for blocking 22 cut against seven-man fronts requires the tight end to block down on the 5 technique, and the backside guard to seal the frontside backer. Therefore, against seven-man fronts, switching the assignments of the tight end and the backside guard will improve the effectiveness of this play. The switch requires the tight end to block the playside backer, and the backside guard logs the 5 technique. This adjustment is called an Iowa scheme: Rip flex 22 Iowa (Figure 3-25). Going left, it would be Liz flex 28 Iowa.

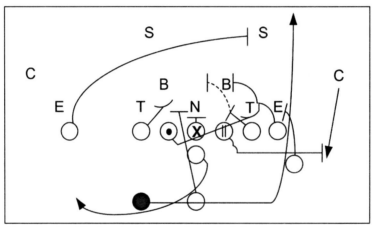

Figure 3-25. Rip flex 22 Iowa against 52 defense

BLOCKING RULES, TECHNIQUES, AND COACHING POINTS
FOR RIP FLEX 22 IOWA

2-Man

Rule: Releases inside and blocks the playside backer.
Coaching Points: He uses a high-pressure control block to wall off the backer. He maintains the block until the whistle blows.

3-Man

Rule: Blocks down or reads up.
Coaching Points: He aims his inside foot for the crotch of a hard man on #4. He makes a vertical release when blocking a backer. If the frontside backer escapes to the outside, he looks to block the backside backer.

4-Man

Rule: Pulls and kicks out first defender outside the right halfback block.
Coaching Points: He gains ground on his first two steps and flattens on his third step. He works for inside-out position on the force man, and blocks him with his right shoulder. He hits on the rise with a wide base and keeps his feet moving. He blocks until the whistle blows.

5-Man

Rule: Blocks man on or over, stepping through the frontside gap.
Coaching Points: If covered by a backer, he sprints for a position where the backer will be when reacting to the play. If open, he steps to and secures the frontside A gap. If the gap is not threatened, he blocks back on the backside backer.

6-Man

Rule: Pulls and logs the 5 technique.
Coaching Points: He pulls as he would if he were trapping the 5 technique. He gains ground into the line of scrimmage and, at the last moment, slips his head to the outside and logs the defender. If the defender reacts correctly, he will log himself. He should not tip off his intentions by altering his course. He approaches his target on the same angle as he does when he traps the 5 technique.

7-Man

Rule: Fills.
Coaching Points: He gets his head in front of a hard man on #6 to prevent him from pursuing the play. He will get help from the fullback. If he is filling on a backer, he aims for a point between the 5-man and the backer, and cuts him off at the pass.

8-Man

Rule: Releases crossfield.
Coaching Points: He should not be deeper than five yards as he block across the hole. He blocks the first defender who crosses his path.

Quarterback

Technique: Same footwork as 21 wham.
Coaching Points: He seats the ball and opens back to the hole. His first step with his left foot is slightly over the middle linebacker to allow the fullback to pass by him. As the fullback passes, he gives him a quick hand fake, and then brings both hands back to the ball in his pouch. On his second step, he steps slightly under the midline with his right foot. On his third step, he steps over the midline with his left foot and turns his shoulders on a 45-degree angle to the line of scrimmage. He hands the ball to the left halfback with his left hand. Turning his shoulders will start his momentum toward the flank, and will facilitate the bootleg. He puts both hands to his outside hip, lowers his right shoulder, bends at the waist, and fakes the bootleg with speed. He checks the reaction of the contain man.

Left Halfback

Technique: Receives ball from the quarterback as he comes square across the backfield. Cuts up the inside block of the 4-man.
Coaching Points: As he receives ball from quarterback, he places it in his right arm and keys on the block by #4. He runs at controlled speed and is prepared to make a sharp 90-degree cut under the block.

Fullback

Technique: Aims for the left foot of #5. Accepts a fake from the quarterback, and secures the backside A gap.
Coaching Points: After receiving a hand fake from the quarterback, he fills in the backside A gap and blocks the first defender to cross his face at the line of scrimmage or at the second level.

Right Halfback

Technique: Blocks the first defender on or outside the 2-man.
Coaching Points: He steps with his left foot for the crotch of the man on or outside the 2-man. He aims his left shoulder pad for the left thigh pad of the 2-man. He will probably make contact with his near hip. He widens his base as he hits and rises, keeps the defender between his feet, and blocks until the whistle blows. (Note: The reference point for a blocker blocking down on a defender inside of him will continue to be the near thigh pad. The desired contact point is the near hip. Because blockers always seem to hit their targets above the reference point, aiming for the thigh pad will place the blocker where he should be—with his inside shoulder and forearm into the near hip of the defender.)

Another problem in running the traditional wing-T sweep is when a force man aligns on the line of scrimmage, and attacks the frontside guard deep in the backfield. He attempts to "wrong-arm" the guard forcing the running back to bounce outside. This technique also blocks the path of the backside guard, eliminating him as a blocker. Consequently, the running back is on the perimeter with no blocker: that is exactly what the defense wants. To further complicate matters, the geometry of the play makes it difficult for the back to bounce outside without loosing speed. It's not easy to come square across the backfield, start a 90-degree cut, and then bounce outside. If the play were run from an I-Formation, a talented tailback, receiving the ball six to seven yards deep in the backfield, is able to bounce outside without losing speed. In either situation, the backside guard would have to have the savvy and agility to do the same, or the back would still be naked on the perimeter.

The way to counter a wrong-armed tactic is to run a predetermined bounce play off sweep action. The play is called Rip flex 22 bounce (Figures 3-26 and 3-27). Running left, the play is Liz flex 28 bounce. The frontside guard will now log the force man, the backside guard will pull around the log and lead the play outside, and the back will dip in and bounce out on the perimeter. This approach not only gets the back outside, but also gets the backside guard leading him down the field.

The ideal way to run the play is for the guards and running back to react to what the force man does. If he uses a wrong-arm technique, the frontside guard logs him, the backside guard bows around the log, and the back flows to the outside. If no wrong-arm technique is employed, the frontside guard kicks out the force, the backside guard seals, and the running back cuts on 90 degrees and hits the hole. In this way, only a single play is needed to counter the wrong-arm technique. However, it is next to impossible to get all players on the same page—seeing and reacting to the same thing. The predetermined play works best. It removes all doubt and indecision, and players are more aggressive when they know what they are doing and where the ball is going.

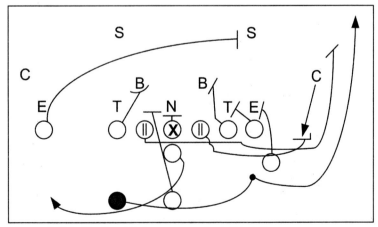

Figure 3-26. Rip flex 22 bounce against 52 defense

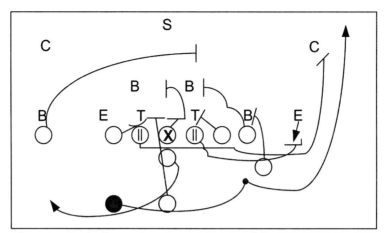
Figure 3-27. Rip flex 22 bounce against 44 defense

BLOCKING RULES, TECHNIQUES, AND COACHING POINTS
FOR RIP FLEX 21 BOUNCE

2-Man

Rule: Blocks gap, reads up.
Coaching Points: If the hard man on #3 disappears, he reads up to the backer level.

3-Man

Rule: Blocks down or reads up.
Coaching Points: If the hard man on #4 disappears, he reads up to the backer level.

4-Man

Rule: Pulls and logs force man.
Coaching Points: He pulls as he does on 21 Iowa, and logs the force man.

5-Man

Rule: Blocks man on or over, stepping through the frontside gap.
Coaching Points: If open, he seals the playside A gap. If that gap is not threatened, he goes up and blocks the backside backer.

6-Man

Rule: Pulls and bows around the log block. Leads upfield
Coaching Points: He pulls flat until he passes #5. Then, he bows his course outside the log block by #4. He leads the left halfback on the perimeter and blocks the first defender to cross his face.

7-Man

Rule: Fills.
Coaching Points: Same as 21 Iowa.

8-Man

Rule: Releases crossfield.
Coaching Points: Same as 21 Iowa.

Quarterback

Technique: Same as 21 Iowa.
Coaching Points: Same as 21 Iowa.

Left Halfback

Technique: Receives the ball from the quarterback, bends inside, and then bounces outside the log block.
Coaching Points: He starts as he would in 21 Iowa. He receives ball from the quarterback and places it in his right arm. He bends his path into the original position of #2, gets within two yards of the line of scrimmage, and then bounces around the log block by #4 and gets out on the perimeter.

Fullback

Technique: Same as 21 Iowa.
Coaching Points: Same as 22 Iowa.

Right Halfback

Technique: Same as 21 Iowa.
Coaching Points: Same as 22 Iowa.

Rip Flex 24 Trap

The next play to the tight-end/wingback side is the traditional trap play. The formation is Rip flex, and the play is 24 trap (Figures 3-28 and 3-29). To the left, the play is Liz flex 24 trap, and the blocking assignments are reversed. The trap is another traditional wing-T play that has retained its effectiveness over the years. It is a part of nearly every contemporary offensive system, on both the college and high school levels. Again, the old adage, "If it ain't broke, don't fix it" applies to the trap play. However, no discussion of the wing-T would be complete without mention of this hallmark play. The same counter plays—26 counter trap and 26 counter sting—can be run to the wingback/tight-end side of the formation, and those plays are novel ideas. The 24 wham trap can only be run to the flexed-end side with a halfback in his deep position.

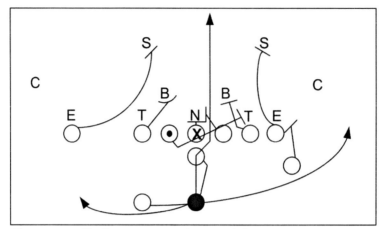

Figure 3-28. Rip flex 24 trap against 52 defense

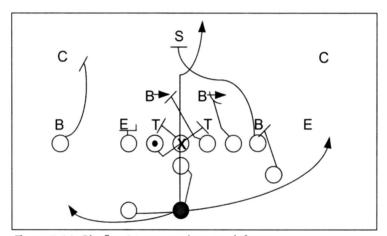

Figure 3-29. Rip flex 24 trap against 44 defense

BLOCKING RULES, TECHNIQUES, AND COACHING POINTS FOR RIP FLEX 24 TRAP

2-Man

Rule: Releases. Blocks the deep-third or deep-half defender to his side.
Coaching Points: He breaks down and uses the stalk block on the safety or deep-half defender. He keeps contact until the whistle blows.

3-Man

Rule: Blocks the first backer on or inside.
Coaching Points: Against a wide-tackle 6, he blocks across the hole to the backside backer. He makes an inside release and gets his body between the backer and the fullback. He uses a high-pressure control block to wall off the backer.

4-Man

Rule: Leads to the center's post, cracks back or influences, and blocks out.
Coaching Points: Against all even fronts, if the alignment of the hard-man on he prevents he from blocking the middle/inside backer, drop step and block the first man to his outside.

5-Man

Rule: Posts the man on or blocks back.
Coaching Points: When he blocks back, he uses all the fundamentals of a sound drive block to complete his assignment. Above all, he keeps his feet moving and gets them out of the hole, and out of the fullback's way.

6-Man

Rule: Pulls and traps the first defender past #5.
Coaching Points: He bears into the line of scrimmage as he approaches the trap area. He assumes the 5 technique will close down, and he will have to dig him out. He gets his head inside the defender and uses his right shoulder to complete the block.

7-Man

Rule: Walls off the backside backer. Fills against an Eagle look.
Coaching Points: Against an Eagle front, he gets his head in front of the 3 technique as he executes a fill technique. He will end up on all fours in a scramble block. He gets his head and left arm across the inside leg of the 3 technique and works to move his shoulders from a 45- to a 90-degree angle to the line of scrimmage.

8-Man

Rule: Retains and releases. Against a backer, retains block. Against a hard man, releases.
Coaching Points: If flexed position, he blocks the deep defender to his side—the corner against a three-deep, and a safety man against a two-deep. If tight position, he walls off the backer in a 44 or Eagle defense, and fills against a 52 defense—gets his head between the 5 technique and the fullback.

Quarterback

Technique: Same footwork as 21 wham. Gives the ball to the fullback, and fakes the bootleg at the 9 hole.
Coaching Points: He makes sure his right hand is to the rear tip of the ball as he makes his handoff to the fullback. After the handoff, he brings both hands to his belt and makes an open-hand fake to the left halfback with his left hand. He puts both hands to his left hip and makes a great bootleg fake at the 9 hole.

Left Halfback

Technique: Fakes 21 wham.
Coaching Points: After the fake from the quarterback, he puts both hands to his outside hip, bends at the waist, dips his left shoulder, and carries out his fake all the way to the perimeter.

Fullback

Technique: Aims for the left leg of #5. Receives handoff from the quarterback and adjusts course according to defense spacing.
Coaching Points: He checks to see if #5 is covered or open. If covered, he runs up his tail and makes a chair move to the right (runs north and south). If #5 is open, he runs straight ahead and splits the backers. He keeps both arms around the ball until he passes the line of scrimmage.

Right Halfback

Technique: Same assignment as 21 sweep. Blocks down.
Coaching Points: When he is a wing to the tight-end side of the formation, he blocks down as he would on 22 cut or 21 bounce. If 24 trap is run to a flexed end, he fakes a wham block and continues across the line of scrimmage. He looks outside-in for a corner or a deep halfback to wall off. Against a 53 front, the stacked backer is considered to be the corner or force man. If the backer crosses his path as the right halfback crosses the line of scrimmage, he blocks the backer.

Rip 28 Counter

The final two plays in the 20 series can be traced back to the late 1940s. The formation for these two plays is the same formation used 50 years ago: two tight ends and a wing. The first play is Rip 28 counter (Figures 3-30 and 3-31), a wingback counter play off 20-series action. It is illustrated as it was run in the 1940s. To the left, the play is Liz 22 counter, and the blocking assignments are reversed.

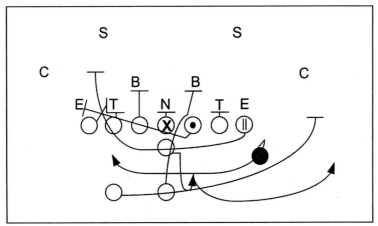

Figure 3-30. Rip 28 counter against 52 defense

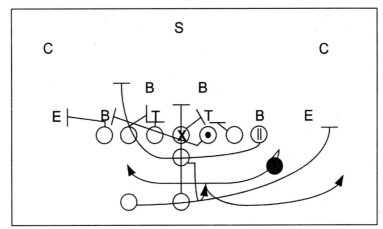

Figure 3-31. Rip 28 counter against 44 defense

BLOCKING RULES, TECHNIQUES, AND COACHING POINTS FOR RIP 28 COUNTER

2-Man

Rule: Pulls flat and leads up the hole.
Coaching Points: He pulls flat down the line and turns up the hole, hugging the double-team block. Against seven-man fronts, he looks outside for a defender to block. Against eight-man fronts, he looks inside for a defender to block.

3-Man

Rule: Blocks a hard man on. If open, stabs the hard man inside him and hinges.
Coaching Points: If open, he takes a slide step with his left foot and gets his left

shoulder into the outside number of the hard man inside of him. He should make sure the 5-man can block him before he hinges. Against an Eagle front, he uses a fill technique to block the hard man to his inside.

4-Man

Rule: Pulls flat and traps the first man past #7.
Coaching Points: He pulls flat across #5, and then takes as much of the line of scrimmage as his offensive line will allow. He bears in off the double-team block and gets inside-out position on the man he is trapping. He hits on the rise with his left shoulder, keeps a wide base, keeps his feet moving, and blocks until the whistle blows.

5-Man

Rule: Blocks the hard man on him. If open, he blocks back to his right.
Coaching Points: When blocking a hard man on him, he should give the man a chance to react to the flow of the play, and then wall him off by positioning himself between the defender and the ballcarrier. When blocking back on a hard man, he must prevent him from penetrating the line of scrimmage.

6-Man

Rule: Retains a hard man on him, blocks area, or posts if the frontside tackle is open.
Coaching Points: When #7 is open, he becomes the post man.

7-Man

Rule: Posts a hard man on him or leads to the 6-man's post.
Coaching Points: He posts a hard man on him, or leads to the 6-man's post if he is open.

8-Man

Rule: Leads to the 7-man's post or influences and blocks out.
Coaching Points: When he blocks out, he uses a high-pressure control block and a wall-off technique. He maintains contact until the whistle blows.

Quarterback

Technique: Opens back to the hole. Makes an inside handoff to the wingback, and fakes a bootleg at one.
Coaching Points: He reverses out back to the hole. He seats the ball and takes his first step with his left foot over the midline. No fake is made to the fullback. His second

step is with his right foot, across and parallel to the midline. With the ball still seated, he maneuvers his hands so that his left hand is at the back tip of the ball. On his third step, he step toward the wingback with his left foot and gives him a one-handed handoff with his left hand. Then, he brings both hands to the front of his right hip, bends at the waist, lowers his left shoulder, and fakes a bootleg with speed at the 1 hole.

Left Halfback

Technique: Fakes 21 sweep and seals the last defender on the line of scrimmage.
Coaching Points: After a proximity fake of 21, he turns toward the line of scrimmage and aggressively attacks the last defender on the line. He drives his left shoulder into the defender's left thigh pad and attempts to knock him down. He should not hesitate in his approach. His block should be made on, or as close as possible to, the line of scrimmage.

Fullback

Technique: Fills over #4.
Coaching Points: He checks to see if a hard man is on #5. If so, he aims for the tail of #5. He gets within a few feet of him before veering his course to the right over the 4-man. If the center is open, he aims for his left foot and seals the frontside A gap.

Wingback

Technique: Open-steps and takes the inside handoff from the quarterback. Follows #2 through the hole.
Coaching Points: He pivots on his right foot and drop-steps with his left foot so his shoulders are at a right angle to the line of scrimmage. He runs a course toward the quarterback that will allow him to cross in front of the quarterback as the quarterback turns in his direction. He uses controlled speed as he receives the handoff and begins to curve his course so he that can hit as square as possible off the double-team block.

Rip 28 counter is a good play against an overhang front like the 44, and it could be a good play against 7-man fronts as well. A problem with 7-man fronts occurs when the defender playing over #8 closes down and stymies the pulling guard. This situation creates a logjam and denies the pulling 2-man access through the 8 hole. The force man can use this tactic because no outside threat occurs with the quarterback bootlegging to the same side as the counter—the quarterback is moving away from the play. The 40 series counter crisscross presents the contain man with a more complicated problem.

Here, the quarterback is faking a bootleg in the same direction as the counter play, and the force man is confronted with an inside and outside threat. The merits of the counter crisscross will be illustrated and discussed in Chapter 4. Therefore, a sound coaching strategy regarding 28 counter against 7-man fronts is to add the word "bounce" to the play when it is warranted. In other words, if the contain man is stuffing 28 counter, run Rip 28 counter bounce (Figure 3-32). To the left, the play is Liz 22 counter bounce, and the blocking assignments are reversed.

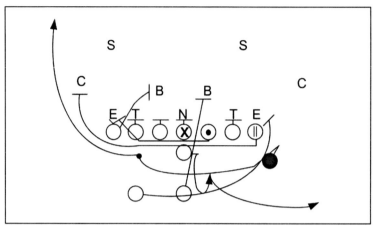

Figure 3-32. Rip 28 counter bounce against 52 defense

Everyone would have the exact same assignments as they do on 28 counter, with the exception of the pulling guard, the pulling end, and the ballcarrier. It is much easier to bounce the counter outside when it is a predetermined play. Even if the contain man is not closing, as long as he is not chasing as deep as the backs, the bounce play has a good chance of being successful. Consider calling 28 counter bounce against 7-man fronts and adjusting the play according to the play of the contain man. If he starts chasing as deep as the backs, change to 28 counter. 28 counter bounce adds to the offense a reverse play that hits outside the 2 and 8 holes—another innovation to the wing-T.

BLOCKING RULES, TECHNIQUES, AND COACHING POINTS FOR 28 COUNTER BOUNCE

2-Man

Rule: Same as 28 counter.
Coaching Points: He pulls flat and stays on that course until he passes the 5-man. Then, he begins to bow his course so he can get around the log block by #4. Once outside, he looks to log the corner to the inside of the field so the wingback can utilize the sideline.

3-Man

Rule: Same as 28 counter.
Coaching Points: Same as 28 counter.

4-Man

Rule: Same as 28 counter.
Coaching Points: He uses his usual pull-and-trap techniques. He should not tip off his intentions by not bearing into the line of scrimmage. At the very last moment, he puts his head to the outside and blocks with his right shoulder. He should not turn the defender too quickly. He may lose him to the inside if he does. He drives the defender a few steps and secures the block by keeping the defender between his feet. Then, he logs him to the inside. If the defender is really intent on bouncing the play by wrong-shouldering him, the defender will log himself.

5-Man

Rule: Same as 28 counter.
Coaching Points: Same as 28 counter.

6-Man

Rule: Same as 28 counter.
Coaching Points: Same as 28 counter.

7-Man

Rule: Same as 28 counter.
Coaching Points: Same as 28 counter.

8-Man

Rule: Same as 28 counter.
Coaching Points: Same as 28 counter.

Quarterback

Rule: Same as 28 counter.
Coaching Points: Same as 28 counter.

Left Halfback

Rule: Same as 28 counter.
Coaching Points: Same as 28 counter.

Fullback

Rule: Same as 28 counter.
Coaching Points: Same as 28 counter.

Right Halfback

Rule: Same as 28 counter.
Coaching Points: Same as 28 counter.

Wingback

Rule: Same as 28 counter.
Coaching Points: He runs his course just the same as he would on 28 counter. He can even dip toward the double-team before bouncing to the outside to set up the guard's load block. Once outside, he stays on the boundary and makes all defenders come to him.

Rip 28 Counter Bootleg

The companion play to Rip 28 counter is Rip 28 counter bootleg (Figures 3-33 and 3-34). To the left, the play is Liz 22 counter bootleg, and the blocking assignments are reversed. This misdirection and deceptive play-action pass play is a great play with "big play" potential. It begins with the threat of the counter and ends up with the quarterback on the perimeter with a pass/run option—a characteristic and great advantage of wing-T play-action passes.

BLOCKING RULES, TECHNIQUES, AND COACHING POINTS
FOR RIP 28 COUNTER BOOTLEG
(Note: All interior linemen block to the pass against all heavy fronts.)

2-Man

Rule: Inside releases and runs a deep flag route.
Coaching Points: Against a three-deep secondary, he runs a deep flag route. Against a three-deep secondary, he converts to a bench route. Against a two-deep, he converts to a bench route. Against man coverage, he uses a double move to get to the flag.

3-Man

Rule: Same as 28 counter.
Coaching Points: All interior linemen must be cautioned not to cross the line of scrimmage.

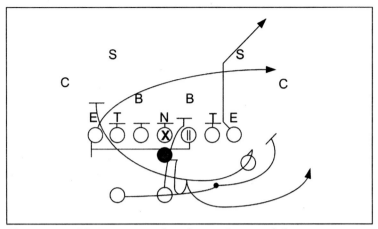

Figure 3-33. Rip 28 counter bootleg against 52 defense

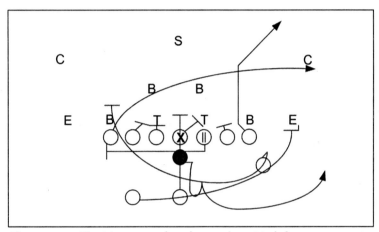

Figure 3-34. Rip 28 counter bootleg against 44 defense

4-Man

Rule: Same as 28 counter.
Coaching Points: All interior linemen must be cautioned not to cross the line of scrimmage.

5-Man

Rule: Same as 28 counter.
Coaching Points: All interior linemen must be cautioned not to cross the line of scrimmage.

6-Man

Rule: Same as 28 counter.
Coaching Points: All interior linemen must be cautioned not to cross the line of scrimmage.

7-Man

Rule: Same as 28 counter.
Coaching Points: All interior linemen must be cautioned not to cross the line of scrimmage.

8-Man

Rule: Inside releases and runs a crossing route.
Coaching Points: The depth of his crossing route will depend on what the secondary defender in the flat area is doing. His normal route is from seven to 12 yards deep. He should aim for a position that will put him behind a shallow flat defender, and in front of one that gets depth. If the flat defender is 12 yards deep, he should be six yards deep. If the flat defender is five to seven yards deep, he should be 12 yards deep.

Quarterback

Technique: Uses the same footwork and technique as he does on 28 counter, except he keeps the ball for a pass/run option.
Coaching Points: He starts his pivot as he does on 28 counter, except he moves the ball to the front of his right hip and holds it with his right hand. He fakes to the wingback with his left hand and allows it to swing back in the direction of the wingback. He bends at the waist, lowers his left shoulder, and shifts the ball from the front to the side of his right hip and sprints into his bootleg course. Immediately, he looks downfield to see if #2 is open on the flag route. If he is, he throws for the touchdown. If not, he looks for #8 on his crossing route. If no one is open, he exercises his run option and runs with the ball.

Left Halfback

Technique: Same as 28 counter.
Coaching Points: He has the key block on this play. As was mentioned in the 28 counter coaching points, he should not hesitate on making his block. It must be made on or as close to the line of scrimmage as possible. He puts the last man on the line of scrimmage down on the ground.

Fullback

Technique: Same as 28 counter.
Coaching Points: Same as 28 counter.

Wingback

Technique: Same as 28 counter, except he will not get the ball.
Coaching Points: Same as 28 counter. He will not get the ball. He carries out his fake and

runs through the line of scrimmage. Both 28 counter and 28 counter bootleg can also be run with the halfback in his halfback position. In this case, the halfback takes a crossover step with his left foot, followed by a lead step with his right foot. The halfback gains ground toward the line of scrimmage on both steps. When his right foots hits the ground, he breaks on it and leans his chest over his right thigh just long enough so the timing of the play is exactly the same as when he runs the play from the wingback position.

Rip Flex 23 Counter Trap

Before leaving the 20 series, the fullback trap play needs to be examined against two troublesome fronts: the 44 and the 53 stack. Both defenses have four players aligned inside the B gaps, and outnumber the offensive blockers by a 4-to-3 ratio. Running a 6- or 4-hole trap against these fronts is difficult at best. Also, the 4i alignment of the tackles in a 53 stack makes it difficult for the frontside tackle to get an inside release to block the middle backer. An innovative idea that will keep the trap play alive against these two fronts is to run it one hole wider, and with counter action. Rip flex 23 counter trap illustrates this point (Figures 3-35 and 3-36). To the left, the play is Liz flex 37 counter trap, and the blocking assignments are reversed. This play changes the frontside tackle's assignment from releasing inside to block the inside backer, to releasing outside to block the backer over the tight end. And, the counter action of the backs facilitates the block of the tight end on the inside backer.

BLOCKING RULES, TECHNIQUES, AND COACHING POINTS
FOR RIP FLEX 23 COUNTER TRAP

2-Man

Rule: Against a 44, cracks back on the frontside backer. Against a 53, cracks back on the middle backer.
Coaching Points: He may have to head fake or use a swim move to get inside to block the middle linebacker.

3-Man

Rule: Against 44, leads to the 4-man's post. Against 53, influences and blocks the backer on #2.
Coaching Points: Against a 44, he and #4 must get good movement on the 3 technique. He drives him inside on a course as parallel to the line of scrimmage as possible. Against a 53, he vertical releases through the frontside C gap and block the frontside backer.

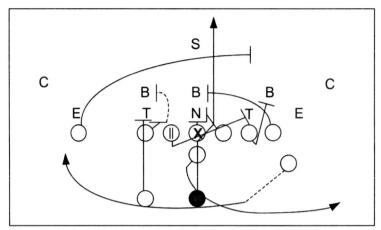

Figure 3-35. Rip flex 23 counter trap against 53 defense

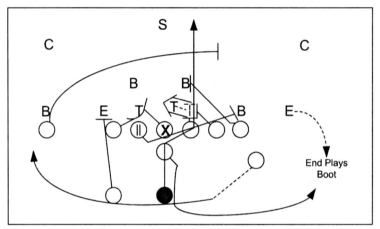

Figure 3-36. Rip flex 23 counter trap against 44 defense

4-Man

Rule: Against 44, posts the 3 technique. Against 53, leads to the 5-man's post.
Coaching Points: Against the 3 technique, he swings his body after posting and drives the defender down the line of scrimmage.

5-Man

Rule: Against a 44, co-op blocks with #7 to account for the 3 technique and the backside backer. Against a 53, posts.
Coaching Points: Against a 44 stack, he starts the co-op block with #7, and when #7 has control of the 3 technique, he goes up to the second level and blocks the backside backer.

6-Man

Rule: Against a 44, pulls and traps the first man past #4. Against a 53, pulls and traps the first man past #4.
Coaching Points: He bears in on his trap course. He anticipates the defender reacting to the down block and closing down.

7-Man

Rule: Against a 44, co-op blocks with #5 to account for the 3 technique and the backside backer. Against a 53, releases through the B gap to cut off the backside backer.
Coaching Points: Against a 44, he takes over the block of the 3 technique so #5 can get up on the backside backer. Against a 53, he makes a vertical release and walls off the backer.

8-Man

Rule: Against a 44, releases crossfield. Against a 53, releases crossfield.
Coaching Points: He crosses the hole no deeper than five yards from the line of scrimmage, and blocks any defender who crosses his path.

Quarterback

Technique: Same as 24 trap.
Coaching Points: Gives the fullback the midline. The fullback has to make a sharp cut against the 44, so he should try to get him the ball as deep in the backfield as possible.

Left Halfback

Technique: Same as 29 wham.
Coaching Points: He blocks as he would on 21 wham. He should be aggressive with the load block.

Fullback

Technique: Aims for the tail of #5. Veers outside the double-team block.
Coaching Points: Against a 44, he takes as much of the midline as the quarterback allows. He shifts the ball to the right arm as he executes a chair move over #4. He runs north and south after the chair move. Against a 53 stack, his course is for the tail of #5, and his chair move is not as extreme as it is against a 44 stack.

Right Halfback

Technique: Motions to the halfback spot and fakes 29 wham.
Coaching Points: He comes in motion and makes a good 29 wham fake.

4

The 30 Series

The 30 series (belly series) features a quick fullback slant play to either side of the formation. It is the base play in the series and sets up the companion run and pass plays in the 30 series. Besides 24 and 26 fullback trap, it hits faster than any other wing-T play. The play is blocked like the traditional belly, except for the wingback/halfback block; the back blocks the corner instead of the frontside backer. This little nuance sets up the pitch play off the belly action. Both plays look exactly the same to the defense. The play is called Rip 33 down, and it is illustrated in Figures 4-1 and 4-2. When run to the left, the play is Liz 37 down, and the blocking assignments are reversed. Rip 33 down is a basic gap read-up blocking scheme with the frontside guard pulling to kick out the first defender past #3. A unique aspect of Rip 33 down is that it can be mirrored to the tight-end side (Rip 37 down, shown in Figures 4-3 and 4-4)—another distinguishing characteristic from the traditional play.

BLOCKING RULES, TECHNIQUES, AND COACHING POINTS FOR RIP 33 DOWN

2-Man

Rule: Blocks down on the first defender inside him, on or off the line of scrimmage.

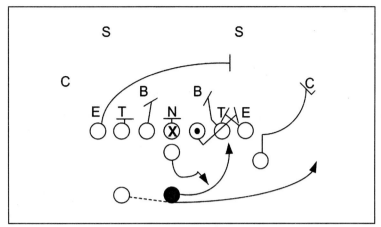

Figure 4-1. Rip 33 down against 52 defense

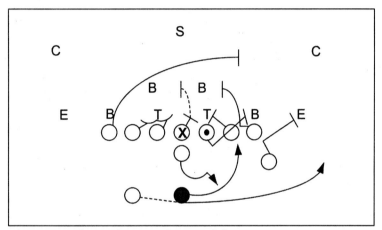

Figure 4-2. Rip 33 down against 44 defense

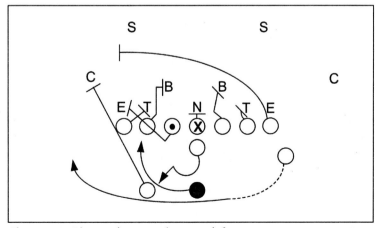

Figure 4-3. Rip 37 down against 52 defense

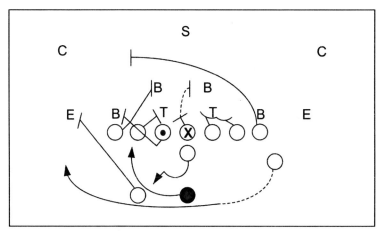

Figure 4-4. Rip 37 down against 44 defense

Against heavy fronts (53, 62, 65), blocks the backer over him.

Coaching Points: Against a hard man on #3, he takes a short, six-inch step with his left foot for the crotch of the defender and whips his arms to a cocked position. He should not rise up as he rotates his trunk on his hips; his chest should be on his left thigh. He aims for the near thigh pad of the defender, and drives his left shoulder into it. He brings up his left forearm on contact and begins to drive the defender down the line of scrimmage. He widens his base and keeps the defender between his feet. He rises up on the block to get his feet out of the hole. If the defender slants to the inside, he pushes off his left foot, goes up to the second level, and walls off any backer in pursuit.

Against a 44 front, he uses a rip technique to release inside a 6 or 6i technique, and aims for a point where he can seal the frontside backer to the inside. He blocks him above the waist with his left shoulder. He should not get knocked back into the hole. He keeps a wide base, hits on the rise, and keeps his feet moving.

3-Man

Rule: Blocks down on the first defender inside him, on or off the line of scrimmage. Against heavy fronts (53, 62, 65), blocks the hard man on him.

Coaching Points: Against a hard man on #4, he uses the same technique as described for #2 against a hard man on #3. Against a backer on #4, he makes a vertical release by taking a short lateral step with his inside foot and rips his right arm through the 5-technique defender. Then, he drives his right foot upfield on a 90-degree angle to the line of scrimmage. He should try to be outside the backer when he arrives at his level. He uses his left shoulder, and blocks above the waist. If he cannot wall off the backer, he keeps contact with him and takes him by the hole. The important thing is to keep contact so the fullback can run off his block. If the 5-technique player crosses his face, he washes him down the line of scrimmage. His job is to protect the frontside B gap.

4-Man

Rule: Pulls and kicks out first defender past #3 on the line of scrimmage.

Coaching Points: He pivots on his left foot and take a drop-step with his right foot. As he does so, he whips his arms, rotates his trunk on his hips, and gets his chest on his right thigh. Both feet should be on a 45-degree angle to the line of scrimmage. He pushes off his right foot, and bears into the line of scrimmage close to the tail of #3. He works inside-out to trap the first defender past #3. He blocks with his right shoulder and gets his head between the defender and the fullback. He bends his knees before contact, widens his base, and hits on the rise. He rolls his hips on contact and arches his back. He straddles the defender between his feet and keeps driving until the whistle blows.

5-Man

Rule: Blocks man on or over, stepping through the frontside gap. Scoops a 53 stack with the 6-man. Against heavy fronts (62, 65) reaches the hard man on #4.

Coaching Points: Against a nose man, he takes a short, six-inch step with his right foot and strikes the frontside number of the nose man with the palms of his hands. He works to position himself between the fullback and the nose man. Against a bandit or chase front, he and #6 must zone block to secure both A gaps. He punches the frontside number of the nose man with palm of his left hand. He steps through the frontside A gap and blocks any threat to that gap. It could be the strong safety in the chase position, or the middle backer in a 53 front. If the nose crosses his face, he blocks him; if not, he continues up to the backer level and blocks the chase man or the 53 middle backer. He uses his hands to wall them off.

6-Man

Rule: Blocks man on or over, stepping through the frontside gap. Scoops a 53 stack with the 5-man.

Coaching Points: Against a hard man, he steps with his right foot for the frontside number of the defender and blocks him with his hands. If the defender slants inside, he hustles down the line and gets his head in front of the defender to cut him off. If necessary, he goes to an all-fours posture to get his head and inside arm past the defender's far knee. He scramble blocks the defender to keep him from reaching the fullback. Against a backer, he aims for a spot where the backer will be when he reaches the backer level. He uses his hands to wall him off. He stays on his feet, and keeps contact until the whistle blows. Against a chase or bandit front zone, he blocks with #5 to secure both A gaps. He starts a co-op block with #5 by stepping with his right foot for the backside number of the nose man. He gains control of the nose so #5 can go up on the backer. If the nose slants to the frontside, #5 will block him and he continues up to backer level and blocks the chase man or the middle backer.

7-Man

Rule: Blocks man on or over, stepping through the frontside gap. He is responsible for the backside B gap. Against heavy fronts (53, 62, 65), he vertical releases and walls off backside backer.

Coaching Points: Against a hard man or a backer, he uses the same techniques as described for the 6-man. He should treat a 44 look as he would a stack. He uses a co-op block with #6 to account for the 3 technique and the backer. He will need to take over the 3 technique if the stacked backer blitzes the backside A gap.

8-Man

Rule: Inside releases and blocks across the hole.

Coaching Points: He should not be any deeper than five yards as he crosses the formation. When he passes the middle of the formation, he blocks the first defender that crosses his face. He gets his head in front of the defender, and he does not clip.

Quarterback

Technique: Reverse pivots with his back to the hole. Gives the ball to the fullback on his second step, and fakes a pitch to the left halfback.

Coaching Points: He seats the ball and reverse pivots with his back to the hole. He crosses the midline on his first two steps, and places both hands to the rear tip of the ball to facilitate a two-handed handoff to the fullback. He reaches back and fully extends his arms as he meshes with the fullback. His left foot will slide toward his right foot as he reaches for the fullback. Both feet should be parallel to the line of scrimmage and about 18 inches apart. He arm-rides the fullback to the midline of his body, gives him the ball, and retracts both hands to chest level. He should not step toward the line of scrimmage with his left foot as he rides the fullback—the ride is with the arms only. This action will keep him a couple of yards off the line of scrimmage and facilitate the companion play to 33 down. After the handoff, he steps with his right foot toward the left halfback and fake a pitch to him.

Left Halfback

Technique: Starts motion that will enable him to be slightly behind and one yard away from the fullback when the ball is snapped. Fakes a 31 pitch.

Coaching Points: He motions to the position mentioned in the blocking rules and gets into a pitch relationship with the quarterback. The pitch relationship is four yards to the side and two yards in front of the quarterback.

Fullback

Technique: Steps with his right foot and aims for the outside foot of #3. After he receives the ball, he squares his shoulders to the goal line and runs to daylight.

Coaching Points: He steps with his right foot and runs a slant course for the outside foot of #3. He receives ball from the quarterback with his inside arm up and begin to work his shoulders parallel to the line. He moves ball into his right arm and crosses the line going north and south. He runs to daylight.

Right Halfback

Technique: For wingback alignment, blocks first defender outside #2, on or off the line of scrimmage.

Coaching Points: As a wing, he steps with his left foot to the defender on #2 to influence the defender. He can punch his outside shoulder with the palm of his left hand to alert him to a possible down block. This action will facilitate the kickout block by #4. Then, he pushes off his left foot and sprints downfield to block the corner to his side of the field. He gets inside-out position on the corner. (Note: against a 44 front, the force man will be on the line of scrimmage.) From a halfback alignment, he aims for a spot one yard outside of the last man on the line of scrimmage. He runs a straight line to that reference point until he gets to the line of scrimmage. At the line, he veers off into the flat area and blocks the frontside corner or deep-third defender.

Rip 31 Down Pitch

The first companion play to 33 down is Rip 31 down. It is illustrated in Figures 4-5 and 4-6. To the left, the play is Liz 39 down, and the blocking assignments are reversed. 31 down can also be run to both sides of the formation without any changes in blocking assignments. Rip 39 down is illustrated in Figures 4-7 and 4-8.

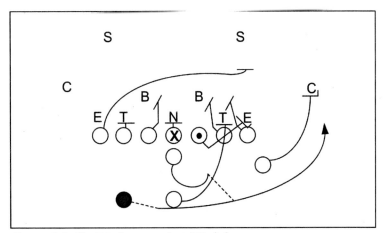

Figure 4-5. Rip 31 down against 52 defense

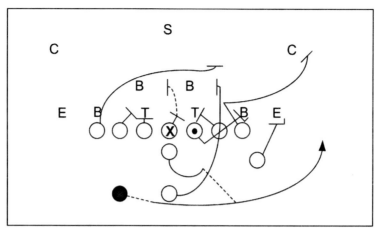

Figure 4-6. Rip 31 down against 44 defense

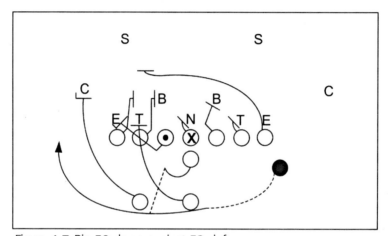

Figure 4-7. Rip 39 down against 52 defense

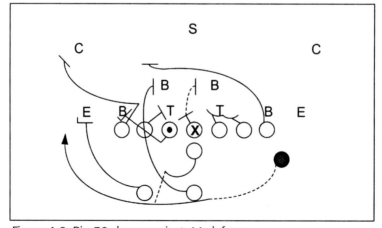

Figure 4-8. Rip 39 down against 44 defense

31 down is a predetermined pitch play to the left halfback. It starts out looking just like 33 down. The play is designed to get the ball outside, and it is used in lieu of an option play. As with 33 down, 31 down can be run to a wingback/tight-end side, or back to a single tight end. Blocking assignments remain the same. Some wing-T teams use the option play off the belly series to get the ball outside. Option plays are best executed from open formations, and they are more compatible with finesse-type offenses. The many nuances of option football demand a serious commitment of time. It would behoove the wing-T coach to spend valuable practice time working to perfect play-action passes rather than on perfecting the option play. However, it is necessary to have a running play off the belly to get the ball outside: 31 down is one of the answers.

BLOCKING RULES, TECHNIQUES, AND COACHING POINTS FOR RIP 31 DOWN PITCH

2-Man

Rule: Blocks the first backer on or to his inside.
Coaching Points: He uses a high-shoulder block to block the backer. (Note: Against a 44 front, he releases outside of the man on him and blocks the frontside deep-third defender. He and the wingback/halfback switch assignments.

3-Man

Rule: Blocks the first man inside on or off the line of scrimmage.
Coaching Points: Same techniques as 33 down.

4-Man

Rule: Pulls and logs the first man past #3 on the line of scrimmage.
Coaching Points: He approaches his target on the same course that he would if he were going to kick the target out with his right shoulder. He should not reveal his intentions by bowing his course. The only difference between trapping and logging is that he will use his left shoulder when he logs the defender. He should not try to turn his target immediately. He drives a few steps before he wheels him to the inside.

5-Man

Rule: Blocks man on or over, stepping through the frontside gap. Scoops a 53 stack with the 6-man. Against heavy fronts (62, 65), reaches the hard man on #4.
Coaching Points: Against a 53 stack, he steps with his right foot into the frontside A gap as he punches the nose man's frontside number with the palm of his left hand. Doing so will give the 6-man a chance to fit into the nose man. He tries to get up on the middle backer. If the nose crosses his face, he locks on the nose and keeps his

body between the nose and the left halfback. Against a 2 or 2i technique, he aims his helmet for a spot outside of the defender's far knee. From an all-fours position, he begins to scramble block the defender, taking him off the line of scrimmage on a 45-degree angle. He tries to work his head and shoulders parallel to the goal line.

6-Man

Rule: Blocks man on or over, stepping through the frontside gap. Scoops a 53 stack with the 5-man.
Coaching Points: Against a 53 stack, he replaces the 5-man's left foot with his right foot and punches into the backside number of the nose man. If the nose man slants to him, or plays into the 5-man, he takes over the block on the nose man. If the nose slants away from him, he goes up and blocks the middle backer.

7-Man

Rule: Blocks man on or over, stepping through the frontside gap. Against heavy fronts (53, 62, 65), vertical releases and walls off backside backer.
Coaching Points: Against heavy fronts (53, 62, 65), he uses a vertical release and walls off the backside backer. He steps into the backside B gap, and gets an inside-out position on the backside backer. He uses a high-pressure block to wall him off.

8-Man

Rule: Releases crossfield.
Coaching Points: He should not be any deeper than five yards as he crosses the formation. He blocks the first defender to cross his face after passing the middle of the formation.

Quarterback

Technique: Same as 33 G, except pulls ball from the fullback and pitches to the left halfback.
Coaching Points: Everything is the same as 33 down. He makes his reverse pivot, reaches the ball to the fullback, makes a quick arm-ride, and retracts the ball to his chest. He steps with his right foot to the left halfback and pitches him the ball. The pitch is a soft, basketball-type pitch.

Left Halfback

Technique: Acts as the ballcarrier. Same footwork as 33 G, except the quarterback will pitch the ball to him.
Coaching Points: He runs at controlled speed and gets into pitch phase with the quarterback. Pitch phase is four yards away from and two yards outside of the

quarterback when he pitches him the ball. He begins to bow his course as he gets to the fullback position. He looks the pitch into his hands. He should not let the ball get to his body; rather, he catches it with his hands going toward the line of scrimmage. After the catch, he secures the ball in his right arm and tries to get outside the block of the right halfback. He keeps the ball on the perimeter as he circles the defense.

Fullback

Technique: Fakes over the tail of #3 and blocks any defender in the area. Uses a load block. *Coaching Points:* He should not slow down to make a fake; the fake is a proximity fake. His job is to get to the line of scrimmage as quickly as possible and to drive his left shoulder pad into the outside thigh pad of the first defender to cross his path.

Right Halfback

Technique: Same as 33 G.
Coaching Points: From the wing or his halfback position, he gets outside-in position on the first defender outside of #2. He uses a high-pressure control block and does not get overextended. He keeps his feet moving and blocks until the whistle blows. Against a 44 defense, the corner will line up on the line of scrimmage, and he and the tight end will switch assignments. He blocks the end man on the line, and the tight end releases for the frontside third defender. If he cannot hook the defender, he keeps contact with the defender through the duration of the play, and lets the running back run off his block.

Rip Flex 33 Down Keep

The second way to get the ball outside using the 30 series is with the keep pass. Rip 33 down keep is illustrated in Figures 4-9 and 4-10. To the left, the play is Liz 37 down keep, and the blocking assignments are reversed. Rip 33 down keep is the traditional way to run the keep pass. It is a vertical stretch pattern with the wingback in the flat, the tight end to the flag, and the backside end on a crossing route. The halfback in the flat comes open quickly, and the quarterback must be ready to deliver the ball on his fifth or sixth step. The crossing and flag routes take a little more time to come open. The tight end usually is covered against a three-deep secondary. He does come open when the three-deep levels the corner into the flat and rolls the safety over the top. This situation amounts to a two-deep look, and the tight end will convert his flag route to a bench route.

BLOCKING RULES, TECHNIQUES, AND COACHING POINTS
FOR RIP FLEX 33 DOWN KEEP

2-Man

Rule: Makes an inside release and starts on a flag route. Reads the safety for an

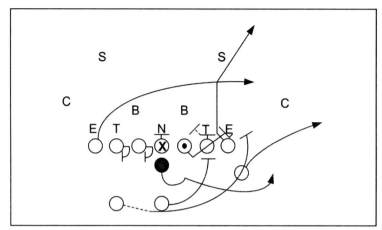

Figure 4-9. Rip 33 down keep against 52 defense

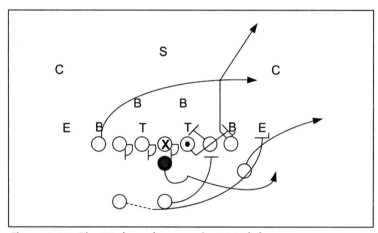

Figure 4-10. Rip 33 down keep against 44 defense

adjustment in his route. On a wheel call, runs a 12- to 15-yard out route.

Coaching Points: As he drives downfield, he reads the reaction of the secondary. If it is a three-deep look, he runs his flag route. If he sees a level technique (i.e., the corner levels and the safety takes him), he converts his route into a bench and runs away from the safety. He should be 18 to 20 yards deep on the sideline. Against man cover, he makes a double-flag move. Against a two-deep, he reverts to the bench route. On a wheel call, he runs a 12- to 15-yard out.

3-Man

Rule: Same as 32 down, but does not cross the line of scrimmage. Protects the B gap.
Coaching Points: If # 4 is open, he slams the hard man on him before he slides down to the frontside B gap. He keeps his shoulders square to the line. He is responsible for any defender entering the frontside B gap. He should not cross the line of scrimmage.

4-Man

Rule: Same as 32 down, but logs the first defender past #3.
Coaching Points: He uses the same approach as he does on 32 belly. He should not bow his path. He strikes the first defender past #3 with his inside shoulder and gets his head outside of the defender. He should not attempt to turn the defender immediately. He drives a few steps and then tries to wheel him to the inside. Against a 44 front, the first man past #3 is a backer. If the backer gets off into pass coverage, the 4-man continues for the last man on the line, who is the defensive end (the left halfback is also blocking this man). If the backer remains on the line of scrimmage, the 4-man blocks him.

5-Man

Rule: Steps to the frontside gap and hinges.
Coaching Points: Against a nose man, he takes a flat six-inch step with his right foot into the frontside A gap. He punches into the frontside number of the nose man and keeps his body between the nose and the quarterback. He should not allow the nose to beat him inside. If the nose slants away, he hinges and protects the frontside A gap. He should block any defender who enters it. If he has no one to block, he gets depth and blocks the widest rusher from the backside.

6-Man

Rule: Steps to the frontside gap and hinges.
Coaching Points: Against a hard man, he uses the same technique as #5. He is responsible for the backside A gap. He should not allow any defender to beat him through that gap. If he is open, he takes a six-inch lateral step with his right foot and hinges. He blocks any defender threatening the backside A gap. If he has no one to block, he comes out the back door and blocks the widest backside rusher. Against a 44 defense, he co-op blocks with #7 to account for the hard man on him and the stacked backer.

7-Man

Rule: Steps to the frontside gap and hinges.
Coaching Points: Against a hard man, he uses the same technique as the 5- and 6-men. Against a 44 front, he co-op blocks with #6; he and #6 are responsible for the two-man stack on #6. Against a bandit or 62 look, he takes a short, six-inch slide step with his right foot into the backside B gap. If the backer blitzes, he blocks him. If not, he hinges and blocks the first man to his outside.

8-Man

Rule: Inside releases and runs a crossing route. On a wheel call, runs a four- to five-yard drag route.

Coaching Points: He inside releases and runs a crossing route that will put him halfway between #2 and the fullback. He should be alert and adjust his depth if #2 changes his route from a flag to a bench. On a wheel call, he runs a four- to five-yard crossing route.

Quarterback

Technique: His first two steps are like 33 down. He does not arm-ride on the keep pass. The fake is a flash fake with his left hand, and he does not slow down; his objective is to get to the flat quickly enough to deliver the ball on his fifth or sixth step. *Coaching Points:* He reverse pivots and breaks the midline with his first two steps as he does on 33 down. He moves the ball to the front of his right hip and holds it with the fingers of his right hand on the laces. He stays low as he pivots to conceal the ball, and he heads towards his reference point—the spot where the right halfback would normally line up. This spot is where the he would run through on a rollout pass. He should think of the keep pass as a rollout pass—one continuous movement to the flank without delay. As the fullback passes in front of him, he extends his left hand and simulates a flash fake to him. He does not mesh with or ride the fullback. Breaking contain on the keep pass is paramount, and a prolonged fake would militate against it. The wingback gets into the flat so quickly that the quarterback would never be able to deliver the ball on time if he made a ride fake to the fullback. The quarterback should sprint through his reference point, gaining a depth of five to six yards off the line of scrimmage. Then, he begins to bow his course into the line of scrimmage, and runs with his chest moving towards the intended receiver. If he is running at a receiver, he will be able to pass with equal facility, sprinting to his left or right. This pass is always thrown on the run. Although the crossing and flat routes are most likely to be open, his read is: deep, crossing, flat, run.

Left Halfback

Technique: Same as 33 down. Arcs his course as he passes the fullback and blocks the last man on the line of scrimmage.
Coaching Points: Same motion spot as 33 down. He sprints behind the fullback's spot and runs an arc course into the line of scrimmage. His shoulders should be parallel to the line, and he should load the last man on the line of scrimmage. He drives his inside shoulder pad into the outside thigh pad of the last man. He should not hesitate if the defender is passive. This block must be aggressive and made at the line of scrimmage.

Fullback

Technique: Sprints for the outside leg of #3 and blocks the defender in that area
Coaching Points: He dives for the outside leg of #3 and load blocks any defender in the area. He should not bow his course and should not hesitate. His assignment is a full sprint to his reference point. He should not be concerned about making a fake; the

quarterback will simulate a handoff to him. He concentrates on getting to his reference point as quickly as possible, and making his block.

Right Halfback

Technique: On a wingback alignment, takes a short jab step at the defender over #2 and runs his four- to five-yard flat route. On a wingback wheel call, releases immediately into the flat area. Gains five to seven yards of width, turns upfield, and takes off. Looks for the ball over his inside shoulder if the quarterback releases it inside of his position.
Coaching Points: He runs a four- to five-yard flat route. He gains width quickly and anticipates a quick pass. On a wheel call, he will switch routes with #2. He turns his flat route into a wheel route, and #2 runs a 12- to 15-yard out route. On the wheel route, after he gains five to seven yards of width, he turns upfield and sprints for the goal line.

Good backers who quickly recognize the keep pass can run under the crossing end. In a three-deep, the safety is also is in good position to run with the crossing receiver. Thus, this route is covered underneath by the backer and over the top by the safety man. Thus, an adjustment in the conventional route is warranted. This can be achieved by switching the routes of the three receivers. The wingback changes from a flat to a wheel route, the tight end changes from a flag to a 12- to 15-yard out route, and the backside end changes from a crossing to a drag route. The play is called Rip 33 down keep wingback wheel, and it is illustrated in Figures 4-11 and 4-12. To the left, the call is Liz 37 down keep wingback wheel, and the blocking assignments are reversed. (Note: All interior linemen block to the pass against all heavy fronts.)

The blocking assignments and techniques on this play are exactly the same as 33 down keep. The only changes are with the routes of the three receivers. The quarterback read is still the same: he looks deep for the wingback, then for the deep out, and finally to the shallow drag route. His last choice is to run with the ball.

Liz 33 H

The next two belly plays are run exclusively to the tight-end side and are innovative ideas. They feature a strong off-tackle play, and also have the ability to threaten the perimeter. The first one is the base play, Liz 33 H, and it is illustrated in Figures 4-13 and 4-14. To the left, the play is Rip 37 H, and the blocking assignments are reversed.

The letter H is used because the halfback will either kick out at the hole, or lead through the hole. The defensive spacing dictates the blocking scheme to be used, and the quarterback calls the play at the line of scrimmage. If the defense had a 5-technique player, the double-team scheme would be used; if no 5-technique player is

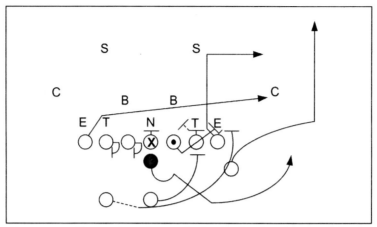

Figure 4-11. Rip 33 down keep wingback wheel against 52 defense

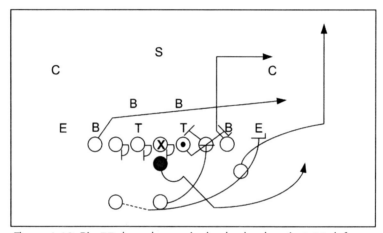

Figure 4-12. Rip 33 down keep wingback wheel against 44 defense

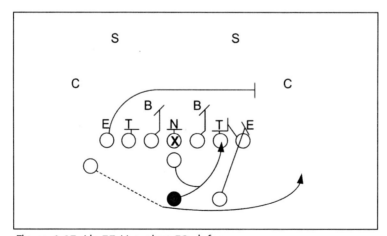

Figure 4-13. Liz 33 H against 52 defense

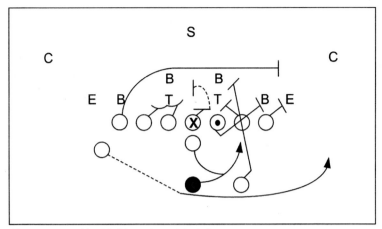

Figure 4-14. Liz 33 H against 44 defense

employed, the cross-block scheme would be used. This concept is consistent with the basic wing-T objective of getting either a double-team or an angle block at the point of attack. The quarterback's huddle call is 33 H or X at the line. If a 5-technique player is to the frontside, the quarterback says 233 H, and 33 H is run on two. If no 5-technique player is present, he calls 233 X, and 33 X is run on two. Remember, all audible calls are run on the second "go."

BLOCKING RULES, TECHNIQUES, AND COACHING POINTS FOR LIZ 33 H

2-Man

Rule: If #3 is covered by a hard man, leads to his post. If #3 is open, makes an arc release and blocks the frontside corner.
Coaching Points: If #3 is covered by a hard man, he uses the double-team techniques already explained. If #3 is open, he arcs on the corner and gets inside-out position. The arc is a bowed path that will place him inside the corner. He uses a wall-off block to keep the corner from the fullback. (Note: Against a 44 front, he turns out on the man to his outside.)

3-Man

Rule: If covered by a hard man, posts. If open, blocks down on the hard man on #4.
Coaching Points: If covered by a hard man, he uses the 20-series post techniques explained in Chapter 3. If open, he uses down-block techniques already explained in the coaching points for 33 down.

4-Man

Rule: If #3 is covered by a hard man, blocks the man on or over him. If #3 is open, pulls and traps the first defender past #3.
Coaching Points: When trapping, he uses the drop-step technique already explained in the coaching points for 33 down.

5-Man

Rule: Blocks man on or over, stepping through the frontside gap. Scoops a 53 stack with the 6-man. Against heavy fronts (62, 65, goal line), reaches the hard man on #4.
Coaching Points: Against a 53 stack and heavy looks, he uses the heavy blocking scheme and techniques already explained in the coaching points for 33 down.

6-Man

Rule: Blocks man on or over, stepping through the frontside gap. Scoops a 53 stack with the 5-man.
Coaching Points: Against a 53 stack, he uses techniques already explained in the coaching points for 33 down.

7-Man

Rule: Blocks man on or over, stepping through the frontside gap. Against heavy fronts (53, 62, 65, goal line), vertical releases.
Coaching Points: Against heavy fronts, he uses techniques already explained in the coaching points for 33 down.

8-Man

Rule: Releases crossfield.
Coaching Points: He uses the crossfield technique already explained in the coaching points for 33 down.

Quarterback

Technique: Same technique as 33 down. Gives the ball to the fullback.
Coaching Points: He uses the same technique already explained in the coaching points for 33 down.

Left Halfback

Technique: Same motion and technique as 33 down.

Coaching Points: He uses the same technique already explained in the coaching points for 33 down.

Fullback

Technique: Acts as the ballcarrier. Same technique as 33 down.
Coaching Points: He uses the same technique already explained in the coaching points for 33 down.

Right Halfback

Technique: If #3 is covered by a hard man, kicks out the first defender past #3. If #3 is open, leads for backer on or inside #3.
Coaching Points: He uses the same technique already explained in the coaching points for 33 down.

Liz 31 H

The companion play to Liz 33 H, Liz 31 H is a pitch play that gets the ball outside in a hurry. It is illustrated in Figures 4-15 and 4-16. To the left, the play is Rip 39 H, and the blocking assignments are reversed. If a 5 technique is aligned on the frontside tackle, the frontside guard pulls and leads the play outside. If the frontside tackle is open, the guard pulls and logs the first defender past the frontside tackle.

BLOCKING RULES, TECHNIQUES, AND COACHING POINTS FOR LIZ 31 H

2-Man

Rule: If #3 is covered by a hard man, he walls off the backer on or to his inside. If #3 is not covered by a hard man, he arc releases and blocks the frontside corner.
Coaching Points: His arc course should be wide enough to catch the corner inside the arc. He should not allow the corner to beat him to the inside. He uses a stalk-type block to engage the corner. (Note: Against a 44 front, he releases outside of the man on him and blocks the deep-third defender to his side.)

3-Man

Rule: Makes an inside release and blocks the first defender to his inside, on or off the line of scrimmage.
Coaching Points: He uses a vertical release when blocking backers and the same down-blocking techniques already explained in the coaching points for 33 down.

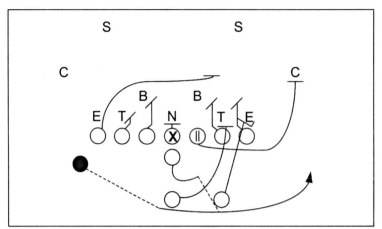

Figure 4-15. Liz 31 H against 52 defense

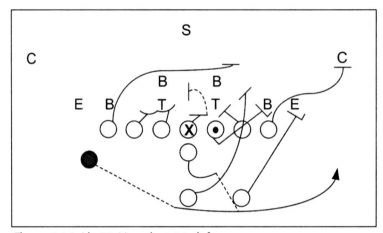

Figure 4-16. Liz 31 H against 44 defense

4-Man

Rule: If #3 is covered by a hard man, pulls and leads the pitch outside. If #3 is open, pulls and logs the first man past #3.

Coaching Points: When he pulls to lead the play, he pulls flat, close to the line of scrimmage, to prevent a collision with the fullback. He should not try to get depth until he passes #3. He gets outside position on the corner man, and he should be under control as he executes a high-pressure control block, making sure to hit up and not out on the corner. He should not be overextended.

5-Man

Rule: Blocks man on or over, stepping through the frontside gap. Scoops a 53 stack with #6. Against heavy fronts (62, 65, goal line), reaches the hard man on #4.

Coaching Points: He uses the reach and scoop techniques already explained against the heavy fronts in the coaching points on 33 down.

6-Man

Rule: Blocks man on or over, stepping through the frontside gap. Scoops a 53 stack with #5.
Coaching Points: He uses the same techniques against heavy fronts explained in the coaching points on 33 down.

7-Man

Rule: Blocks man on or over, stepping through the frontside gap. Against heavy fronts (53, 62, 65, goal line), vertical releases.
Coaching Points: He uses the same techniques against heavy fronts explained in the coaching points on 33 down.

8-Man

Rule: Releases crossfield.
Coaching Points: He uses the same techniques described in the coaching points for 33 down.

Quarterback

Technique: Same technique as 31 down.
Coaching Points: He uses the same techniques as described in the coaching points for 31 down.

Left Halfback

Technique: Same technique as 31 down.
Coaching Points: He uses the same techniques as described in the coaching points for 31 down.

Fullback

Technique: Same technique as 31 down.
Coaching Points: He uses the same techniques as described in the coaching points for 31 down.

Right Halfback

Technique: If #3 is covered by a hard man, he logs the first man past #3. If #3 is open, he leads through the hole—running over the tail of #3—and blocks the first frontside backer on or inside #3. The one exception to his rule is against a 44 defense; he blocks the last man on the line of scrimmage.

Coaching Points: He uses the same techniques as described in the coaching points for 33 H. When he is loading the man over #2, he runs the same course as he does when he kicks him out. He should not bow his course and tip off his intentions. Most of the time, the defender will close down and he will log himself. When leading over the tail of #3, he blocks the backer with his left shoulder.

Rip 36 Counter No Mo

The 30 series counter play was very effective in the past. However, over time, defensive recognition of counter action has diminished its big gain potential. Most wing-T teams run it with the ballcarrier in his halfback position, or motion him from a wing to the halfback position. Rip 36 counter no mo is a wingback counter play without wingback motion. It is illustrated in Figures 4-17 and 4-18. To the left, the play is Liz 34 counter no mo, and the blocking assignments are reversed.

When the counter is run from the wing without motion, the quarterback adds the words "no mo" to the play call. Running the counter from the wing without wingback motion is contrary to the traditional method of running it, and gives the counter a new look. The counter play has to be kept alive because it sets up a play-action pass play in this series that is still a big gainer for wing-T teams.

BLOCKING RULES, TECHNIQUES, AND COACHING POINTS FOR RIP 36 COUNTER NO MO

2-Man

Rule: Releases crossfield, makes an inside release, and blocks across the hole.

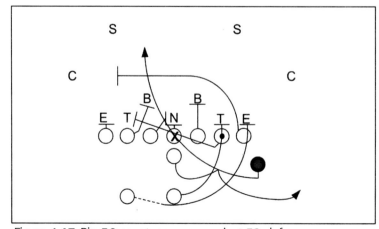

Figure 4-17. Rip 36 counter no mo against 52 defense

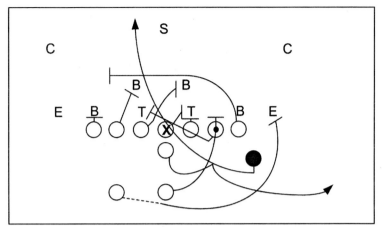

Figure 4-18. Rip 36 counter no mo against 44 defense

Coaching Points: He should not be any deeper than five to six yards from the line of scrimmage as he executes his crossfield assignment. He blocks the first defender across the hole in any direction. He blocks high and doesn't clip. He stays on the block until the whistle blows.

3-Man

Rule: Pulls and traps first defender past #5.
Coaching Points: He pivots on his right foot and takes a short six-inch 45-degree step with his left foot. His arms should be cocked, and his trunk should be over his right thigh. He stays low and approaches his target with his arms pumping and his feet apart. He bears into and takes as much of the line of scrimmage as he can. Just prior to contact, he bends his knees, keeps his head up, and explodes into the first defender to show past #5. He gets his head inside the defender, and blocks with his left shoulder.

4-Man

Rule: If #5 is open, posts the hard man on him. If not, he blocks the man on or over him. Against a 53 stack (bandit), blocks the middle backer.
Coaching Points: Against a 53 stack (bandit), he is assigned to the middle linebacker. The flow of the play should draw him across his face. He aims for a spot inside the backer's initial alignment and walls him off.

5-Man

Rule: If covered by a hard man, posts. If not, leads to #4's post.
Coaching Points: He follows his rule and uses the post and lead techniques already explained in the coaching points for 24/26 trap.

6-Man

Rule: If #5 is covered by a hard man, leads to his post. If not, he either cracks back on the middle or backside backer, or he influences and blocks out.
Coaching Points: If #5 is open, the alignment of the hard man on him will determine his assignment. If the hard man is in a 2 or 3 alignment, he releases inside to block the middle or backside backer. If the hard man is in a 2i alignment, he makes a switch call to #7 and influences and blocks out. If he doesn't feel he can get inside a 2 alignment, he makes the same switch call and blocks #7's man.

7-Man

Rule: Blocks the frontside backer on or to his inside.
Coaching Points: If #6 makes a switch call, he cracks the middle linebacker. Against a 53 stack or 62 tight, he makes a vertical release and blocks the frontside backer.

8-Man

Rule: Blocks the man on or over him.
Coaching Points: He has a key block on the counter play. He steps with his right foot for the inside number of the defender over him. He gets his head inside the defender, and works to position his body between the defender and the ballcarrier.

Quarterback

Technique: Reverse pivots, as on 32 belly. Makes proximity fake with fullback and gives an inside handoff to the right halfback. Fakes a keep at the 1 hole.
Coaching Points: As he begins his reverse pivot, he seats the ball and moves his left hand to the back tip of the ball. His first two steps are just like 32 belly. His third step is with his left foot, which is when he makes a one-handed inside handoff to the right halfback. After the handoff, he brings both hands to the outside hip and uses all the techniques already explained to execute a keep fake.

Left Halfback

Technique: Same assignment and technique as on 32 keep.
Coaching Points: He runs the same course as he does on 32 keep, and aggressively attacks the last man on the line of scrimmage with a load block. He drives his inside shoulder pad into the outside thigh pad of the last man.

Fullback

Technique: Dives for the inside leg of #3 and loads any defender in the area.

Coaching Points: His first step is with his right foot. His aim point is the inside leg of #3. He load blocks any defender in the area with his right shoulder.

Right Halfback

Technique: Receives an inside handoff from the quarterback and hits over #5 or #4. He can be in a wingback or halfback position on 36 counter. (See coaching points for backs for footwork from both alignments.)
Coaching Points: In a wingback alignment, he steps back off the line of scrimmage with his right foot, pivots on it, opens his hips, and runs an arc course to the hole. In a halfback alignment, he rocks his weight to his right foot and starts a course with his left foot that will allow him to hit over the left leg of #5 (or the left leg of #4). His aim point will depend upon who is the post man. If #5 is the post, he runs over #5's left leg; if #4 is the post, he runs over #4's left leg. He heads north and south as he crosses the line of scrimmage.

Liz 36 Counter FB @ 4

The second idea that will help to keep the counter play alive is to slip the ball to the fullback and fake the counter. The play is called Liz 36 counter FB @ 4. It is illustrated in Figures 4-19 and 4-20. To the left, the play is Rip 34 counter FB @ 6, and the blocking assignments are reversed. 36 counter FB @ 4 is a nuisance that will add another problem for teams that depend on play recognition to stifle the counter play. Slipping the ball to the fullback will slow down defensive reaction and increase the productivity of the counter play. On Liz 36 counter FB @ 4, the wing comes in motion as he does on 36 counter. For both plays, the counter and the FB @ 4 should look identical to the defense. Like the sting plays already mentioned, the fullback special is designed primarily against a 52 and 44 defensive front.

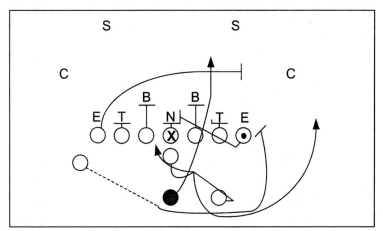

Figure 4-19. Liz 36 counter FB @ 4 against 52 defense

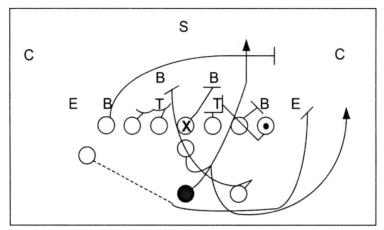

Figure 4-20. Liz 36 counter FB @ 4 against 44 defense

BLOCKING RULES, TECHNIQUE, AND COACHING POINTS
FOR LIZ 36 COUNTER FB @ 4

2-Man

Rule: Against a 52, pulls and traps the man on #5. Against a 44, pulls and traps the man on #6.

Coaching Points: He closes his split to one foot and hustles to his assignment. The fullback should not have to slow down for him to cross his face. He drop-steps with the frontside foot, and bears into the line of scrimmage. Against a 52, he traps the nose; against a 44, he traps the 3 technique. In both cases, he aims his left shoulder pad for the near hip of the defender. He should be in a good football position on contact and drive the defender to the inside. He hits on the rise, widens his base, and keeps his feet moving until the whistle blows.

3-Man

Rule: Against a 52, blocks the man on him. Against a 44, blocks out on the defender on #8.

Coaching Points: He has the key block against a 52 front. He takes a maximum split of three feet, and aims his outside shoulder pad for the frontside number of the 5 technique. He should not try to drive the defender back off the line. He rises quickly on his block and works his tail into the hole. He blocks high and walls off the 5 technique. Against a 44, he aims his outside shoulder pad for the near hip of the defender on #2. He should be in a good fundamental hitting position when he makes contact. He hits on the rise, brings up his blocking surface, widens his base, and drives the defender to the outside.

4-Man

Rule: Against a 52, blocks the backer over him. Against a 44, posts the man on him.
Coaching Points: Against a 52, he uses a high-pressure control block to wall off the backer. Against a 44, he should be aggressive on his post block on the 3 technique— he should not be knocked back off the line of scrimmage. He fronts the defender on the line of scrimmage, and sets him up for the block by #2.

5-Man

Rule: Against a 52, posts the man on him. Against a 44, steps to the frontside A gap and seals it.
Coaching Points: Against a 52, he posts the man on him by stepping with his frontside foot first. He secures the frontside A gap. Against a 44, he steps to the frontside A gap, and blocks a backer who attempts to run through it. If no threat, he goes up late and walls off the frontside backer.

6-Man

Rule: Against a 52, blocks the backer over him. Against a 44, co-op blocks with #7 and protects the backside A gap.
Coaching Points: He walls off a backer against a 52. He stays up on the block and works his tail into the hole. Against a 44, he starts the co-op block, but he should be ready to protect the backside A gap if the backside backer attempts to run through it.

7-Man

Rule. Against a 52, blocks the man on him. Against a 44, co-op blocks with #6
Coaching Points: He uses his hands against a 5 technique and gets his body between the defender and the backside B gap. He closes his split to one foot against a 44, and co-op blocks with #4 on the 3 technique. He should be ready to take over the 3 technique if #4 has to get off the co-op block to block a blitzing backer.

8-Man

Rule: Against a 52 or a 44, makes an inside release and blocks across the hole.
Coaching Points: He should not be deeper than five yards from the line of scrimmage as he crosses the field.

Quarterback

Technique: Same footwork as 36 counter, except slips the ball to the fullback.
Coaching Points: He reverse pivots on his right foot, seats the ball, and gains ground

with his left foot as he steps to the fullback and crosses the midline. His right foot follows, also crossing the midline and pointing to the fullback. He gives the ball to the fullback with his left hand. He takes a short step with his left foot past the fullback, and makes a two-handed fake to the left halfback as he fakes the counter. After the fake, he puts both hands on the outside of his right hip and fakes a bootleg at one. He uses the same bootleg mechanics explained in the 20 series.

Left Halfback

Technique: Same as 36 counter bootleg.
Coaching Points: He comes into motion, and he should be about one foot behind and one foot from the fullback. On the snap, he curves his path so his shoulders are square to the goal line, and he load blocks the last man on the line of scrimmage. He blocks as he would on 36 counter bootleg. He drives his inside shoulder through the outside thigh pad of the defender.

Fullback

Technique: Same as 36 counter, except he will receive the ball.
Coaching Points: Against a 52 defense, he steps with the right foot and aims for the tail of #4. He receives the ball and runs to an open area. Against a 44 defense, his aim point is the inside foot of #3. He squares his shoulders to the goal line as he crosses the line of scrimmage.

Right Halfback

Technique: Same footwork as 36 counter.
Coaching Points: On the snap, he shifts his weight to his left foot and allows the fullback to cross in front of him. He steps with his right foot for the right foot of #5. He makes a good fake and hits squarely into the backside A gap. He blocks any defender in the area.

Liz 36 Counter Bootleg

The counter bootleg has been a signature play of the wing-T offense since its inception. Liz 36 counter bootleg is illustrated in Figures 4-21 and 4-22. To the left, the play is Rip 34 counter bootleg, and the blocking assignments are reversed. The idea of using the play-action pass as part of the running game is the wing-T's strongest suit. Efficiency in executing the keep and counter bootleg passes in this series is essential to the success of the wing-T offense. These plays get the quarterback outside containment with a pass/run option: the most optimal position for a wing-T quarterback to demonstrate his skill. It is just as important for the wing-T quarterback to have success with the pass/run option on the perimeter as it is for the option quarterback to have success on the line of scrimmage with the pitch/keep option. The big plays in the 30 series come off the keep pass and the counter bootleg pass. They should be scripted into the game plan and used often. The inside belly and counter plays should be run just enough to make the defense respect the inside plays.

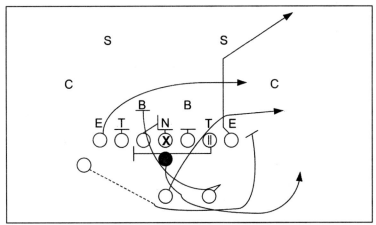

Figure 4-21. Liz 36 counter bootleg against 52 defense

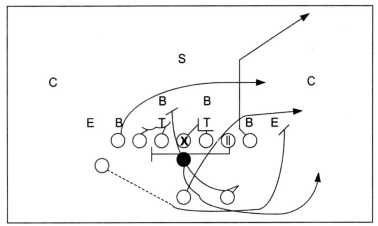

Figure 4-22. Liz 36 counter bootleg against 44 defense

BLOCKING RULES, TECHNIQUES, AND COACHING POINTS FOR LIZ 36 COUNTER BOOTLEG

2-Man

Rule: Inside releases and runs a deep flag route.
Coaching Points: Against a three-deep secondary, he reads the safety for an adjustment in his flag route. If the safety levels, he flattens out his route and runs toward the sideline and away from the safety. Against a two-deep, he converts the flag

into a bench route. In both adjustments, he should be 20 to 25 yards deep. Against man cover, he uses a double move.

3-Man

Rule: Pulls flat to his left and blocks the first free defender past #5.
Coaching Points: He should be alert to deepen his path to block a wide rushing defender, and to make a quick block against a Bear look.

4-Man

Rule: Same rule as 36 counter. He should not cross the line of scrimmage.
Coaching Points: He uses a high-pressure control block against a hard man. If open, he steps to the nose man and fakes a lead block. He keeps his eyes on the backer over him. If the backer rushes, he blocks him.

5-Man

Rule: Same rule as 36 counter. He should not cross the line of scrimmage.
Coaching Points: Against a hard man, he aims for the hard man's playside number when he posts him. If the hard man slants away, he stays square to the line of scrimmage and protects the frontside A gap. He blocks any defender running through that gap.

6-Man

Rule: If #5 is covered by a hard man, leads to his post. If not, blocks the man on him. He should not cross the line of scrimmage.
Coaching Points: Against a hard man, he aims for his frontside number. He uses his hands to position himself between the defender and the quarterback. He is responsible for protecting the backside A gap.

7-Man

Rule: Blocks a hard man on or inside him. Does not cross the line of scrimmage.
Coaching Points: Against a hard man, he aims for his frontside number. He uses his hands to position himself between the defender and the quarterback. He is responsible for the backside B gap. Against a 44 stack, he takes a lateral step with his right foot and co-op blocks the 3 technique with #6.

8-Man

Rule: Inside releases and runs a crossing route.

Coaching Points: On his crossing route, he positions himself halfway between #2 and the fullback. He throttles down when he crosses the field, and settles in an open area. He uses a hump move against man coverage.

Quarterback

Technique: Same technique and footwork as 36 counter, except fakes the ball to the right halfback and executes a keep maneuver at the 1 hole.
Coaching Points: On his second step, he controls the ball with his right hand and begins to shift it to the front of his right hip. On his third step—with his right foot—he gives the right halfback a hand fake and moves the ball to the side of his right hip. From there, he executes the fundamentals of a keep action at the 1 hole.

Left Halfback

Technique: Same assignment as 36 counter.
Coaching Points: He has the key block on 36 counter bootleg. As he passes the fullback position, he sharply arcs his course into the line of scrimmage. He should be running north and south as he load blocks the last man on the line of scrimmage. He should not hesitate; he should make an aggressive block on the line. He drives his left shoulder pad through the outside thigh pad of the last man and put him on the ground.

Fullback

Technique: Aims for outside hip of #3 and continues into the flat. Runs a four- to five-yard fan route.
Coaching Points: He steps with his right foot directly toward the outside foot of #3. If the 3 technique crosses his face, he blocks him. Otherwise, he continues into the flat and runs a four- or five-yard fan route. He throttles down in an open area and makes himself an easy target for the quarterback. If he catches the ball, then he stays on the perimeter and uses the sideline. He stays on the move against man coverage.

Right Halfback

Technique: Fakes 36 counter and blocks any free defender in the area.
Coaching Points: If #5 is the post man, he fills over #5's left leg. If #5 is a lead blocker, he fills over #5's tail. In either case, he blocks the first defender to show in the area.

Liz 36 Counter Bootleg Switch

In the past, the crossing end in the counter bootleg was difficult to cover, and the fullback in the flat was almost always open. However, defenses are beginning to react to the play much better because they see it so often. In two-deep defenses, the frontside safety takes the deep flag route, the backers run under the crossing route, and the corner sits in the flat and waits for the fullback. In three-deep defenses, the safety covers the crossing end, the deep corner covers the flag, and the frontside backer runs with the fullback in the flat. Again, a simple innovation that will give the counter bootleg a new look, and make it tougher to defend, is to switch the assignment of the ends. Liz 36 counter bootleg end switch is illustrated in Figures 4-23 and 4-24. To the left, the play is Rip 34 counter bootleg end switch, and the blocking assignments are reversed.

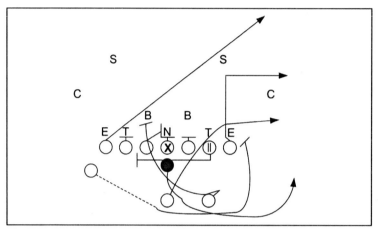

Figure 4-23. Liz 36 counter bootleg end switch against 52 defense

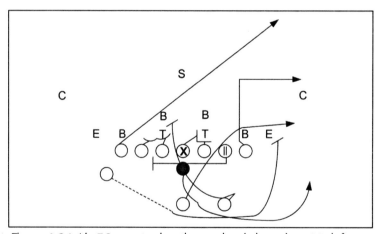

Figure 4-24. Liz 36 counter bootleg end switch against 44 defense

The frontside end runs a 12- to 15-yard out, and the backside end runs a deep crossing route. The fullback stays with his three- to four-yard flat route. The assignments of the interior linemen and the backs are not affected by the switch call; only the 2-man and the 8-man make the switch adjustment.

BLOCKING RULES, TECHNIQUES, AND COACHING POINTS FOR LIZ 36 COUNTER BOOTLEG SWITCH

2-Man

Rule: Same as 36 counter bootleg.
Coaching Points: He makes an inside release and runs an out route at 12 to 15 yards downfield. He gets his head around quickly and cruises at controlled speed through the open area. Against man coverage, he starts an inside post move at eight yards deep. He takes three or four steps to the post, and breaks sharply back to the outside. His depth will still be about 15 yards. He stays on the move and runs away from coverage.

3-Man

Rule: Same as 36 counter bootleg.
Coaching Points: Same as 36 counter bootleg.

4-Man

Rule: Same as 36 counter bootleg.
Coaching Points: Same as 36 counter bootleg.

5-Man

Rule: Same as 36 counter bootleg.
Coaching Points: Same as 36 counter bootleg.

6-Man

Rule: Same as 36 counter bootleg.
Coaching Points: Same as 36 counter bootleg.

7-Man

Rule: Same as 36 counter bootleg.
Coaching Points: Same as 36 counter bootleg.

8-Man

Rule: Same as 36 counter bootleg.
Coaching Points: He inside releases and runs a diagonal route behind the frontside deep defender. He runs to a landmark that will put him 25 to 30 yards from the line of scrimmage. He should be deep enough so the deep defender cannot cover him on the diagonal and #2 on his 12- to 15-yard out. He should not get closer than 10 yards

from the sideline. If he has to, he drifts deep when he arrives at his landmark (if the ball has not yet been thrown).

The deep diagonal route makes it improbable for backers to run under that deep of a crossing route. The safety in a three-deep (or the corner) will have to defend the diagonal route. If the safety covers #8, the corner has to sink deep to cover #2 on the out. This situation would leave the fullback open in the flat. The counter fake should hold the backers long enough for the fullback to beat them into the flat area.

Quarterback

Technique: Same footwork and techniques as 36 counter bootleg.
Coaching Points: He has the same vertical stretch into the sideline, with #8 and #2 switching levels—#8 becomes the deep receiver, and #2 becomes the middle-level receiver. The fullback remains the short receiver. As he starts his bootleg, he gets his eyes downfield, and his progression read is still deep, medium, and short receiver. If he has the deep pass, he takes it; if not, he checks down to the middle and short receivers. His last option is to run the ball.

Left Halfback

Technique: Same as 36 counter bootleg.
Coaching Points: Same as 36 counter bootleg.

Fullback

Technique: Same as 36 counter bootleg. Stays with his three- to four-yard flat route.
Coaching Points: Same as 36 counter bootleg.

Right Halfback

Technique: Same as 36 counter bootleg.
Coaching Points: Same as 36 counter bootleg.

Liz Flex 37 Roll-Away

Before leaving the 30 series, two more innovative ideas deserve some attention. The first one is a misdirection pass. The pass is run from a Liz flex formation, and it is illustrated in Figures 4-25 and 4-26. It is called Liz flex 37 roll-away. To the left, the play is Rip flex 33 roll-away, and the blocking assignments are reversed. Roll-away action is like a bootleg, except—as a security measure—the backside guard pulls and logs the last man on the line of scrimmage.

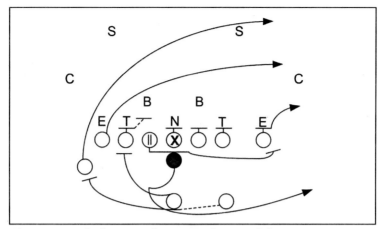

Figure 4-25. Liz flex 37 roll-away against 52 defense

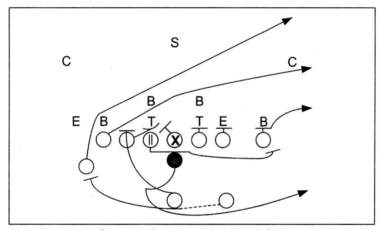

Figure 4-26. Liz flex 37 roll-away against 44 defense

BLOCKING RULES, TECHNIQUES, AND COACHING POINTS FOR LIZ FLEX 37 ROLL-AWAY

2-Man

Rule: Blocks the man on him for two counts and releases into the flat at a depth of three to four yards.
Coaching Points: He uses a high-pressure control block to keep the defender on the line of scrimmage long enough for #6 to log the defender.

3-Man

Rule: Blocks the man on or over him.
Coaching Points: Against a Bear or wide-tackle 6 look, he eyeballs the backer as he steps down to help #4. If the backer rushes the frontside B gap, he blocks the backer.

4-Man

Rule: Blocks the man on or over him.
Coaching Points: If he is open, he eyeballs the backer as he blocks the man on #5. If the backer rushes the frontside A gap, he blocks him. He co-op blocks with #5 against a 53 front.

5-Man

Rule: Blocks the man on or over him.
Coaching Points: If open, he takes a controlled step to the backside A gap. If the backer flows with the play, he blocks the defender in the backside A gap. If the backer rushes either A gap, he blocks the backer. Against a 53 front, he co-op blocks with #4.

6-Man

Rule: Pulls and logs the last man on the line of scrimmage.
Coaching Points: He pulls flat until he cross #5. Then, he gains ground and logs the last man on the line of scrimmage. If a defender sifts through the line before the 6-man gets to his assignment, he blocks the defender.

7-Man

Rule: Fills
Coaching Points: If the 6-man is covered by a backer, he slams the hard man on him before he seals the backside B gap. If #6 is covered by a hard man, he gets his head and inside arm beyond the hard man, and goes to all fours as he scramble blocks the 3 technique.

8-Man

Rule: Runs a 12- to 15-yard crossing route.
Coaching Points: He finds a soft spot in the zone defense and throttles down so he is an easy target for the quarterback to hit. He makes a hump move against man coverage.

Quarterback

Technique: His first two steps are the same as if he were running 37 down. He pivots on his left foot and crosses the midline with his right foot. On his second step with his left foot, he extends his arms and meshes with the fullback. He drags his right foot so it is about 18 inches from his left foot. The toes of both feet face the fullback. He arm-rides the fullback to his left hip and pulls the ball. He pushes off his right foot to begin his roll-away maneuver.

Coaching Points: His fake to the fullback is with the arms only. He should not slide his right foot towards the line of scrimmage as he ride the fullback. He wants to be as far off the line as possible to facilitate his roll-away technique. He should not put the ball deep into the fullback's pocket. Instead, he puts it on his near hip so he can easily retract it. His depth on the roll-away is the same as bootlegs—about six yards from the line of scrimmage. It is important for him to get outside of the log block so the pass/run option is viable. Once on the perimeter, he should have a choice between the crossing receiver and the flat receiver. If the safety covers the crossing route, he should have a good chance of hitting the left halfback behind him. His progression is to check the deep receivers first, and then to check down to the flat receiver.

Left Halfback

Technique: Runs a deep crossing route.
Coaching Points: His crossing route should take him behind the frontside deep-third defender. He should be 25 yards from the line of scrimmage when he arrives in the frontside third of the field. He makes a hump move against man coverage.

Fullback

Technique: Fakes 37 down.
Coaching Points: He concentrates on making his block at the line of scrimmage. He forms a pocket as he heads for his reference point, and allows the quarterback to put the ball on his hip and arm-ride him. He should not close his arms on the ball. When he get to the line, he puts his outside shoulder pad on the inside thigh pad of the defender in the area.

Right Halfback

Technique: Blocks the last man on the line of scrimmage.
Coaching Points: His action is the same as it would be on 37 keep. He sprints toward the line of scrimmage and load blocks the last man on the line. He puts his inside shoulder pad on the outside thigh pad of the last man.

Rob Double 33 Reverse @ 9

The second innovative idea is a reverse play off the 30 series. It can be run from a variety of formations with no changes in the blocking assignments. The reverse can be directed to a tight end or a split end. The ballcarrier can be aligned in a slot, as a wing, or in his halfback position. From the halfback position, he would have to take a few steps to the outside before reversing his course to receive the handoff from the quarterback. For variety purposes, a Rob double formation will be used for the reverse.

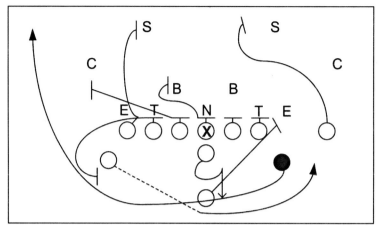

Figure 4-27. Rob double 33 reverse @ 9 against 52 defense

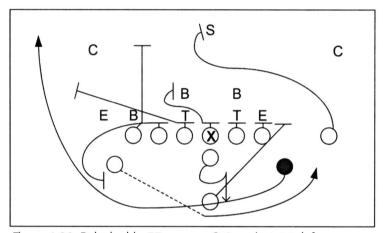

Figure 4-28. Rob double 33 reverse @ 9 against 44 defense

The play Rob double 33 reverse @ 9 is illustrated in Figures 4-27 and 4-28. To the left, the play is Len double 37 reverse @ 1, and the blocking assignments are reversed.

BLOCKING RULES, TECHNIQUE, AND COACHING POINTS FOR ROB DOUBLE 33 REVERSE @ 9

2-Man

Rule: From a tight or split alignment, blocks the deep-third or the deep-half defender to his side. Makes an inside release when he aligns as a tight end.
Coaching Points: He sprints to a spot that will give him inside-out position on the deep defender. The flow of the play should help him to get inside his target. He uses a stalk block to wall off the defender.

3-Man

Rule: Blocks the man on or over him. He is responsible for the backside B gap.
Coaching Points: Against all heavy fronts, he must prevent penetration in the backside B gap. He eyeballs the backside backer as he stabs the inside number of the hard man on him with his right hand. He simultaneously takes a six-inch slide step with his left foot, and checks the backside backer. If the backer is rushing the backside B gap, he blocks him. If not, he continues to block the hard man covering him.

4-Man

Rule: Blocks the man on or over him. He is responsible for the backside A gap.
Coaching Points: He prevents penetration in the backside A gap. Against a 44 front, he blocks the inside number of the 3 technique, but he should be aware of the backside backer. If the backer rushes the backside A gap, he blocks him. If not, he stays on the 3 technique.

5-Man

Rule: Steps to the frontside A gap and stops the penetration of any defender he encounters. Follows #6 and turns upfield to wall off the frontside backer.
Coaching Points: Against a hard man, he jolts the hard man to stop his penetration, and as the hard man reacts to the flow of the play, the 5-man releases for the frontside backer. He sprints inside the frontside backer to a spot outside the 3-man's pre-snap position before turning to block the backer.

6-Man

Rule: Releases inside a hard man, and follows #7 toward the sideline. Continues toward the flank, and blocks the force man. He can kick him out, or log him in—whatever is the easiest block to make.
Coaching Points: He stays close to the line of scrimmage as he works toward the sideline. If the force man reacts quickly, he may have to kick him out. Staying close to the line will help his block. If the force man is retreating or moving with the flow of the play, he tries to log him to the inside.

7-Man

Rule: Inside releases, and works back to the outside. He should be about one yard past the line of scrimmage as he works back toward the sideline. As he passes the tight-end area, he peels back, gaining ground behind the line of scrimmage. He should be as deep as necessary to block the last man on the line as the last man reacts to the reverse.

Coaching Points: As he peels back to block the last man on the line of scrimmage, he makes sure he doesn't clip the last man. If a defender is reacting inside-out to the ball, he waits for him to turn his numbers to him before blocking him. He should be as deep in the backfield as is necessary to make his block.

8-Man

Rule: From a tight or spread alignment, blocks the deep-third, or deep-half defender to his side. Makes an inside release when he is aligned as a tight end.
Coaching Points: He uses a stalk block on the secondary defender to the 8-man's side of the formation. He keeps contact, and stays on his feet until the whistle blows.

Quarterback

Technique: Same footwork and technique as 33 keep. After a flash fake to the fullback, starts his keep course and reaches back to hand the ball to the right halfback on his fourth step. After the handoff, continues to the flank, faking the keep.
Coaching Points: He reverse pivots with his back to the hole. He crosses the midline with his left foot on his first step. His second step with his right foot should be pointed at the right-halfback position. He makes a flash fake to the fullback on that step. He takes a short balanced step with his left foot, and pushes off it as he reaches back for the right halfback. He hands the ball to the halfback and continues to the flank, faking a keep pass.

Left Halfback

Technique: Comes in quick motion and should be tandem with the fullback when the ball is snapped. Arcs his course so the right halfback has plenty of room to run under him. Attacks the last defender on the line as he would on 33 keep.
Coaching Points: He should be deep enough to allow the right halfback to pass under his course without the threat of colliding with the right halfback. He aggressively attacks the last man on the line as if the quarterback had the ball.

Fullback

Technique: Aims for the outside leg of #3, and seals the backside C gap.
Coaching Points: He heads for the outside foot of #3 and seals the backside C gap. He loads any defender in the area. He should not worry about making a good fake. He forms a pocket, and runs a straight line to his reference point.

Right Halfback

Technique: Makes a reverse pivot on his left foot with his back to the line of scrimmage. Runs a controlled course through his halfback position and the area where the fullback initially lines up.

Coaching Points: As he works back through his halfback position, he should be under control and time his arrival so the quarterback can hand him the ball after his flash fake to the fullback. The timing should allow the quarterback to hand him the ball and flow to the perimeter in one continuous motion. When he receives the ball, he keys the block by #7 on the contain man. He may have to give some ground to get around the contain man. Once he gets outside, he stays on the perimeter.

5

The 40 Series

The 40 series is a fast-flow series featuring sweep plays, power plays, counter plays, and play-action-pass plays. The counter plays are an excellent antidote for fast pursuing teams, and the play-action passes discourage defenses from committing eight and nine defenders to the line of scrimmage to stop the run game. All of these plays will be illustrated in this chapter.

The power plays in the 40 series are characterized by a blocking scheme that has the fullback as the lead or kickout blocker, the backside guard as the seal blocker, and the frontside guard blocking solid. The sweep plays have both guards pulling with the fullback as a lead blocker.

A unique characteristic of the 40 series is that the center, the frontside guard, and the frontside tackle use zone blocking on the power plays and the arc sweep—the backside guard, tackle, and end block by rule. The zone scheme is the answer to troublesome heavy fronts that pose a blitz threat to every gap along the line of scrimmage. It also accounts for slanting linemen and scraping backers. A zone scheme is best executed when blockers use their hands, rather than their shoulders—another deviation of traditional wing-T techniques. Players not involved in the zone scheme still use traditional shoulder blocks.

The chapter on the 40 series begins with some new ideas that will improve the traditional wing-T sweep. Three different sweep plays, each of which is a little different from the traditional wing-T sweep, will be illustrated. What these sweeps have in common with the traditional wing-T sweep is that they are mirrored—they are run to both sides of the formation. This feature is essential to prevent defenses from ganging up on the formation side. Running the traditional sweep away from formation against 7-man fronts is no problem. The problem is running the sweep away from formation against 8-man fronts that have an overhang player lined up outside the tight end. Later in this chapter, a formation will be illustrated that allows the 40-series sweep to be run to both sides of the formation—irrespective of whether the defense is a seven- or eight-man front. That important innovation will keep the sweep alive to and away from formation.

Rip B 41

The first sweep is Rip B 41 base, a traditional wing-T sweep to the formation side. It is illustrated in Figures 5-1 and 5-2. To the left, it is Liz B 49 base. As mentioned in the chapter introduction, the sweep is a mirrored play and can be run to both sides of the formation. The block by the wingback/halfback has a much better chance of success against a seven-man front than it does against an eight-man front.

The sweep away from the formation is Rip 49 sweep, and it is illustrated in Figures 5-3 and 5-4. To the left, it is Liz 41 sweep. The unique features of this sweep are the blocking variations that are made against a 50 defense and all heavy fronts. These variations make the base sweep a stronger play against a 50 front, and keep it viable against all heavy fronts.

Against a 50, an Iowa call changes the assignments of the frontside tight end and the backside guard. This same Iowa scheme was introduced in Chapter 2. Rip B 41 Iowa (Figure 5-5) is illustrated to the formation side, and Rip 49 Iowa is shown away from the formation (Figure 5-6). The adjustments for heavy fronts will be discussed in Chapter 7.

Instead of blocking down on the 5 technique, the tight end blocks the frontside backer; instead of sealing for the frontside backer, the backside guard logs the 5 technique. By alignment, the tight end is in better position than the backside guard to seal the frontside backer. Since the backers are the toughest defenders to block on sweep plays, the Iowa scheme—with the tight end blocking the frontside backer— improves the efficiency of the play.

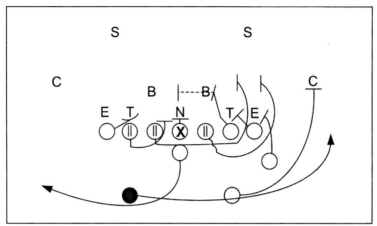

Figure 5-1. Rip B 41 base against 52 defense

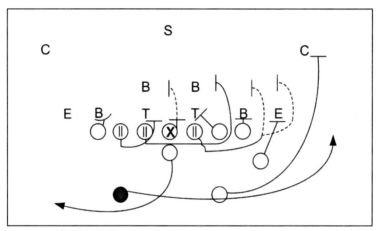

Figure 5-2. Rip B 41 base against 44 defense

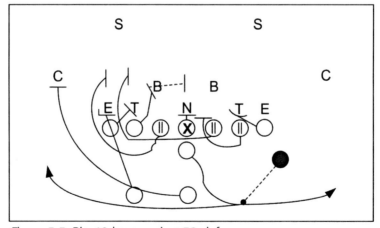

Figure 5-3. Rip 49 base against 52 defense

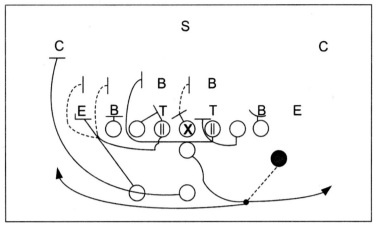

Figure 5-4. Rip 49 base against 44 defense

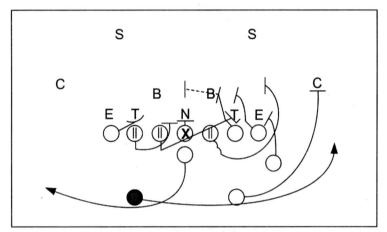

Figure 5-5. Rip B 41 Iowa against 52 defense

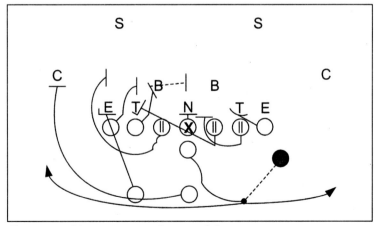

Figure 5-6. Rip 49 Iowa against 52 defense

BLOCKING RULES, TECHNIQUES, AND COACHING POINTS FOR RIP B 41

2-Man

Rule: Blocks down on the first man inside, on or off the line of scrimmage. On a heavy call, blocks the man on or over him. On an Iowa call, blocks the frontside backer.

Coaching Points: He steps with and aims his inside foot for the crotch of the hard man on #3. He aims his left shoulder for the outside thigh pad of the defender. On contact, he brings up his left arm to increase his blocking surface, widens his base, pumps his off arm, and drives the defender to the inside. If the defender disappears to the inside, he goes up to the next level and blocks the frontside backer. If the first defender to his inside is a backer, he uses a vertical release and positions himself between the defender and the ballcarrier. He uses a high-pressure control block to wall off the backer. On an Iowa call, he makes an inside release and blocks the frontside backer.

3-Man

Rule: Blocks down on the first man inside, on or off the line of scrimmage. On a heavy call, blocks the man on, over, or inside him.

Coaching Points: When blocking a hard man or a backer to his inside, he uses the same techniques as described for the tight end. An Iowa call does not change his assignment, but a heavy call does. It requires him to block the man on, over, or inside of him.

4-Man

Rule: Pulls and seals frontside backer. Turns upfield outside of the wingback/halfback's block. On a heavy call, reads wingback's block to determine his course—goes around the wingback if the wingback hooks last man on line of scrimmage, goes inside the wingback if the defender skates outside.

Coaching Points: His objective is to seal the frontside backer. He gains depth on his first two steps and keys the block of the wingback or halfback. He should be just deep enough to get around that block. He looks to the inside to pick up the frontside backer, and blocks him with a left shoulder block. He keeps his body between the backer and the ballcarrier. On a heavy call, the back will be blocking the last man on the line of scrimmage, and depending on the play of the defender, his course can be inside or outside the wingback/halfback block. If the defender skates to the outside, the 4-man turns up just outside of where the tight end normally lines up, and he blocks the frontside backer. If the wingback/halfback hooks his man, the 4-man bends outside of the back's block and blocks the backer.

5-Man

Rule: Blocks man on or over, stepping through the frontside gap.

Coaching Points: If he is blocking a nose man, he steps with his frontside foot and aims for his frontside number. If the nose slants away, he goes to the next level and blocks the middle or backside backer. If the backer plays into his block, he gets his head between the defender and the ballcarrier and walls him off. If he is uncovered, he reaches a 2- or 2i-technique player on the frontside guard. If the defender on the frontside guard is in a 3 technique, he steps to the frontside A gap and blocks any defender threatening that gap. If no threat is present, he goes up to the backer level and walls off the backside backer.

6-Man

Rule: Pulls flat down the line of scrimmage and blocks the first man to penetrate to the frontside. If no penetration occurs, turns up the first opening past #3 and blocks inside pursuit.
Coaching Points: His first objective is to block any penetration to the frontside. He pulls as flat as the frontside linemen will allow him to, and he expects to make contact immediately as he passes #5. If no penetration occurs, he turns up the first opening past #3 and blocks inside pursuit. On an Iowa call, his assignment changes, and he logs the frontside 5 technique.

7-Man

Rule: Full scoops.
Coaching Points: He gains ground on his first two steps as he pulls to the near hip of #5. His third step should be on his right foot. He pivots on that foot and levels his shoulders to the line of scrimmage. He scoops any defender in the backside A and B gaps. He may have to chase a 2i-technique player down the line of scrimmage. He throws his head and inside shoulder past the defender and tries to execute a running scramble block.

8-Man

Rule: Fills.
Coaching Points: If #7 is covered by a hard man, the 8-man is responsible for cutting off the hard man on him. If #7 is open, the 8-man blocks the first backside backer on or to his inside.

Quarterback

Technique: Opens back to the hole. His first step with his left foot is slightly under the midline. His next two steps are also slightly under the midline. Hands the ball to the left halfback on his third step, and fakes a bootleg at the 9 hole.
Coaching Points: He receives and seats the ball. He pushes off his right foot and steps

back with his left foot slightly under the midline. He slides his left hand to the rear tip of the ball to facilitate the handoff to the left halfback. His next two steps are also under the midline, and his shoulders begin to turn toward the sideline. He should complete the handoff, with his left hand as he takes his third step. After the handoff, he brings both hands to the front of his left hip, bends at the waist, drops his right shoulder, and sprints toward the 9-hole area. He runs an arc course that will take him five to six yards away from the line of scrimmage. He checks the reaction of the contain man to determine if a bootleg can be run to that side.

Left Halfback

Technique: Acts as the ballcarrier. Open-steps with his right foot and comes flat across the backfield. Receives the handoff from the quarterback and runs a sweep at the 1 hole.
Coaching Points: Acts as the ballcarrier. He open-steps with his right foot and comes across the backfield parallel to the line of scrimmage. He receives the ball from the quarterback, and positions himself on the outside hip of his lead blocker: the fullback. He watches the block of the fullback, and uses it to get inside or outside of the man he is blocking. He can help the block of the fullback by faking inside and bouncing back to the outside.

Fullback

Technique: Runs an arc course outside the block of the wingback/halfback, and blocks the first perimeter defender to cross his path. Blocks the defender in any direction he can.
Coaching Points: He is the lead blocker on 41/49 base. He open-steps with his right foot and comes across the backfield parallel to the line of scrimmage. When he gets to the tight end, he arcs his course outside the block of the wingback/halfback. His objective is to get outside the block of the wingback/halfback and block the first secondary player he meets. The only time he will come under the wingback/halfback block is if the man the wingback/halfback is blocking skates to the outside and a defensive back is coming under the block to stop the run. He comes under the block and blocks the defensive back. He should be under control when he makes his block. He gathers himself before contact by bending his knees and lowering his center of gravity. He explodes into the defender, hitting on the rise and keeping a wide base. He stays on his feet as he follows through, and blocks until the whistle blows.

Right Halfback

Technique: Blocks down on the first hard man on or outside of #2. On a heavy call, blocks the last man on the line of scrimmage.
Coaching Points: From the wing position, when he is blocking a hard man on #2, he uses the same blocking techniques described for #2 when #2 blocks down on a hard man on #3. When blocking the last man on the line of scrimmage, he uses the same

high-pressure control technique as #2 when #2 blocks from a flexed position. From the halfback position, he steps with his outside foot and sprints for a spot one yard outside of the last man on the line of scrimmage. He stays on course, unless the defender's position changes before he reaches him. He adjusts his course on the run so he can drive his inside shoulder pad into the outside thigh pad of the defender. He tightens his path if the defender moves inside, and widens it if the defender slides outside. He drives through the defender, and hits with enough force to put the defender on the ground.

Rip Flex 41 Arc

The novel aspect of the next sweep play is that the tight end releases downfield, which is quite a departure from the traditional wing-T sweep. However, it adds to the effectiveness of the play by forcing the secondary to respect the pass. Thus, it slows down their pursuit of the sweep. Rip flex 41 arc is illustrated in Figures 5-7 and 5-8. To the left, it is Liz flex 49 arc.

This play is run to the formation side. Of course, simply releasing an eligible downfield and not throwing him the ball will not keep the secondary in check. A halfback option pass, which will be discussed later in this chapter, is needed to complement the arc sweep.

BLOCKING RULES, TECHNIQUES, AND COACHING POINTS
FOR RIP FLEX 41 ARC

2-Man

Rule: From a closed formation, he inside releases and redirects his course back to the outside. He goes flat down the line of scrimmage two or three yards outside his original

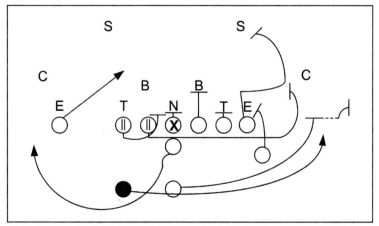

Figure 5-7. Rip flex 41 arc against 52 defense

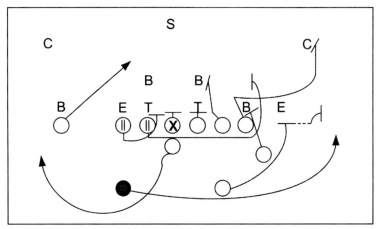

Figure 5-8. Rip flex B 41 arc against 44 defense

position, and he turns upfield to block the deep-third defensive back. From an open formation, he releases upfield and slow-blocks the deep-third defender. Against a funnel man, runs straight at him, jolts him with his outside hand, and goes inside and stalk blocks the deep-third defender.

Coaching Points: He is instructed to make an inside release on the man on or over him. The inside release facilitates the wingback's block. If necessary, he makes a quick head-and-shoulder fake to the outside, and then uses a rip or swim move to release inside. He runs parallel to the line of scrimmage for a point three to four yards outside of his original alignment before turning upfield to block the defensive back. He will try to get outside-in position on the defensive back and seal him to the inside. If the defensive back widens, the tight end will put his head in front of the defensive back and drive him into the sideline. The ballcarrier will turn up inside the tight end's kickout block. If the defender aligns in a 6i technique, or if the tight end feels he cannot make an inside release in time to block a secondary defender, he makes an Omaha call, and he and the wingback exchange assignments. He will block the 6i technique, and the wingback will release upfield to block the secondary defender. The Omaha call is only used when he has a wingback to his side. Without a wingback, the tight end—against a 6i technique—makes an outside release and carries out his assignment.

3-Man

Rule: Blocks zone.

Coaching Points: Against a man on, he short steps with his frontside foot, aiming for the frontside. number of the defender on him. If the defender plays into him or moves outside, he locks on the defender and work his body between the defender and the ballcarrier. If the man on him stunts inside, he passes him off to #4, and goes up to the second level to block the inside backer. Against a backer or open, he short steps with his frontside foot to the C gap. If a defender threatens that gap, he blocks the defender. If not, he goes up to the second level to block the backer or backside pursuit.

4-Man

Rule: Blocks zone.
Coaching Points: Against a man on, he short steps with his frontside foot aiming for the frontside number of the defender on him. If the defender plays into him or moves outside, he locks on the defender and works his body between the defender and the ballcarrier. If the man on him stunts inside, he passes him off to #5 and goes up to the second level to block the middle or backside backer. Against a backer, he short steps with his frontside foot to the B gap. If a defender threatens that gap, he blocks the defender. If not, he goes up to the second level to block the backer or backside pursuit.

5-Man

Rule: Blocks zone.
Coaching Points: Against a man on, he short steps with his frontside foot aiming for the frontside number of the defender on him. If the defender plays into him or moves to the frontside gap, he locks on the defender and works his body between the defender and the ballcarrier. If the man on him stunts to the backside A gap, he passes the defender off to #7, and goes up to the second level to block the backside backer. Against backer or open, he short steps with his frontside foot to the A gap. If a defender threatens that gap, he blocks the defender, and gets his head between the defender and the ballcarrier. If the A gap is not threatened, he goes up to second level to block the backer or backside pursuit.

6-Man

Rule: Pulls flat across the 5-man and seals.
Coaching Points: His first responsibility is to block any seepage in the frontside gaps. His goal is to seal the frontside backer. He should eyeball the backer on his first step (minus seepage), turn up outside the tight end's original position, and log the backer to the inside. If the backer is blocked, he continues upfield and blocks the safety.

7-Man

Rule: Full scoops.
Coaching Points: He scoops any defender trying to penetrate the backside B or A gaps. He must prevent a defender from working down the line of scrimmage and catching the sweep from behind. His technique is to gain depth on his first, second, and third steps. His third step is with his outside foot, and he pivots off that foot and works his head and shoulders into the line of scrimmage, scooping any defender who lines up or stunts into that area. At times, he may have to leave his feet and throw his inside arm and head in front of a defender to cut him off. In that instance, he works his head and shoulders up field from an all-fours position.

8-Man

Rule: Inside releases and blocks the middle-third defender, or fakes a bootleg quick route.
Coaching Points: He sprints to a position that will enable him to block a defensive back in the deep third of the field. As a change of pace, he can fake a bootleg quick to gauge the reaction of the backside defensive back.

Quarterback

Technique: Opens back to the hole, and steps under the midline. Hands the ball to left halfback on his third step and fake bootleg at the 9 hole.
Coaching Points: After receiving the ball from the center, he seats it by bringing the fat part of the ball to his beltline with his elbows close to his body. He simultaneously steps with his left foot, slightly under the midline, in the direction of the left halfback. He takes his second step with his right foot, and slides his left hand to the rear tip of the ball to facilitate the handoff to the left halfback. The third step is with the left foot and a one-handed exchange is completed on this step. The exchange takes place about one yard under the midline. After the handoff, he brings both hands to his outside hip, bends at the waist, dips his right shoulder, and begins the bootleg action. His shoulders are at a right angle to the line of scrimmage, and his depth is five to six yards from it. He will call the bootleg when the contain man does not honor the bootleg fake.

Left Halfback

Technique: Acts as the ballcarrier. Open-steps and comes flat across the backfield. He gets on the outside hip of the fullback, and keys his block on the force man.
Coaching Points: He starts with an open step and runs parallel to the line of scrimmage. As he receives the ball from the quarterback, he runs a course on the outside hip of the fullback, and keep his eyes on the force man. As he approaches the original position of the tight end, he fakes inside to set up the fullback's block. He swings around the fullback and gets out on the perimeter. If the force man will not be logged, the fullback will kick him out, and the ballcarrier will turn up inside the fullback's block. Once across the line of scrimmage, the left halfback will swing to the perimeter and try to get outside the tight end's block on the defensive back.

Fullback

Technique: Open-steps with his frontside foot and runs parallel to the line of scrimmage. Gets the force man inside his arc, and logs him to the inside. If the force man runs upfield, kicks him out.
Coaching Points: He has the key block on 49/41 arc. He is responsible for logging the force man to the inside. This assignment is easier from B backs—especially when the

force man aligns on the line of scrimmage. In B backs, he is closer to the force man and can get him inside his arc on the third or fourth step. The down block of the wingback should influence the force man to close off the wing's tail, and that will help the fullback's block. He shortens his arc course if the force man attempts to come inside and run under his block. If the force man skates outside, the fullback will extend the arc to five yards outside the original position of the force man. At that junction, if the force man cannot be logged, the fullback will kick him out. The ballcarrier will turn up inside the fullback's block. The fullback will kick out the force man only as a last resort. The objective of this sweep play is to get the ball on the perimeter.

Right Halfback

Technique: Blocks the last man on the line of scrimmage.
Coaching Points: On a wingback alignment, down-blocks on the man on or over the 2-man. Aims his inside shoulder pad for the near hip pad of that man and drives him to the inside. If the man stunts inside, he moves up to the second level and blocks the frontside backer. On an Omaha call from the tight end, he and the tight end exchange assignments. He releases and blocks the deep-third or deep-half defender, and the tight end blocks the man on him. See tight end rules for technique on release and blocking downfield. On a halfback alignment, he uses the same technique as explained in the coaching points for 41 base. He will not get an Omaha call when he is aligned in a halfback position.

As stated previously in this chapter, releasing an end downfield and not throwing him the ball will do nothing to minimize secondary pursuit on the sweep play. Therefore, a pass off the sweep—preferably with the halfback throwing the ball—is a play that the wing-T coach has to have in his repertoire. It only has to be used once in a while to send a message to his opponent—and future opponents—that when his tight end releases downfield on sweep action, somebody better cover him. Rip flex 41 arc halfback pass is illustrated in Figures 5-9 and 5-10. To the left, it is Liz flex 49 arc halfback pass. (Note: All interior linemen block to the pass against all heavy fronts.)

BLOCKING RULES, TECHNIQUES, AND COACHING POINTS
FOR RIP FLEX 41 ARC HALFBACK OPTION PASS

2-Man

Rule: Same release as 41 arc. Fakes stalk block and slips past the defender toward the flag.
Coaching Points: On his approach to the secondary defender, he breaks down as he does on the stalk block and tries to sell the run. He should not be in a hurry—he delays for two counts before he run his route. His aim point is about five yards inside the near pylon. He looks over the outside shoulder for the ball. If the defensive back is fooled and runs past him, he gets into his route immediately.

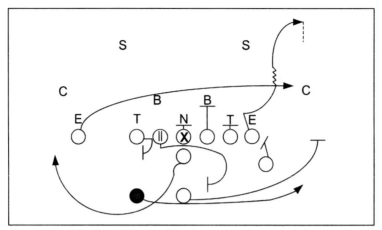

Figure 5-9. Rip flex 41 arc halfback pass against 52 defense

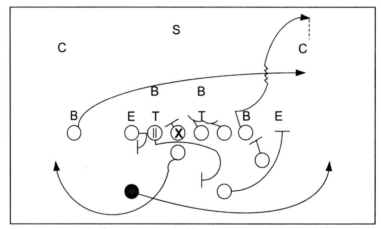

Figure 5-10. Rip flex B 41 arc halfback pass against 44 defense

3-Man

Rule: Blocks man on or inside. He should not go across the line of scrimmage.
Coaching Points: He follows rule.

4-Man

Rule: Blocks man on or inside. He should not go across the line of scrimmage.
Coaching Points: He follows rule.

5-Man

Rule: Blocks on or to his left. He should not go across the line of scrimmage.
Coaching Points: He follows rule.

6-Man

Rule: Pulls flat past #5, and when he gets to #3, pivots away from line of scrimmage, and blocks any defender chasing the play from behind.
Coaching Points: He follows rule.

7-Man

Rule: Full scoops. He should not cross the line of scrimmage.
Coaching Points: He follows rule.

8-Man

Rule: Inside releases, and runs crossing route.
Coaching Points: His crossing route should not be any deeper than 8 to 10 yards. He sprints across the formation, but slows down when he gets to the reception zone—he makes himself an easy target for the left halfback. He settles in the open area and keeps the passing lane open.

Quarterback

Technique: Same as 41 arc.
Coaching Points: It is important for him to make a great bootleg fake. Doing so will hold the contain man to the bootleg side and prevent him from pressuring the halfback's pass play from behind.

Left Halfback

Technique: Same as 41 arc, except he is passing the ball if he has an open receiver.
Coaching Points: When he receives the ball from the quarterback and has it in his pouch, he adjusts it so the laces are on the fingers of his throwing hand. As he starts on his sweep course, his eyes should be downfield, looking at the reaction of the defensive back to the side of the play. He makes a slightly bigger bow on the pass than he does on the run, and begins to come under control, with his momentum headed toward the line of scrimmage. If #2 is open, he throws for the touchdown; if #2 is covered, he looks for #8 crossing. If no one is open, he shouts, "Go," and runs the ball. When in doubt, he shouts, "Go," and runs.

Fullback

Technique: Same as 41 arc.
Coaching Points: He is the personal blocker for the left halfback. He makes the pass play look as much like the run as possible. Against an overhang defender, he attacks

the defender, aggressively driving his left shoulder pad into the defender's left thigh pad. He puts the defender on the ground. Against a corner, he should be a little more cautious, but he should not tip off the pass. He allows the corner to come to him before blocking the corner. If the left halfback shouts, "Go," he sprints upfield and blocks for the left halfback.

Right Halfback

Technique: Same as 41 arc. Blocks aggressively.
Coaching Points: He blocks the pass play as aggressively as he would block for the run. After making contact, he brings up his blocking surface, rolls his hips, keeps the defender between his feet, and rises up on the block. He keeps contact until the whistle blows.

Rip Flex 41 Arc Bootleg Quick

The bootleg quick is a counter play to 41 arc. The play is always run to the tight- or flexed-end side. Rip flex 41 arc bootleg quick is illustrated in Figures 5-11 and 5-12. To the left, the play is Liz flex 49 arc bootleg quick, and the blocking assignments are reversed.

When facing an eight-man front, it is best to run the bootleg to a flexed end. The flexed end forces the overhang player to line up on the tight end and forfeit his position of leverage. Bootlegs off the 40 series get the quarterback outside quicker than bootlegs from any other series. Consequently, the quarterback is ready to pass the ball immediately after the fake of the sweep. He needs a receiver whose route is timed for a quick throw. The timing works best with a tight or flexed end. The bootleg with any counter run or pass play is the perfect antidote against teams with superior foot speed. Get them started in one direction, and then run or pass in the opposite direction. (Note: All interior linemen block to the pass against all heavy fronts.)

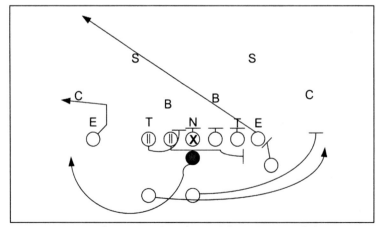

Figure 5-11. Rip flex 41 arc bootleg quick against 52 defense

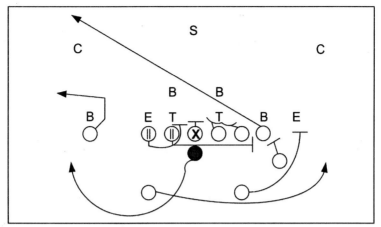

Figure 5-12. Rip flex B 41 arc bootleg quick against 44 defense

BLOCKING RULES, TECHNIQUES, AND COACHING POINTS FOR RIP FLEX 41 ARC BOOTLEG QUICK

2-Man

Rule: Runs a crossing pattern.
Coaching Points: He runs a diagonal route across the formation, aiming for a spot about 15 to 20 yards from the line of scrimmage and directly behind the original position of the defensive back to the side of the bootleg.

3-Man

Rule: Same as 41 arc. He should not cross the line of scrimmage.
Coaching Points: All interior linemen block 41 arc bootleg quick as they would the running play, with the exception—because it is a possible pass play—that no one is allowed to cross the line of scrimmage.

4-Man

Rule: Same as 41 arc. He should not cross the line of scrimmage.
Coaching Points: All interior linemen block 41 arc bootleg quick as they would the running play with the exception—because it is a possible pass play—that no one is allowed to cross the line of scrimmage.

5-Man

Rule: Same as 41 arc. He should not cross the line of scrimmage.
Coaching Points: All interior linemen block 41 arc bootleg quick as they would the

running play with the exception—because it is a possible pass play—that no one is allowed to cross the line of scrimmage.

6-Man

Rule: Pulls flat and kicks out first defender past the 3-man. He should not cross the line of scrimmage.
Coaching Points: All interior linemen block 41 arc bootleg quick as they would the running play with the exception—because it is a possible pass play—that no one is allowed to cross the line of scrimmage. He still pulls, but he kicks out the last man on the line of scrimmage instead of sealing.

7-Man

Rule: Same as 41 arc. He should not cross the line of scrimmage.
Coaching Points: All interior linemen block 41 arc bootleg quick as they would the running play with the exception—because it is a possible pass play—that no one is allowed to cross the line of scrimmage.

8-Man

Rule: Inside releases and runs a short flat route.
Coaching Points: On 41 arc bootleg quick, the 8-man makes an inside release, takes two steps upfield, and runs a slightly bowed route to sideline. The depth of the route is four to five yards. He looks for the ball as he makes his break to the sideline. If the quarterback runs with the ball, he turns upfield and blocks the closest defensive back.

Quarterback

Technique: Same as 41 arc, except he keeps the ball and executes a bootleg quick at the 9 hole.
Coaching Points: The quarterback's first two steps are exactly the same as they are on 41 arc. The change comes on the third step. Instead of handing off the ball, he drops his right shoulder, which shifts the ball to the front of his left hip—no hand or ball fake is made to the left halfback. The fake is insinuated by the proximity of the quarterback and the left halfback. As the left halfback passes him, the quarterback moves the ball to the side of his left hip where it is controlled by his left hand. He drops his right arm (to simulate a handoff), and begins his bootleg maneuver. The quarterback should stay bent at the waist to conceal the ball as he sprints to the perimeter. Speed is necessary to run by an end who is stationary on the line of scrimmage. An end who is chasing the left halfback presents no threat to the quarterback. The bootleg is usually thrown on the run. The bootleg quick is thrown about three to four steps after the quarterback passes the left halfback. Regular bootlegs are thrown later when the quarterback is out

on the perimeter and has a chance to turn his shoulders toward his target. As the left halfback passes, the quarterback uses both hands to bring the ball to his right shoulder. If he has to throw quickly to the frontside end, he will do so with his momentum going nearly parallel to the line of scrimmage. If he is not pressured, he will have time to square his shoulders to the line of scrimmage and throw to the crossing end or run the ball.

The bootleg is a pass/run option play. If the quarterback gets outside the contain man, and can gain as much yardage running the ball as he can by passing it, he should run the ball. When he cannot, he should pass the ball. If he has a deep receiver open for an easy touchdown, he throws for the touchdown. The quarterback will always look for the touchdown pass—regardless of whether a regular, slow, or bootleg quick is called.

Left Halfback

Technique: Same as 41 arc, except he does not get the ball. Makes a great fake by putting both hands on his right hip. Bends at the waist and carries out his fake.
Coaching Points: All backs simulate 41 arc and sell the run by carrying out their fakes until the whistle blows.

Fullback

Technique: Same as 41 arc.
Coaching Points: All backs simulate 41 arc and sell the run by carrying out their fakes until the whistle blows.

Right Halfback

Technique: Same as 41 arc.
Coaching Points: All backs simulate 41 arc and sell the run by carrying out their fakes until the whistle blows.

Liz B Flex 41 Wham

The third and last sweep to be discussed in the 40 series is the wham sweep. It is run from a Rip B and Liz B flex formation. Liz B flex 41 wham is illustrated in Figures 5-13 and 5-14. To the left, it is Rip B flex 49 wham. The wham sweep is always run to the flexed-end side of the formation—another departure from the traditional wing-T sweep play. It can be run from an A or B backfield set. From B backs, it can attack away from the wingback without the use of motion. In Liz B, the fullback lines up as the left halfback, and in Rip B he lines up as the right halfback. The flexed-end formation is tailor-made for the heavy fronts because the split of the tight end forces the overhang player to line up on him. This innovative formation allows all 40 series plays to be run to the tight-end/wingback side, and a pro-style sweep to the flexed end. The split of the flexed end must be wide enough to make an overhang player line up on him—usually between two to four yards. With the wingback/tight end to one side, and the flexed end to the other side, the defense cannot outflank the offense on either side of the formation. This result is a decisive advantage for the offense, and it gives the offense the benefit of running a sweep to either flank with equal facility.

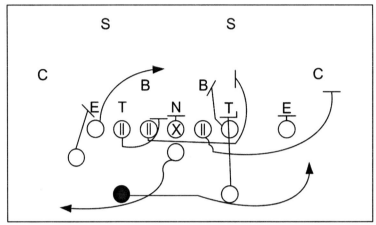

Figure 5-13. Liz B flex 41 wham against 52 defense

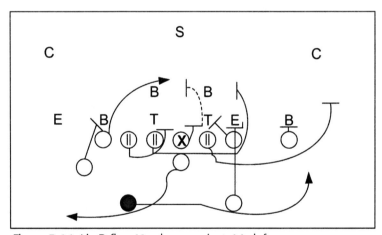

Figure 5-14. Liz B flex 41 wham against 44 defense

All three sweeps mentioned in this chapter can be run from Rip/Liz flex formations. Both 41 base and 41 arc can be run to the tight-end/wingback side against all defensive fronts. They can be mirrored to the single tight-end side against all seven-man fronts, but cannot be run well against heavy fronts. With a Rip/Liz flex formation, the base and arc sweeps can be run to the wingback/tight-end side, and the wham sweep to flexed-end side—and they can be run against all defensive fronts. Thus, Rip/Liz flex formations are the ones with a high utility value. They are innovative formations that gives a wing-T coach the assurance that his team can run a sweep play to or away from the formation against any defense—a crucial innovation in updating and rejuvenating the wing-T.

BLOCKING RULES, TECHNIQUES, AND COACHING POINTS
FOR LIZ B FLEX 41 WHAM

2-Man

Rule: Split three to four yards from 3-man, and uses a high-pressure control block to block the man on him. Takes him in any direction he wants to go.

Coaching Points: He opens his split far enough to force the last man on the line of scrimmage to align on him. A three- to four-yard split is about right. His block is a high-pressure control block—similar to a pass block. He starts with a short step with his outside foot, aimed at the middle of the defender. Simultaneously, he thrusts the heels of both hands into the defender's chest. He should be prepared to shuffle inside if the defender slants in that direction. He must prevent the defender from escaping to the inside. He should not attempt to drive the defender off the line of scrimmage. Upon contact, he widens his feet, arches his back, and keeps his head up, controlling the defender with just enough pressure so that the defender cannot knock him back off the line of scrimmage. He allows the defender to take a side, and then he takes the defender in that direction. He stays high and keeps contact until the whistle blows.

3-Man

Rule: His rule is to block down and read up.

Coaching Points: Against an even front, the 5-man will decide if the can reach the hard defender on #4. If so, the 5-man will make a "me" call, telling him that the 5-man can block his man. In this case, he steps with his left foot for the crotch of the hard man, slams him with his left shoulder, and goes up on the middle or backside backer. On a "you" call from #5, he blocks down on the hard man on the 4-man. Against an odd front, if the 4-man is covered by a backer, the 3-man slams the hard man on him with his right shoulder before going up to block the frontside backer. If the backer escapes to his outside, he blocks the backside backer.

4-Man

Rule: Pulls deep around the wham block by back, and blocks first defender outside the 2-man.

Coaching Points: Pulls, losing ground on his first two steps to get around the wham block by the fullback. As he levels off on his third step, he circles the 2-man at a point three to four yards outside his original position, and leads the sweep downfield. When he arrives at that junction, if the 2-man is engaged with and working the defender to the outside, he turns up inside the 2-man and blocks the first defender in the area.

5-Man

Rule: Against an even front, makes a "me" call if he can reach the hard man on #4.

Makes a "you" call if he cannot reach the hard man. Against an odd front, uses a zone technique to block the hard man on him. He and the 7-man must seal the frontside and backside A gaps.

Coaching Points: On a "me" call, he gets his head and left arm outside the defender's outside knee. He elongates his body by grounding his hands, and begins to scramble block the defender on a 45-degree angle from the line of scrimmage. He tries to work his head downfield so that he winds up with his body at a right angle to the line of scrimmage. On a "you" call, he uses a zone technique to block the hard man on him. He steps for the hard man's playside number and works his head between the hard man and the ballcarrier. If the hard man slants away, he goes up to the second level to block the backside backer.

6-Man

Rule: Pulls flat to the 4-man. Bows around the wham block and seals the frontside backer.
Coaching Points: He pulls flat across the 5-man, and then bows his course to get around the wham block by the fullback. He is assigned to seal the frontside backer, and as he takes his first step he should eyeball the backer. He turns up outside and close to the wham block, looking inside for the playside backer. If that backer crosses his face, he uses a high-pressure control block and keeps contact with the backer until the whistle blows.

7-Man

Rule: Full scoops. Seals the backside A gap.
Coaching Points: He uses a full scoop technique. He uses the same technique that he uses on 41 arc. He and the 5-man are responsible for sealing both A gaps.

8-Man

Rule: Inside releases, and blocks the middle-third defender.
Coaching Points: He inside releases crossfield. He uses the same technique that he uses on 41 arc. On his release, he should not be much deeper than five yards from the line of scrimmage as he crosses the ballcarrier's path.

Quarterback

Technique: Same as 41 arc.
Coaching Points: He follows technique.

Left Halfback/Wingback

Technique: Lines up as a wing left, and blocks the first man on or outside of #8.
Coaching Points: If called into motion, he starts the motion facing the sideline, and when

he gets to the 2-man, he converts to a shuffle and faces the line of scrimmage. He times his motion so that he is about five yards outside the 2-man when the ball is snapped.

Fullback

Technique: Acts as the ballcarrier. Lines up as the left halfback with his toes four yards from the line of scrimmage and slightly outside the feet of the 3-man.
Coaching Points: He comes square across the backfield, and receives the ball from the quarterback just before he arrives at his fullback spot. When he gets to the right-halfback position, he starts a slight bow that will allow him to start upfield, aiming for a spot about three to four yards outside the original position of the 2-man. If the contain man is blocked in, the fullback stays on his outside course; if the contain skates outside, the fullback runs inside of the man. He squares his shoulders to the line of scrimmage so he can take advantage of cutback possibilities.

Right Halfback

Technique: Sprints for the outside hip of 3-man and load blocks anyone in the area.
Coaching Points: In B backs, he remains in the right halfback position. His toes are four yards from the line of scrimmage, and his feet are slightly outside the feet of the 3-man. He is the wham blocker. He starts with his right foot, and aims for the outside foot of the 3-man. He runs a straight line to that spot and blocks the first defender to show up in that area. He blocks low on the defender, aiming his left shoulder pad at the outside thigh pad of the defender. He keeps his head up and drives through his target. He does not bow his course. He keeps his feet moving, and attempts to run through the defender. His objective is to put the defender on the ground.

Liz B Flex X-to-1 41 Wham Halfback Pass

Cross-to motion adds an extra blocker to the wham sweep. The wingback cracking the middle safety adds to the effectiveness of the play. Liz B X-to-1 41 wham is illustrated in Figures 5-15 and 5-16. To the left, it is Rip B X-to-9 49 wham. Blocking assignments remain the same as 41 wham. Cross-to motion also makes the halfback option pass available to the flexed side. Liz B X-to-1 41 wham halfback pass is illustrated in Figures 5-17 and 5-18. To the left, it is Rip B X-to-9 49 halfback pass. Again, the blocking assignments remain the same as 41 wham halfback pass.

BLOCKING RULES, TECHNIQUES, AND COACHING POINTS FOR LIZ B FLEX X-TO-1 41 WHAM HALFBACK PASS

2-Man

Rule: Blocks man on, as he would on 41 wham.

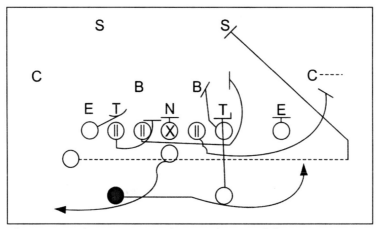

Figure 5-15. Liz B x-to-1 41 wham against 52 defense

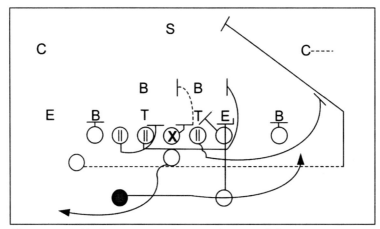

Figure 5-16. Liz B x-to-1 41 wham against 44 defense

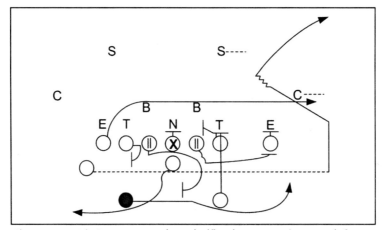

Figure 5-17. Liz B x-to-1 41wham halfback pass against 52 defense

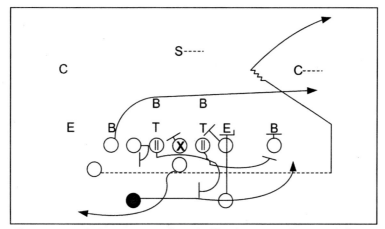

Figure 5-18. Liz B x-to-1 41 wham halfback pass against 44 defense

Coaching Points: He has the responsibility for keeping the defender on him from getting to the passer. He fronts the defender, stays on his feet, and blocks until the whistle blows.

3-Man

Rule: Same as 41 wham.
Coaching Points: He should not cross the line of scrimmage.

4-Man

Rule: Same as 41 wham, but does not cross the line of scrimmage.
Coaching Points: He keys the block of #2 as he pulls to the perimeter. If #2 needs help with his block, he helps him. If not, he continues outside #2 and blocks the corner man. He should not cross the line of scrimmage.

5-Man

Rule: Blocks the man on or in the gap to his left.
Coaching Points: Same as 41 wham, but he should not cross the line of scrimmage.

6-Man

Rule: Pulls flat past #5, and pivots away from line of scrimmage. Blocks the defender chasing from behind.
Coaching Points: He makes his pivot away from the line of scrimmage just before he gets to the 3-man. He gains two to three yards of depth on his pivot. He should not cross the line of scrimmage.

7-Man

Rule: Steps and hinges.
Coaching Points: Against an Eagle front, he fills.

8-Man

Rule: Crossing route of about 8 to 10 yards in depth.
Coaching Points: He settles in an open area and becomes an easy target for the passer.

Quarterback

Technique: 41 sweep mechanics.
Coaching Points: Again, his bootleg fake is needed to prevent backside rushers from chasing the play from behind. He makes a great bootleg fake.

Left Halfback

Technique: Comes in cross-to motion, and gets about five to six yards outside #2 when the ball is snapped.
Coaching Points: He faces the sideline when he begins his motion. When he gets past #3, he goes into a slide step and faces the defense. He times his motion so he is five to six yards outside #2 when ball is snapped. On the snap, he starts upfield and fakes a crackback block on the safety. He breaks down and stutters in place for two counts before breaking for a point five yards inside the pylon to his side. If the safety is fooled by the play-action, he gets into his pattern as soon as the safety commits to the run. Otherwise, he should not hurry the route. He makes a good stalk fake before getting into his pattern.

Fullback

Technique: B backs puts him in the left-halfback position behind #7. He will receive the handoff and execute the pass/run option as he crosses the formation.
Coaching Points: He receives the ball from the quarterback, and starts across the backfield as he would on 41 wham. His eyes should immediately go to the secondary to anticipate if he has a chance to pass for a touchdown. With the ball still in his pocket, he maneuvers it so the fingers of his throwing hand are on the laces. He sells the run for as long as he can before putting the ball in the throwing position. He makes his bow (as on 41 wham), and exercises his pass/run option. If he throws on the run, his body should be moving toward the receiver. If the wingback is open, he throws for the touchdown. If not, he comes down to #8 on his crossing route. If both receivers are covered, he shouts, "Go," and runs the ball. Remember: just because an option pass is called in the huddle, it does not mean that he automatically has to throw the ball. If he has any indecision as to whether or not he should pass the ball, he should run it.

Right Halfback

Technique: Same as 41 wham.
Coaching Points: His wham block is as important on the option pass/run play as it is on the sweep. He executes the fundamentals of the wham block, and he tries to put the 5 technique on the ground.

Rip 42 Power

The power play is a basic wing-T play that hits outside the tight end. It features a double-team block at the point of attack, a kickout block by the fullback, and a block through the hole by the backside guard. It can be run from A or B backs. Rip B 42 power is illustrated in Figures 5-19 and 5-20. To the left, the play is Liz B 48 power. Rip B 42 power is a quintessential wing-T football play. The play is designed to hit wider than the basic off-tackle power play. This scheme allows the quarterback to flow to the frontside and threaten the defense to the outside. The fake puts additional pressure on the force man—threatening him with the power inside and the quarterback keep outside.

BLOCKING RULES, TECHNIQUES, AND COACHING POINTS FOR RIP 42 POWER

2-Man

Rule: Posts or leads. If covered by a hard man, posts; if not, leads to 3-man's post.
Coaching Points: He executes the post technique by taking a six-inch controlled step on a 90-degree angle with his outside foot. Keeping a flat back, he strikes the defender in the chest with the heels of both hands. His forehead follows his hands, and he forms a triangle with his two hands and forehead. This action should get the defender to rise, exposing his outside hip to the lead blocker—the right halfback. The 2-man must not

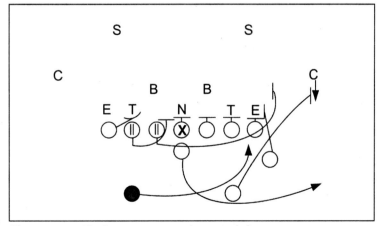

Figure 5-19. Rip B 42 power against 52 defense

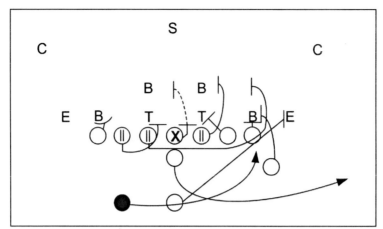

Figure 5-20. Rip B 42 power against 44 defense

knock the defender back with his post technique. If he knocks the defender back, the lead blocker will not be able to make contact on his second step, and the double-team block will break down. He keeps his man on the line of scrimmage until the right halfback makes contact with the defender. If the defender slants inside, he gets his head in front of the defender and uses a reverse shoulder block to block the defender inside. If he is open, he lead blocks to the 3-man's post. Refer to the right halfback assignment description for coaching points on the lead block.

3-Man

Rule: Blocks man on or over, stepping through the frontside gap.
Coaching Points: Against a 44 defense, he and the 4-man will use a co-op block or a horn scheme to block the 3 technique and the frontside backer. This scheme is done by a line call, or by making it a game-plan decision.

4-Man

Rule: Blocks man on or over, stepping through the frontside gap.
Coaching Points: Against a 44 defense, he and the 3-man will use a co-op block or a horn scheme to block the 3-technique and the frontside backer. This scheme is done by a line call, or by making it a game-plan decision.

5-Man

Rule: Blocks man on or over, stepping through the frontside gap.
Coaching Points: Against heavy fronts, he uses the same zone techniques described in preceding chapters.

6-Man

Rule: Pulls and seals.
Coaching Points: The seal technique on 42 power requires the 6-man to begin to bear into the line of scrimmage immediately as he clears the 5-man. Like 41 arc, he should block any seepage that may occur. He is aiming for the tail of the post man, and taking as much of the line of scrimmage as his teammates will allow. He should be tight enough to the double-team block to scrape his inside shoulder on the tail of the lead blocker. No defender should escape between the seal blocker and the double-team block. He looks to the inside, and blocks the frontside backer with a running left shoulder block.

7-Man

Rule: Full scoops.
Coaching Points: Same techniques as described in 41 arc.

8-Man

Rule: Fills.
Coaching Points: He cuts off any defender threatening the backside B gap. If #7 is covered by a hard-man, he must get his head and shoulders past the defender's inside knee and block him on all fours. His main job is to prevent a backside defender from running down the power play from behind. If the 7-man is open, he blocks the man on him with a high-pressure control block. He works to position his body between the defender and the ballcarrier.

Quarterback

Technique: Reverse pivots with his back to the hole. Crosses the midline on the second step, and hands the ball to left halfback behind the 4-man. Fakes a keep at the 1 hole.
Coaching Points: As he receives the snap, he seats the ball and pivots off his right foot. His first step with his left foot is on the midline. On his second step, with his right foot, he crosses the midline. With the ball seated, he moves his left hand to the back tip of the ball, which facilitates the handoff to the left halfback. His third step is with the left foot, and he hands the ball to the left halfback. His shoulders are at a 45-degree angle to the line of scrimmage. After the handoff, he places both hands to his outside hip, lowers his left shoulder, bends at the waist, and sprints to the corner, faking the keep.

Left Halfback

Technique: Acts as the ballcarrier. Receives ball from quarterback, and hits the 2 hole.
Coaching Points: He uses an open step and comes across the backfield parallel to the

line of scrimmage. He receives the ball from the quarterback and heads for the tail of the 2-man. He keeps the ball in his outside arm and runs tight to the double-team block. He runs with good body lean when he crosses the line of scrimmage. He bends at the waist and gives the tacklers the hard parts of his body. He runs with enough body lean so that he will fall forward when tackled. He runs like a sprinter when he gets into the secondary.

Fullback

Technique: Uses a crossover step and heads for the tail of the post man. Kicks out the first man outside the double-team block.
Coaching Points: Starting with a crossover step will put the fullback closer to the line of scrimmage and give him a better angle to kick out a defender lined up on or off the line of scrimmage. His approach is a diagonal one, aimed at the outside hip of the post man. He should stay close to the double-team block, and block the first defender to show outside it. He gets inside-out position on the defender, bends his knees, widens his base, and explodes up and into the force man. He blocks the defender with his outside shoulder, keep his feet moving, and sustains the block until the whistle blows. Emphasis should be placed on the following points: he takes a direct route to the defender, does not bow the course, widens his base prior to contact, hits on the rise with the outside shoulder, and keeps the feet moving.

Right Halfback

Technique: Leads to 2-man's post if the 2-man is covered by a hard man. If not, influences and blocks out.
Coaching Points: He steps with his left foot for the crotch of the defender on #2. He aims his left shoulder pad for the near hip of the posted defender. He hits with a wide base and extends his left forearm into the defender's waist. When the 2-man feels the pressure of the right halfback, the 2-man slips his head inside, and extends his right shoulder and forearm into the defender's waist. Both blockers lock their forearms, work their butts together, and drive the defender off the line of scrimmage on a 45-degree angle. If the man on #2 slants inside, the right halfback goes up to the next level and seals the frontside backer.

Rip 42 Power Bounce

The technique of wrong-shouldering the fullback is a problem that wing-T coaches frequently experience when running the power play. The force man gets across the line of scrimmage quickly and collisions the fullback in the backfield. He hits with his outside shoulder and tries to create a pile that will force the back out of the hole, and cut off the pulling guard. This unexpected move causes the average running back to hesitate before trying to get to the outside. The hesitation causes the back to lose speed, which aids defensive pursuit. Even with a fluid running back who bumps the play outside quickly and smoothly, he is on the perimeter without any blockers. One cannot expect the pulling guard to see the same picture and react as smoothly as a talented running back. An innovative play to combat this strategy is Rip 42 power bounce (Figures 5-21 and 5-22). To the left, it is Liz 48 power bounce. This same adjustment to a wrong-arm technique was mentioned in previous chapters. The bounce concept is applicable in the teen, 20, 30, and 40 series.

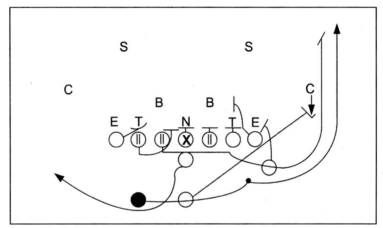

Figure 5-21. Rip 42 power bounce against 52 defense

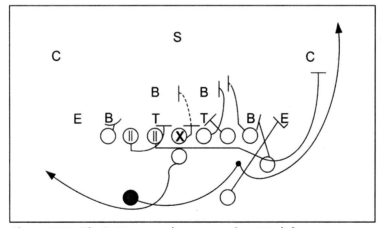

Figure 5-22. Rip B 42 power bounce against 44 defense

The bounce play attempts to take advantage of this wrong-arm strategy by having the fullback log the force man, and the pulling guard swing around the log block and lead the runner upfield. Having a predetermined play puts the pulling guard and the running back on the same page. It also alerts the tight end to release inside and seal the frontside backer—a more efficient way to seal him than using the backside guard to do so. The quarterback fakes a bootleg after handing off to the left halfback, and the left halfback will make a quick fake inside and swing around the fullback's block to the outside. With the exception of the fullback and the backside guard, all assignments for 42 bounce are exactly the same as 42 power.

BLOCKING RULES, TECHNIQUES, AND COACHING POINTS FOR RIP 42 POWER BOUNCE

2-Man

Rule: Inside releases and seals playside backer.
Coaching Points: The 2-man takes the job of the 6-man and seals the playside backer. He can bump the man on him as he releases inside. His block should be a high-pressure controlled block. He should not try to take ground, but simply prevent the backer from getting out to the perimeter.

3-Man

Rule: Same as 42 power.
Coaching Points: He follows rule.

4-Man

Rule: Same as 42 power.
Coaching Points: He follows rule.

5-Man

Rule: Same as 42 power.
Coaching Points: He follows rule.

6-Man

Rule: Pulls as he does on 42 power, and leads the play outside.
Coaching Points: He makes the play look as much like 42 power as possible. He starts to bow his course as he passes the 5-man. He swings around the collision between the fullback and the force man, and leads the left halfback down the field. He is the personal blocker for the left halfback; he blocks the first defender to cross his path.

7-Man

Rule: Full scoops.
Coaching Points: Same as 42 power.

8-Man

Rule: Same as 42 power.
Coaching Points: He follows rule.

Quarterback

Technique: Same as 42 power.
Coaching Points: Because this play is an outside play, you do not want to attract attention to the quarterback by faking a keep. Therefore, on 42 bounce, the quarterback fakes a bootleg at the 9 hole.

Left Halfback

Technique: Same as 42 power.
Coaching Points: He receives the ball from the quarterback, and starts out as he would on 42 power. At the appropriate time, he dips a yard or two into the 2 hole, and then quickly swings outside the block of the fullback. The 6-man will be ahead of him, and he will pick up the 6-man's block as he swings to the outside.

Fullback

Technique: Same as 42 power, except he logs the force man.
Coaching Points: He takes the same approach as he does on 42 power. The force man will log himself by striking the fullback with his outside shoulder. The fullback does not bow his course and tip off his intentions. He blocks high and wheels the force man to the inside.

Right Halfback/Wingback

Technique: Same as 42 power.
Coaching Points: He follows rule.

Rip Flex 42 Keep

The keep is a play-action-pass play that simulates 42 power. It is run to the tight-end/wingback side, and it can be executed from either A backs or B backs. The keep pass is an ideal complement to 42 power. It is another wing-T play that gets the quarterback on the corner with a pass/run option. Rip flex 42 keep is illustrated in Figures 5-23 and 5-24. To the left, it is Liz flex 48 keep.

The basic pattern calls for the 2-man to release inside and run a flag route. The 8-man runs a 12- to 15-yard crossing route, and the fullback runs a five-yard flat route.

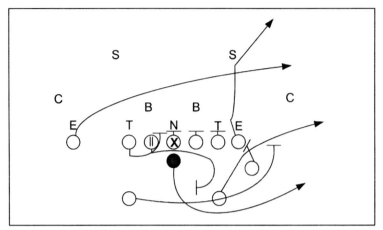

Figure 5-23. Rip B flex 42 keep against 52 defense

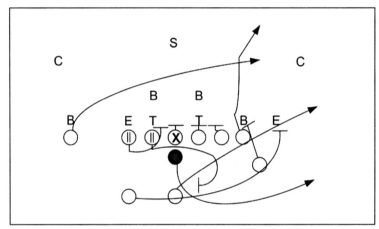

Figure 5-24. Rip flex 42 keep against 44 defense

The line blocking is basically the same as it is on 42 power, except the linemen do not block beyond the line of scrimmage.

BLOCKING RULES, TECHNIQUES, AND COACHING POINTS FOR RIP FLEX 42 KEEP

2-Man

Rule: Inside releases and runs a flag route.

Coaching Points: Against a two-deep secondary, he converts to a bench route. After releasing inside, he drives 15 yards upfield at the deep-half defender, forcing him to retreat into his deep-half responsibility. He breaks to the post for two to three steps and rounds off his route so that he is headed toward the sideline. He should be about 18 to 20 yards deep, and he should get as much separation as possible between himself and the deep-half defender. At 18 to 20 yards, he throttles down in an open area and looks for the ball. Against a three-deep secondary, he inside releases and drives at the outside shoulder of the deep-third defender. If the defender retreats, he drives to the post for three steps, and then breaks on a diagonal route for a spot five yards inside the flag. This course will allow him to catch the ball going across the goal line instead of going across the sideline. If the deep-third defender levels and plays in the flat, he anticipates the safety coming over to cover him, and adjusts his route as he would against a two-deep. Against a man-to-man coverage, he inside releases and drives for a head-on alignment with the defensive back. At about eight yards of depth, he makes a good head-and-shoulder fake to the flag, and drives to the post for three to four steps. Then, he quickly executes his flag route.

3-Man

Rule: Same as 42 power. Does not cross the line of scrimmage.
Coaching Points: He follows rule.

4-Man

Rule: Same as 42 power. Does not cross the line of scrimmage.
Coaching Points: He follows rule.

5-Man

Rule: Same as 42 power. Does not cross the line of scrimmage.
Coaching Points: He follows rule.

6-Man

Rule: Pulls as he does on 42 power. When he get to the 3-man's area, he turns away from the line of scrimmage and blocks the first defender chasing the play from the backside.
Coaching Points: He pulls flat across the 5-man, and begins to bow slightly. As he reaches the original position of the 3-man, he circles to his right and gains four to five yards of depth as he prepares to protect the quarterback by blocking any defender chasing the play from the backside. He should not get beat to the inside.

7-Man

Rule: Same as 42 power. Does not cross the line of scrimmage.
Coaching Points: He follows rule.

8-Man

Rule: Runs a 12- to 15-yard crossing route

Coaching Points: He inside releases and gains depth gradually as he crosses the formation. As he arrives at the flank, he should be aware of the depth of the fullback and the 2-man. He tries to remain equidistant from both receivers. He throttles down in an open area to become an easy target for the quarterback.

Quarterback

Technique: Fakes 42 power, and runs a keep course.
Coaching Points: His execution on 42 keep starts out exactly as 42 power. Instead of handing the ball to the left halfback on his third step (see faking the keep on 42 power), he hips the ball with his right hand, and makes a fake to the left halfback with his left hand. It is imperative that the quarterback not begin the keep action until the left halfback passes him. To do so would ruin the timing and compromise the deception of the play. As the left halfback passes, the quarterback drops his left shoulder, bends at the waist, and sprints for the flank as he eyeballs the contain man. The reaction of the contain man will determine whether he will pass or run with the ball. If the contain man skates, the quarterback will have to pull up and throw the ball. If the receivers are covered, he will have to run the ball inside the contain man. Once outside of the contain man, he looks for the deep receiver. If the receiver is open, he throws for the touchdown; if not, he looks to the 8-man crossing, and to the fullback, in that order. If no one is open, he shouts, "Go," and runs with the ball.

Left Halfback

Technique: Fakes 42 power and seals the first defender outside the wingback's block.
Coaching Points: After faking 42 power, he crosses the formation and bends his course into the line of scrimmage. He blocks the first defender outside the wingback's block. This block is aggressive, and he should not delay in his approach to his target. His block should be made on the line of scrimmage. His technique is to drive his inside shoulder pad into the outside thigh pad of the last defender on the line. He should strike with enough force to put the defender on the ground.

Fullback

Technique: Fakes 42 power. Slips inside the force man and runs a four- to five-yard flat route.
Coaching Points: Up to the point of contact, he does exactly the same thing on 42 keep as he does on 42 power. His approach is the same, but just before contact, he slips inside the force man and runs a four- to five-yard flat route. Once in the flat, he should throttle down and become an easy target for the quarterback. If the pass is thrown to him, he catches the ball and stays on the perimeter. He should take on tacklers from the outside in.

Right Halfback/Wingback

Technique: Blocks the first defender on or over the 2-man's area.
Coaching Points: The wingback should block as he does on 42 power. After contact, he should work up on the defender and seal him to the inside.

Two innovations make the keep play as effective today as it was 40 years ago. Both innovations call for the quarterback to get a little more depth and pull up, rather than continue his path to the perimeter. The first innovation is to have the 8-man start his crossing route and then sharply break back for the flag. With the flow of the play going in one direction, and the 8-man running a route in the opposite direction, the play becomes a misdirection pass and puts considerable pressure on defensive backs. Rip flex 42 keep throwback-to-8 is illustrated in Figures 5-25 and 5-26. To the left, it is Liz flex 48 keep throwback-to-2. The blocking assignments are the same as for 42 keep for everyone except the fullback. He blocks an overhang player instead of running his flat route. If no overhang player exists, he fakes his flat route and blocks the corner late.

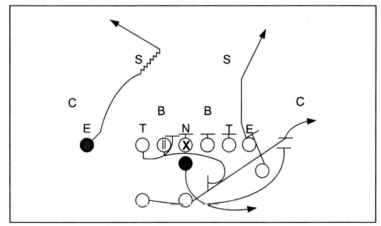

Figure 5-25. Rip flex 42 keep throwback-to-8 against 52 defense

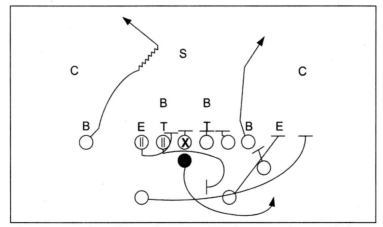

Figure 5-26. Rip B flex 42 keep throwback-to-8 against 44 defense

The second innovation is a play that Syracuse University used so effectively inside their opponents 10-yard line. It looks just like 42 keep. The frontside linemen block the man on or in their inside gap, and the backside linemen hinge block. The 2-man blocks to the inside, pretends to loose his balance and falls down. After a count or two, he recovers and runs a crossing route to the opposite pylon. At times, he is so open that he actually turns to the quarterback and backpedals to the pylon. Yale University used this play as a two-point conversion play for many years. Assignments and technique for the tight-end delay pass were covered in Chapter 1. The play is just as effective when executed from the 40 series. Rip flex 42 keep throwback to 2 is illustrated in Figures 5-27 and 5-28. To the left, it is Liz flex 48 keep throwback to 8. (Note: All interior linemen block to the pass against all heavy fronts.)

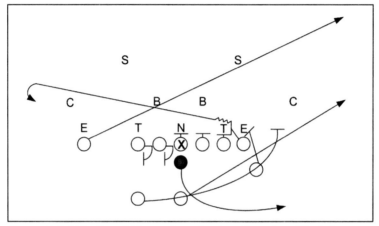

Figure 5-27. Rip flex 42 keep throwback to 2 against 52 defense

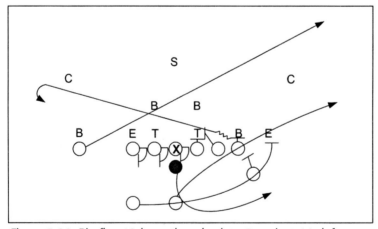

Figure 5-28. Rip flex 42 keep throwback to 2 against 44 defense

Liz 43 Counter Crisscross

The counter crisscross is a perfect complement to 41 bootleg. Liz B 43 counter crisscross is illustrated in Figures 5-29 and 5-30. To the left, it is Rip B 47 counter crisscross. It can best be executed from a closed formation, and it is run from A or B backs. The threat of the bootleg puts great pressure on the contain man in seven-man fronts. He is faced with an inside release by the tight end—alerting him to the possibility of a run off-tackle—and is simultaneously threatened outside by the possibility of the quarterback bootleg. This situation creates a dilemma for him: he can come upfield to contain the quarterback, or he can close off the tail of the tight end and defend the off-tackle play. If he comes upfield, he is vulnerable to the off-tackle play; if he closes the off-tackle hole, he is vulnerable to the bootleg. The backer in an eight-man front—if he aligns over the tight end—sees the tight end move to his outside on both 42 counter crisscross and 49 bootleg quick. If he widens with the tight end, he is vulnerable to the counter crisscross; if he closes on the influence by the tight end, he is unable to cover the tight end in the flat on the bootleg quick. The pressure the counter crisscross puts on the contain man is reason enough to have it as part of the wing-T offense.

BLOCKING RULES, TECHNIQUES, AND COACHING POINTS FOR LIZ 43 COUNTER CRISSCROSS

2-Man

Rule: Leads to a post by the 3-man. If the 3-man is not covered by hard man, influences and blocks out.

Coaching Points: If the 3-man is covered by a hard man, he leads to his post. If the 3-man is not covered by a hard man, he influences the man on him and blocks the first defender to the outside. He should not come off his influence block too soon. The

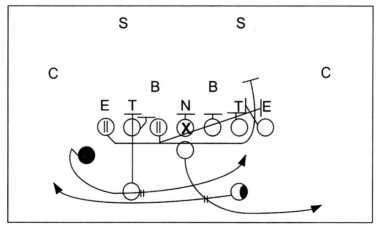

Figure 5-29. Liz B 43 counter crisscross against 52 defense

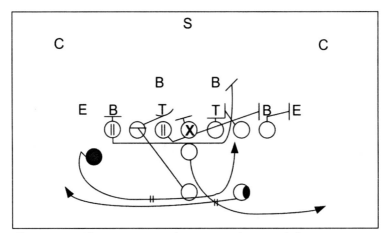

Figure 5-30. Liz 43 counter crisscross against 44 defense

overhang player has contain responsibility, and that player will be checking the quarterback. He has time to set up the man on him for the kickout block by the 6-man.

3-Man

Rule: Posts or leads.
Coaching Points: He posts a hard man on him. If he is not covered by a hard man, leads to the post of the 4-man.

4-Man

Rule: Blocks area solid. He may be the post man. He should not get driven back.
Coaching Points: If he has a backer over him, he shows the pass and blocks his area. If the 3-man is not covered by a hard man, he becomes the post man and the 3-man becomes the lead blocker.

5-Man

Rule: Blocks a hard-man on him with his left shoulder. If no hard man is on him, blocks the man in the backside A gap with his right shoulder. He should not get driven back into the line of scrimmage.
Coaching Points: If he is blocking a hard man, he moves him off the line of scrimmage. He should not get driven backwards or allow a 2 or 2i player to penetrate the line of scrimmage. Penetration will disrupt the play by cutting off the pulling guard and the tight end.

6-Man

Rule: Pulls flat for the tail of the 2-man and kicks out the first man past the double-team block.

Coaching Points: He pulls flat across the 5-man. As he passes him, he begins to bear into the line of scrimmage. He takes as much of the line of scrimmage as he can. He kicks out the first defender to show outside of the double-team block. He blocks him with his right shoulder, using all the techniques of a good trap block already explained. If the contain man goes upfield to contain the quarterback, he turns up the hole and blocks downfield.

7-Man

Rule: Seals the backside B gap.
Coaching Points: He should not be in a big hurry to slam/release a hard man on him unless a backer is shooting his inside gap. In that case, he blocks the backer. Penetration from a hard man or a backer will cut off the path of the pulling 8-man.

8-Man

Rule: Pulls flat down the line of scrimmage and turns up outside the double-team block. Looks for the playside backer. If the backer is blocked, leads the left halfback upfield and blocks a deep defender.
Coaching Points: He closes his split so he can reach the hole as quickly as possible. He uses his arms to facilitate his pull. He whips his right arm back and through his left arm across his body. He keeps his chest on his right thigh as he takes his first step. He should not begin to rise until his third step. He bows his course slightly to facilitate turning up the hole. He stays close to the double-team, and gets as square as possible as he crosses the line of scrimmage. He looks inside for the frontside backer, who is the man he is assigned to block. If the backer is blocked, he continues upfield and blocks a secondary defender. He does not stop to block, but keeps moving. He should not get in the runner's path and clutter the hole.

Quarterback

Technique: Same footwork as 49 base. Hands the ball to the right halfback, and fakes a bootleg at the 1 hole.
Coaching Points: He executes the counter crisscross exactly the same as he would on 49 base. This play should be called when he has had success with the bootleg, and the contain man finally decides to "search" the quarterback on all bootleg fakes.

Right Halfback

Technique: Same footwork as 49. Receives ball from quarterback, and then makes an inside handoff to wingback. After the exchange, fakes 49 sweep.
Coaching Points: He starts the counter crisscross just like 49 base. As he receives the ball from the quarterback, he runs at controlled speed and bends at the waist. He begins to

adjust the ball to facilitate the exchange with the wingback. He places his right hand on the back tip of the ball and makes an inside handoff to the wingback with his right hand. After the exchange, he puts both hands on his left hip and carries out his fake to the flank.

Fullback

Technique: Heads for the tail of the 7-man, and blocks any defender in that area.
Coaching Points: He sprints for the inside leg of the 7-man, and drives his left shoulder pad into the inside thigh pad of any defender in the area. He gets to his landmark ahead of the 2-man. The 2-man should not have to bow his course to get around his block.

Wingback

Technique: Comes from his wing position on a course that will enable him to receive the inside handoff from the right halfback.
Coaching Points: From a wingback alignment, he jab steps with his left foot and then begins to bow back and run a parallel course across the formation just inside the crossing right halfback. The exchange between him and the right halfback should take place in an area between the 7-man and the 6-man. After he gets the ball, he rolls into the hole, hugging the double-team block. He tries to hit the hole with his shoulders parallel to the line of scrimmage. Doing so will enable him to make cuts in all directions. From a halfback alignment, he starts by taking a crossover step with his right foot, followed by a lead step with his left foot. Both steps are aimed at the tail of the 8-man. His second step should put him about three yards from the line of scrimmage. He breaks on the second step and pushes off it to start himself back on a course that will facilitate the exchange from the right halfback.

Liz 42 Counter Crisscross Keep

The keep off the counter crisscross is the third and last play that stems from the bootleg. It too can be run from A or B backs. Liz 43 counter crisscross keep is illustrated in Figures 5-31 and 5-32. To the left, it is Rip 47 counter crisscross keep. The keep should be run only after both the bootleg and counter crisscross plays have been successfully run. These three plays confront the contain man with defending a bootleg by the quarterback, a counter inside the bootleg, and a pass off the counter fake—quite a chore for any defender. (Note: All interior linemen block to the pass against all heavy fronts.)

BLOCKING RULES, TECHNIQUES, AND COACHING POINTS FOR LIZ 42 COUNTER CRISSCROSS KEEP

2-Man

Rule: Runs a flag route behind the defensive back.

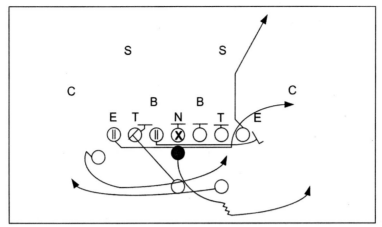

Figure 5-31. Liz 43 counter crisscross keep against 52 defense

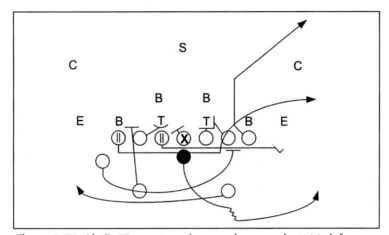

Figure 5-32. Liz B 43 counter crisscross keep against 44 defense

Coaching Points: He steps with his left foot and simulates a lead block. He pushes off that foot, drives upfield, and runs his flag route. He adjusts his route to coverage as he does in 42 keep.

3-Man

Rule: Same as 42 counter crisscross. Does not cross the line of scrimmage.
Coaching Points: He follows rule.

4-Man

Rule: Same as 42 counter crisscross. Does not cross the line of scrimmage.
Coaching Points: He follows rule.

5-Man

Rule: Same as 42 counter crisscross. Does not cross the line of scrimmage.
Coaching Points: He follows rule.

6-Man

Rule: Same as 42 counter crisscross. Does not cross the line of scrimmage.
Coaching Points: He logs the contain defender if the defender is playing the counter, and kicks him out if he is playing the quarterback.

7-Man

Rule: Same as 42 counter crisscross. Does not cross the line of scrimmage.
Coaching Points: He follows rule.

8-Man

Rule: Same as 42 counter crisscross, except when he turns up the hole, he runs a five-yard flat route.
Coaching Points: He pulls as he does on 42 counter crisscross. As he runs through the hole, he bends his route into the flat area at about five to six yards deep. He settles in the open area and runs at controlled speed so he becomes an easy target for the quarterback.

Quarterback

Technique: Fakes 48 counter crisscross and reads the reaction of the contain man. Pulls up if he comes upfield. Continues to flank if he plays the counter.
Coaching Points: The keep by the quarterback is best described as a delayed bootleg. He begins by faking to the right halfback with both hands on the ball. He then draws the ball to his right hip, holding it in his right hand, and allows his left hand to dangle free at his side. After the fake, he retreats two to three yards, watching the reaction of the contain man. The retreat gives him time to see if the contain man is defending the counter play, or coming upfield to contain him. If he is playing the counter, he continues his path to the flank and executes his pass/run option. If the contain man comes upfield, he pulls up and allows the 6-man to kick him out. In either case, he is looking to see if the defensive back has allowed the 2-man to get behind him. He is always looking to pass for a touchdown. If the 2-man is covered, he looks for the 8-man in the flat. If no one is open, he yells. "Go," and he runs with the ball.

Left Halfback/Wingback

Technique: Fakes 42 counter crisscross.

Coaching Points: After faking the counter crisscross, he blocks any defender to cross his face in the 2-hole area.

Fullback

Technique: Same as 42 counter crisscross.
Coaching Points: He follows rule.

Right Halfback

Technique: Fakes 42 counter crisscross.
Coaching Points: He fakes an exchange to the wing, places both hands to his outside hip, and carries out his fake at the 9 hole.

Rip 43 Power

The final play in this chapter is the tighter off-tackle power play Rip 43 power, which is illustrated in Figures 5-33 and 5-34. To the left, it is Liz 47 power. This off-tackle power play is a signature wing-T play. Like 42 power, it features a double-team at the point of attack, a kickout block, and a block through the hole. The defensive spacing dictates where the double-team will occur. If the tackle is covered by a hard man, the double-team will be between the tackle and the tight end. If he is not covered by a hard man, the double-team is between the tackle and the frontside guard. In both cases, the ballcarrier has a tighter hole to hit, and the play is better executed with the quarterback making a bootleg rather than a keep fake. The keep fake can force the ballcarrier too wide—especially when the double-team is with the tackle and the guard. The bootleg action allows the ballcarrier to flow smoothly into the off-tackle hole. Of course, 43 bounce can be run off 43 power action. Only the fullback, the left halfback, and the pulling guard would have to make an adjustment.

BLOCKING RULES, TECHNIQUES, AND COACHING POINTS FOR RIP 43 POWER

2-Man

Rule: Leads or cracks back.
Coaching Points: If #3 is covered by a hard man, he uses his post/lead techniques to double-team the man on #3. He steps with his inside foot for the crotch of the defender. He keeps his chest on his left thigh pad, and aims his left shoulder for the near thigh pad of the defender. Upon contact, he broadens his blocking surface by bringing up his left forearm, and widens his base so the defender is between his feet. He works his left hip next to the 3-man's right hip and begins to drive the defender down the line of scrimmage. If the 3-man is open (as in a 4-3 or 44 front), he rips

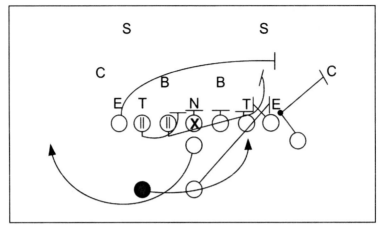

Figure 5-33. Rip 43 power against 52 defense

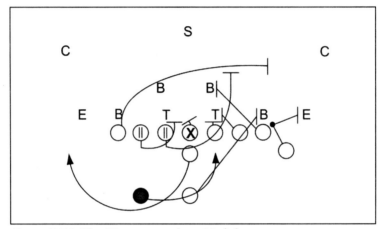

Figure 5-34. Rip 43 power against 44 defense

inside the man on him and blocks the inside backer. He uses a shoulder block to try to collapse the backer to the inside.

3-Man

Rule: Posts or leads.

Coaching Points: If he has a hard man on him, he posts the hard man. He takes a short step with his right foot into the middle of the defender's body, and punches both palms of his right and left hands into the hard man's numbers. His job is to get the defender upright so the 2-man can get a good shot at his exposed near hip. When he feels the pressure of the 2-man, he turns his body to the left so he and #2 lock forearms and are hip-to-hip. He drives the defender down the line of scrimmage.

4-Man

Rule: Blocks man on or over, stepping through the frontside gap.
Coaching Points: If #3 is open, the 4-man becomes the post man. He uses the same post techniques as described for the 3-man. Otherwise, he follows his rule.

5-Man

Rule: Blocks man on or over, stepping through the playside gap.
Coaching Points: He follows his rule. If uncovered (as in a 44, or 62 front), he reaches through the frontside A gap and blocks any defender who threatens that gap.

6-Man

Rule: Pulls and leads through hole.
Coaching Points: He pulls flat down the line of scrimmage and bears into the line as much as possible. He should be close to the double-team when he turns up the hole (no daylight should be seen between him and the double-team). He blocks the first defender to cross his face with a running left shoulder block.

7-Man

Rule: Full scoops.
Coaching Points: He pulls and gains ground on his first three steps. When his right foot hits the ground on his third step, he whips his body into the line of scrimmage and blocks anyone threatening the backside A gap. If the A gap is not threatened, he turns back and picks off any backside pursuit.

8-Man

Rule: Releases crossfield.
Coaching Points: He should not be any deeper than five yards as he crosses the hole. He blocks the first defender to cross his face.

Quarterback

Technique: Same footwork and techniques as 41 arc.
Coaching Points: He follows technique.

Left Halfback

Technique: Starts like 41 arc. Receives the ball running at controlled speed, and bends toward the line of scrimmage so he can hit directly over the double-team block.

Coaching Points: He crosses the formation at controlled speed. Once he gets the handoff from the quarterback, he turns sharply toward the line of scrimmage, squares his shoulders to the goal line, and accelerates over the tail of the post man. If #4 is the post man (as in a 44), he will have to make a very tight cut into the line to run over the post man.

Fullback

Technique: Kicks out the first defender outside the double-team block.
Coaching Points: From his fullback position, he starts a crossover step with his left foot and aims for the outside leg of #3. He uses his right shoulder to block the first defender outside the double-team block. Hw widens his feet before contact, lowers his center of gravity, and hits on the rise. He brings up his right forearm to increase his blocking surface, pumps his off arm and his feet, and maintains contact until the whistle blows.

Right Halfback

Technique: Blocks first man outside #2.
Coaching Points: In a wingback alignment, his job is to make the defender over #2 believe that he is down blocking on the defender. He steps to the defender and strikes the defender's near shoulder with his left shoulder pad. Then, he blocks out on first defender to the outside. He uses a wall-off block on the outside defender. In halfback alignment, he sprints for a spot one yard outside the first man outside #2. He runs a straight line to that reference point and fakes a load block on the defender. At the last moment, he veers outside and walls off the corner defender.

6

The 50 Series

The lead play in the 50 series is a quick toss to the fullback. It can attack the flank quicker than any other play in the wing-T repertoire. It is a traditional wing-T play, and it is used in many other offensives systems. Several innovations will be introduced in this chapter that enhance and improve the plays in the 50 series. The innovations will deal with formations, blocking schemes, cross-to motion, and an adjustment on the bootleg pass.

Rip Flex 51 Easy

The fullback toss play is run with an easy scheme to a wingback/tight-end or halfback/tight-end side of the formation. Rip 51 toss is illustrated to the wingback/tight-end side (Figures 6-1 and 6-2), and Liz 51 toss is illustrated to the single tight-end side (Figures 6-3 and 6-4).

The easy scheme is so named because of the ease with which the tight end is able to seal the frontside backer against seven-man fronts. The frontside backer always aligned inside the tight end, which makes it easy for him to seal the backer. Against

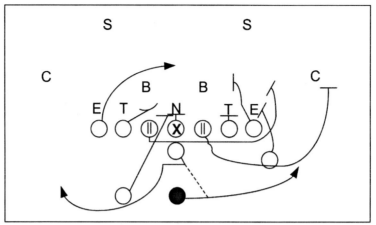

Figure 6-1. Rip 51 toss to wingback/tight-end side easy scheme against 52 defense

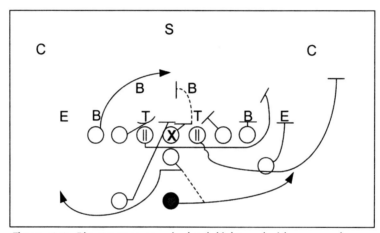

Figure 6-2. Rip 51 toss to wingback/tight-end side easy scheme against 44 defense

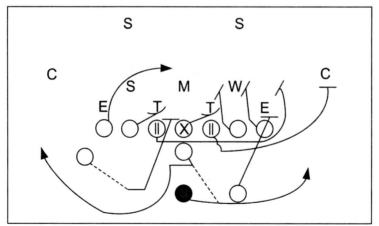

Figure 6-3. Liz 51 toss to tight-end side easy scheme against 43 defense

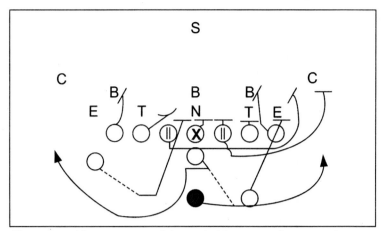

Figure 6-4. Liz 51 toss to tight-end side easy scheme against 53 defense

most defenses, the wingback outflanks the last man on the line of scrimmage, which gives him a great chance to seal that defender.

The fullback toss to the tight-end side is a good play—especially against fronts that do not have an overhang player; however, the play is problematic against fronts that do. To the halfback side, an overhang player can get penetration and force the fullback to bow his course, which hurts the timing of the play. A wing is closer to the overhang player than the halfback, so the wing has a better chance to engage the overhang player on the line of scrimmage. This situation gives the fullback a two-way go, similar to the option block by the flexed end in a wham scheme. From his normal alignment, the fullback has a lead blocker to both sides of any formation: one blocker is aligned as a wing or slot, and the other is in a halfback position. This alignment makes it possible to run the toss to both sides of the formation.

BLOCKING RULES, TECHNIQUES, AND COACHING POINTS FOR RIP FLEX 51 EASY

2-Man

Rule: Blocks the first backer on or to his inside.
Coaching Points: Easy tells the tight end to block the first backer on or inside him. This is a wall-off-type block. The 2-man uses a high-pressure control block and just tries to keep his body between the backer and the ballcarrier. He keeps a wide base, shuffles his feet, and fronts the defender, preventing the defender from escaping inside or outside his block.

3-Man

Rule: Blocks a hard man on or inside him. If a backer is over him—as in a 4-3 front, he chips the 2 technique and goes up on the middle backer.

Coaching Points: In nearly every situation, #3 will be blocking a hard man on or inside of him. The only front that will alter his assignment is a college 4-3. Here, the 3-man will chip off the hard man to his inside and go up to block the middle backer. Whether blocking a backer or a hard man, #3 should just try to get his body between the defender and the ballcarrier.

4-Man

Rule: Pulls with depth and leads the fullback on the perimeter.
Coaching Points: He pulls with depth, gaining ground on his first two steps, and levels off on his third step. He looks for the right halfback or the wingback's block on the last man on the line of scrimmage. He should be deep enough to get outside of that block, and take the force man in any direction he can. The fullback will break off his block.

5-Man

Rule: Blocks man on or over, stepping through the frontside gap.
Coaching Points: In reaching for a 2 or 2i player, he takes a step with his right foot for the crotch of the defender and tries to get his head and inside arm past the defender's outside leg. He elongates his body with his chest on his right thigh, and scramble blocks the defender on all fours. He tries to work his head on a 45-degree angle to the line of scrimmage. Against a base 50 front, if the backer over #4 crowds the line and is threatening to blitz, he avoids the nose man and reach blocks the blitzing backer. The 7-man and left halfback will block the nose man. He and the 7-man are responsible for the frontside and backside A gaps. If he is blocking the nose man, he takes a short step with his right foot to the frontside gap, aiming for the frontside number of the nose man. He gets his body between the defender and the ballcarrier, rises quickly, and walls off the nose man. If the nose man slants away, he goes up to the second level and blocks the backside backer.

6-Man

Rule: Pulls and seals outside the right halfback's block. Eyeballs the playside backer on his first step and is prepared to block the backer if he rushes any frontside gap.
Coaching Points: He pulls flat across #5, and then begins to get deep enough to get around the right halfback or wingback's block. He is responsible for sealing the first defender to show outside of the back's block. If no threat is coming from the inside, he continues downfield and blocks at that level.

7-Man

Rule: Full scoop technique. Same as 51 wham.
Coaching Points: He uses his arms to facilitate his pull, and loses ground on his first

three steps. As he turns into the line, his shoulders should be parallel to it, and he should be running over a spot where the #5 man initially lined up. He seals any defender in the area. If he has to leave his feet and end up on all fours, he does so.

8-Man

Rule: Releases crossfield.
Coaching Points: He uses the same crossfield technique as in 51 wham.

Quarterback

Technique: Reverse pivots with his back to the hole. Makes a two-handed toss to the fullback, fakes a counter to the left halfback, and bootlegs at the 9 hole.
Coaching Points: As he receives the snap, he seats the ball and begin a reverse pivot, using his right foot as the pivot foot. He crosses the midline with his left foot and bends at the waist. His left toe should be pointed at a spot one yard to the right of the fullback's original position. He uses a soft, dead-ball, two-handed pitch to get the ball to the fullback. He leads the fullback so he does not have to wait for the ball or reach back for it. He should not straighten up as he makes the pitch—to do so will cause the pitch to rise and increase the chances of making a bad pitch. After the toss, he brings both hands back to his stomach, pushes off his left foot, and steps with his right foot in the direction of the faking wingback. He fakes to the wingback with his right hand, brings both hands to his left hip, pushes off his right foot, and fakes a bootleg at the 9 hole.

Left Halfback

Technique: Same as 51 wham.
Coaching Points: Same as 51 wham.

Fullback

Technique: Leads with his right foot, and catches the toss from the quarterback. Heads for a spot one to two yards outside the 2-man. Runs inside or outside of his block.
Coaching Points: He steps with his right foot, losing enough ground to allow him to belly around the right-halfback position. He looks to the quarterback immediately, and uses both hands to offer him a target for the toss. His hands should be at waist level with the fingers pointed downward. He catches the toss at the level of his waist (or lower) with his fingers pointed downward. He reverses this position if the toss is above the waist or higher. He should not use his body to catch the toss, but instead catch it with his hands only. Remember, he catches the ball by using two faculties: his hands and his eyes. After he catches the toss, he gets his momentum started upfield, and runs north and south. He aims for a point one to two yards outside the flexed end.

Right Halfback (or Wingback)

Technique: From a halfback position, he sprints for a position one yard outside the last man on the line of scrimmage and executes a load block. From a wingback position, he blocks down on the first man on or outside the tight end.

Coaching Points: From a halfback position, he aims for a spot one yard outside of the last man on the line of scrimmage. He steps with his right foot, and runs a straight line for his reference point. He should not bow his course. This course will allow him to block the end if the end skates out, or tighten his course if the end closes to the inside. At the point of contact, he bends his knees, keeps his head up, and drives his left shoulder pad into the left thigh pad of the defender. He explodes into the block, hits on the rise, and runs through the defender. His block should be forceful enough to knock the defender's outside leg out from under him and put him on the ground. If the defender fails to go down, he continues his block from an all-fours position, and scramble blocks the defender until the whistle blows.

From a wingback position, he steps with his left foot for the crotch of the defensive end. On his second step, he aims his inside shoulder pad for the outside thigh pad of the defensive end. Aiming below the hip will allow for a natural rise by the wing, and contact will be at the break of the hip of the defender. He brings up his blocking surface, bows his neck, widens his base, and drives the defensive end down the line of scrimmage. If he begins to lose the block, he goes to all fours and continues with a scramble block until the whistle blows. Against an overhang player, he uses the same option-block techniques as the flexed end (see coaching points for the flexed end on 51 wham).

Liz Flex 51 Wham

An innovation to the base fullback toss play is to flex the end to the toss side, and run it with a wham scheme. Liz flex 51 wham is illustrated in Figures 6-5 and 6-6. To the left, the play is Rob flex 59 wham, and the blocking assignments are reversed. With a flexed end, and using the wham scheme, the fullback toss can be run against all defensive fronts with overhang players. The unique thing about the wham play—unlike the traditional toss—is that it is an option run for the fullback. The fullback takes the toss, aims for a spot a couple of yards outside the flex end, and simply reads his block. The play has the potential of a power play inside, or a sweep outside. The toss is a great play away from formation when defenses rotate their secondary, overshift their fronts, or slant their line to the formation side. The wham scheme is the most efficient scheme for the fullback toss because it can effectively attack any defensive front. Army/Navy flex formations force overhang players to align on the flexed ends to both sides of the formation. These formations allow the fullback toss play to be run to either flank—even against eight-man fronts. Army/Navy 51 wham formations are illustrated in Figures 6-7 through 6-10. In the Army formation, the play is run to the formation side, and in the Navy flex formation, it is run to the flexed end and away from the formation.

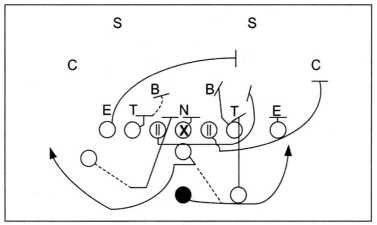

Figure 6-5. Liz flex 51 toss to flexed-end side wham scheme against 52 defense

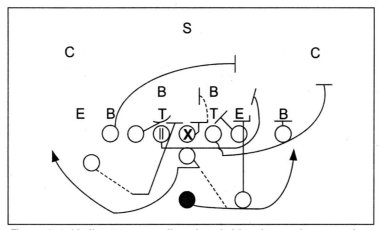

Figure 6-6. Liz flex 51 toss to flexed-end side wham scheme against 44 defense

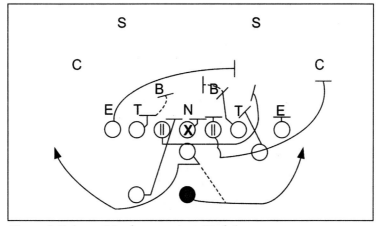

Figure 6-7. Army 51 wham against 52 defense

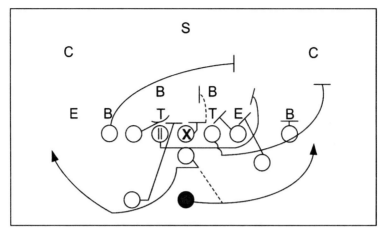

Figure 6-8. Army 51 wham against 44 defense

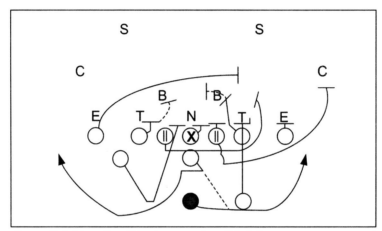

Figure 6-9. Navy flex 51 wham against 52 defense

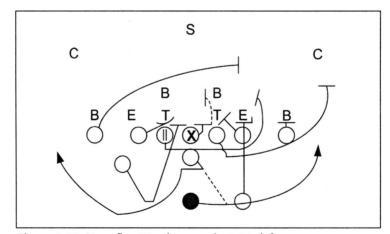

Figure 6-10. Navy flex 51 wham against 44 defense

Cross-to motion is another variation that can strengthen the play by adding another blocker at the point of attack. It also slows down secondary support by the release of an eligible receiver (WB) downfield. Liz flex X-to-1 51 wham is illustrated in Figures 6-11 and 6-12. To the left, the play is Rip flex X-to-9 59 wham, and the blocking assignments are reversed.

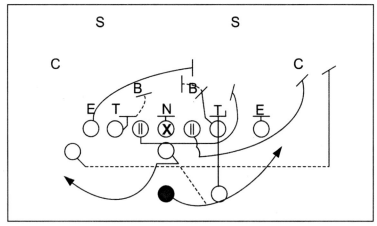

Figure 6-11. Liz flex x-to-1 51 wham against 52 defense

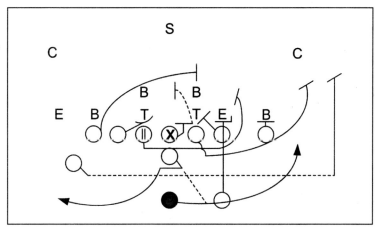

Figure 6-12. Liz flex x-to-1 51 wham against 44 defense

Slide-to motion is a good scheme when the backside guard is having trouble blocking the frontside backer. It can help the play by putting the motion man in a better position than the backside guard to seal the inside backer. In slide-to motion, the wingback ends up outside of the frontside backer when the ball is snapped, which puts him in a perfect position to seal the backer. Liz flex slide-to-3 51 wham is illustrated in Figures 6-13 and 6-14. To the left, the play is Rip flex slide-to-7 59 wham, and the blocking assignments are reversed. With the nuances previously mentioned, Army/Navy formations, cross-to motion, and slide-to motion can also be used with the wham-blocking scheme in the 40 series.

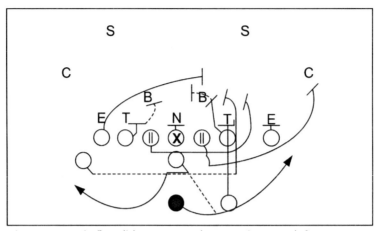

Figure 6-13. Liz flex slide-to-3 51 wham against 52 defense

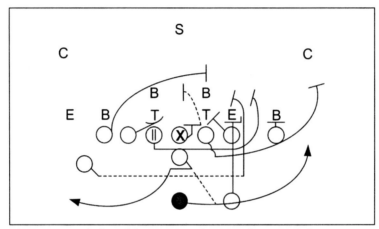

Figure 6-14. Liz flex slide-to-3 51 wham against 44 defense

BLOCKING RULES, TECHNIQUES, AND COACHING POINTS FOR LIZ FLEX 51 WHAM

2-Man

Rule: Flexes three to four yards, wide enough to force an overhang player to line up on him. Blocks the defender on him with a high-pressure control block.

Coaching Points: His block is similar to a pass-protection block. He starts with a short step, with the outside foot aimed at the middle of the defender. Simultaneously, he thrusts the heels of both hands into the defender's chest. He should be prepared to shuffle inside if the defender slants in that direction. He must not lose him to the inside. He should not attempt to knock him off the line of scrimmage, but remain content with keeping him on the line. Upon making contact, he widens his feet, arches his back, keeps his head up, and controls the defender with just enough pressure so that the defender does not knock him back off the line. He allows the defender to take a side, and then he aggressively blocks the defender in that direction. He stays high and keeps contact until the whistle blows.

3-Man

Rule: Blocks gap, reads up.
Coaching Points: Against an even front, #5 will decide if he can reach the hard man on #4. If so, #5 will make a "me" call, telling the 3-man that #5 can block the man in his inside gap. In this case, #3 steps with his left foot for the crotch of the hard man, slams him with his left shoulder, and goes up to the second level to block the middle or backside backer. Against an odd front, if a backer covers the 4-man, #3 slams the hard man on him with his right shoulder before going up to block the backer. If the backer escapes to his outside, he blocks the backside backer.

4-Man

Rule: Pulls deep around the wham block and leads the fullback outside or inside the 2-man's block. Leads the fullback downfield.
Coaching Points: He pulls, losing ground on his first two steps to get around the wham block by the right halfback. As he levels off on his third step, he circles #2 at a point three to four yards outside of #2's original position, and blocks the first support defender to cross his face. If #2 is engaged with and working the defender to the outside, the 4-man turns up inside #2 and blocks the first defender in the area. He should not go beyond four to five yards of #2's initial alignment before he turns upfield.

5-Man

Rule: Blocks man on or over, stepping through the frontside gap.
Coaching Points: Against an even front, he makes a "me" call if he can reach the man on #4. When he reaches, he uses a scramble-block technique to get his head and left arm outside the defender's outside knee. He stays on all fours and works the defender off the line of scrimmage on a 45-degree angle. If he cannot reach the man on #4, he makes a "you" call and blocks the man on or over him. Against a nose man, he takes a short step with his right foot for the frontside number of the nose man, and works his head between the nose and the ballcarrier. If the nose man slants away, #5 goes up to the second level and blocks the backside backer. He and #7 must seal the frontside and backside A gaps. Against a backer, he steps to the frontside A gap and blocks any defender threatening it. If no threat is present, he goes to the second level and blocks the backside backer.

6-Man

Rule: Pulls and seals the frontside backer.

Coaching Points: He pulls flat across #5, and then bows his course to get around the wham block. He is assigned to seal the frontside backer. He eyeballs the backer as he takes his first step, and he is prepared to block if the backer should run through any frontside gap. He turns up outside and close to the wham block, looking inside for the frontside backer. If the backer is moving to the flank, he gets his head past his outside shoulder and runs with him. He keeps contact until the whistle blows.

7-Man

Rule: Full scoops. Seals the backside A gap.
Coaching Points: His job is to prevent any lineman working down the line, or a backer trying to penetrate the backside A gap, from catching the play from behind. He pulls, gaining depth on his first three steps. When his right foot strikes the ground on his third step, he pivots off it and works his head and shoulders into the line of scrimmage, scooping any defender who is caught in his arc. At times, he may have to leave his feet and throw his inside arm and head in front of a defender, and work on all fours to cut off backside pursuit.

8-Man

Rule: Releases crossfield.
Coaching Points: He releases inside and sprints across the formation, just behind the backers, and blocks the first defender in to cross in his path. He should not be any deeper than five yards from the line of scrimmage.

Quarterback

Technique: Same as 51 easy.
Coaching Points: Same as 51 easy.

Left Halfback (or Wingback)

Technique: Fakes 24 counter.
Coaching Points: He times his motion so his right foot hits the left-halfback position when the ball is snapped. He bends his chest over his right knee to break his momentum, then pushes off the right foot and heads for the tail of #5. The quarterback will give him a hand fake. He makes a good fake and blocks any defender in the backside A gap.

Fullback

Technique: Same as 51 easy.
Coaching Points: Same as 51 easy.

Right Halfback

Technique: Sprints for the outside hip of #3, and blocks any defender in the area.
Coaching Points: He starts with his right foot and sprints for his reference point: the outside leg of #3. He stays low, and does not bow his course. He runs a straight line to his reference point. He blocks the first defender in the area. He drives his inside shoulder pad into the outside thigh pad of the defender. He explodes into the defender and attempts to run through the defender. His block should be executed with enough thrust to knock down an interior lineman on contact.

Liz Flex 54 Counter

The fullback toss play has two companion plays. The first one is a counter play. Liz flex 54 counter is illustrated in Figures 6-15 and 6-16. To the left, the play is Rip flex 56 counter, and the blocking assignments are reversed. The counter plays are designed to slow down the backers and delay their pursuit when the fullback carries the ball on 51-59 toss. These plays set up the play-action passes in this series, and also keep the 5 technique in a 50 front from overplaying the wham block. He sees the same blocking pattern on 51 toss as he does on 54 counter. The counter plays are blocked with a traditional trap-blocking scheme.

BLOCKING RULES, TECHNIQUES, AND COACHING POINTS FOR LIZ FLEX 54 COUNTER

2-Man

Rule: From a flex position, inside releases crossfield. From a tight position, same rule as flex position.
Coaching Points: He inside releases and blocks across the hole. He should not be much deeper than five yards from the line of scrimmage. He blocks the first defender past the hole.

3-Man

Rule: Inside releases and blocks the first backer to his inside.
Coaching Points: If he is blocking the backer in a 50 or 44 front, his approach to the backer should be with his shoulders square to the line of scrimmage. The fake to the fullback may draw the backers across the hole. He should try to front them with a high block and maintain contact. The back will run off his block. He stays on his block until the whistle blows.

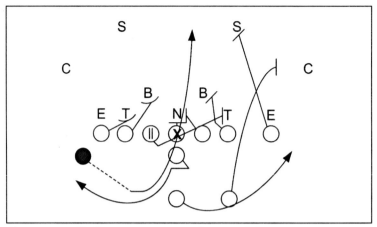

Figure 6-15. Liz flex 54 counter against 52 defense

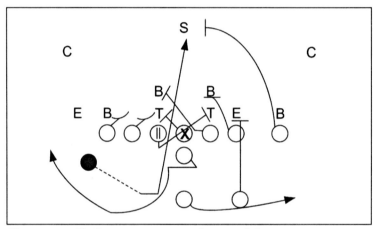

Figure 6-16. Liz flex 54 counter against 44 defense

4-Man

Rule: Leads if #5 is covered by a hard man. Against a 3-technique, blocks across the hole to the backside backer. Against a 2 or 2i technique, influences and blocks out.
Coaching Points: If #5 is covered by a hard man, leads to his post. Takes a short, six-inch step with his left foot for the crotch of the defender. He keeps his chest on his left thigh and aims his left shoulder pad for the defender's near hip. Upon contact, he brings up his blocking surface, widens his base, and begins to rise slowly. He pumps his right arm and moves his feet in short, choppy steps. Against an even front and a 2 or 2i defender on him, he pivots on his left foot, and drop-steps with his right foot. Both feet should be at a 45-degree angle to the line of scrimmage, with his arms cocked and his trunk bent at the waist. He pushes off his left foot and crosses the line right off the tail of #3. He kicks out the first unblocked defender.

5-Man

Rule: Posts if he has a hard man on him; blocks back to his left if not.
Coaching Points: He posts a hard man playing over him. He takes a short, six-inch step with his right foot, and keeps his chest close to his right thigh and his head up. He punches the heels of both hands into the defender's chest and gets the defender to rise up. The 4-man will block the defender's near hip, and he and the 4-man will work together and drive the defender off the line on a 45-degree angle. If he is open, he blocks back to the left. He takes a short, six-inch step with his left foot for the crotch of the defender, and aims his left shoulder pad for the defender's near thigh pad. On contact, he brings up his blocking surface, widens his base, pumps his right arm, and rises slowly, taking short, choppy steps.

6-Man

Rule: Pulls and traps the first defender past #5.
Coaching Points: He uses his arms to assist him in his pivot. He whips back his right arm and throws his left arm forward as he pivots on his left foot and drop-steps with his right foot. After the pivot, both feet should be placed at a 45-degree angle to the line of scrimmage. He proceed into the line, coming close to the double-team. This angle will allow him to get his head inside a defender who does not penetrate across the line of scrimmage. He stays low and keeps a wide base as he approaches his target. Prior to contact, he lowers his center of gravity by bending his knees, and he explodes up and into the defender, aiming his right shoulder into the defender's center of mass. He rises slowly, keeps his base wide, and rapidly moves his feet, using short, choppy steps.

7-Man

Rule: Fills or cuts off.
Coaching Points: He secures the backside B gap by blocking a man on, over, or to his inside. Against a 44 look, he fills on the 3-technique player in the B gap. Against a Bear look, he may have to throw his head and left arm past the inside leg of the 3-technique and scramble block him on all fours. He takes a split that will allow him to complete that block.

8-Man

Rule: Fills or cuts off.
Coaching Points: If #7 is covered by a hard man, he takes a short, six-inch step with his right foot and aims it for the crotch of the defender. On that step, his arms should be cocked and his chest on his right thigh. He explodes off his right foot and throws his inside arm and head past the hard man on #7. He elongates his body and scramble

blocks the defender on all fours. He works the defender off the line on a 45-degree angle. If #7 is open, he takes a slide step inside and seals the C gap.

Quarterback

Technique: Same as 51 toss, except hands the ball to the left halfback.
Coaching Points: He checks to see if a hard man is on #5. If #5 is covered by a hard man, he must give the midline to the left halfback. He should be a good yard off the midline when he hands the ball to the left halfback. Doing so will allow the left halfback to hit over the right leg of #5. If #5 is not covered by a hard man, he can be on the midline when he makes his handoff. In this case, the left halfback will hit over the left leg of the #5. His footwork and technique on 54 counter is the same as it is on 51 wham or easy. However, instead of pitching the ball to the fullback, he fakes the pitch, and makes a two-handed handoff to the left halfback. After the handoff, he places both hands to his left hip, bends at the waist, and begins his bootleg fake at the 9 hole.

Left Halfback

Technique: Same as 51 toss, except he is getting the ball.
Coaching Points: From a wing position, the wingback times his motion so that his right foot hits the left-halfback spot when the ball is snapped. He bends at the waist to stop his momentum, allows the quarterback time to fake to the fullback, and aims for the tail of #5. From a halfback position, he just takes a lateral timed step with his right foot, keeps his shoulders parallel to the line of scrimmage, and runs over his reference point. If the 5-man is covered by a hard man, he approaches the hole on a course that will allow him to hit over his right leg and run in a north-and-south plane. He hugs the double-team block, and breaks into an open area. If #5 is open, his reference point is his left foot. Again, he hits the hole running north and south.

Fullback

Technique: Same as 51 toss, except he is not getting the ball.
Coaching Points: He does exactly what he does on 51 wham. When the quarterback fakes him the toss, he simulates catching it, puts both hands on his right hip, bends at the waist, and swings outside the 2-man. He carries out the fake until the whistle blows.

Right Halfback (or Wingback)

Technique: Same as 51 toss, except he bypasses the 5-technique and blocks downfield.
Coaching Points: He starts his wham course as he does on 51. He avoids contact with the 5-technique player and continues to the second level, blocking any defender in the

area. If no defender is in the area, he continues to the secondary level and blocks the first defender to cross his face. Against a 44 front, he load blocks the hard man on #3.

Liz Flex 54 Counter Sting

As mentioned in Chapter 2, some variations in blocking schemes are necessary against teams that key the guards and that are good at reading blocking patterns. The same "sting" blocking schemes used in the 20 series against a 50 and 44 defense can be used in the 50 series. Liz flex 54 counter sting is diagrammed in Figures 6-17 and 6-18 against a 52 and 44 defense. To the left, the play is Rip flex 56 counter sting, and the blocking assignments are reversed.

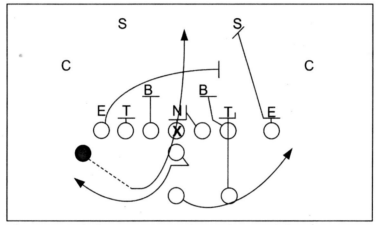

Figure 6-17. Liz flex 54 counter sting against 52 defense

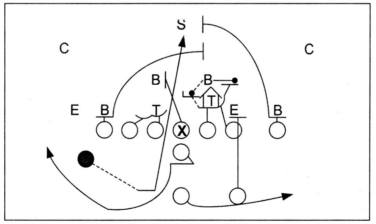

Figure 6-18. Liz flex 54 counter sting against 44 defense

BLOCKING RULES, TECHNIQUES, AND COACHING POINTS FOR LIZ FLEX 54 COUNTER STING

2-Man

Rule: Inside releases and blocks the secondary man in the deep third or half of the field.
Coaching Points: He sprints downfield and gets in front of the defensive back he is blocking. He breaks down three to four yards from the defensive back and gathers himself. He uses a stalk block, and keeps contact until the whistle blows.

3-Man

Rule: Against a 50 front, inside releases, keeping his shoulders parallel to the line of scrimmage, and blocks frontside backer. Takes the backer in the direction he chooses to go. Against a 44-front, co-op blocks with #4 on the 3-technique defender.
Coaching Points: Numbers 3 and 4 step with their near foot into the crotch of the 3-technique player in a 44 front. They drive the near shoulder into the near number of the 3 technique, get in a good football position, and begin to take the 3 technique straight off the line of scrimmage. Both men simultaneously eyeball the playside backer, anticipate coming off the block of the hard man, and go up to block the backer. If the backer pressures the frontside A gap, #4 will come off the block and block the backer, while #3 will take over the block on the hard defender and wall him off. If the backer moves outside the 3 technique, #4 will take over the block of the hard man, and #3 will go up to wall off the backer. The 3-man should not be in a great hurry to come off the double-team block. He should wait for the backer to cross his face before doing so. If neither man leaves the co-op block, but does a good job of blocking the hard man, the back still has a good chance of running by the frontside backer.

4-Man

Rule: Against a 50 front, leads to the 5-man's post. Against a 44 front, co-op blocks the 3 technique with #3.
Coaching Points: Same as the 3-man.

5-Man

Rule: Against a 50 front, posts the nose man. Against a 44 front, blocks the backside backer in any direction the backer chooses to go.
Coaching Points: Against a 50 front, he uses basic post techniques already explained. Against a 44, he goes to the backside backer immediately and blocks him with his left shoulder.

6-Man

Rule: Against a 50 front, blocks the backside backer. Tries to wall him off. Against a 44 front, double-teams the 3 technique with #7.
Coaching Points: The double-team block by #6 and #7 starts out exactly the same as the co-op block by #3 and #4. The difference is that neither blocker attempts to come off the double-team block. The objective is to drive the 3 technique straight back off the line of scrimmage and maintain contact until the whistle blows.

7-Man

Rule: Against a 50 front, blocks the hard man on him. Walls him off. Against a 44 front, double-teams the 3 technique with #6.
Coaching Points: Same coaching points as described for 6-man.

8-Man

Rule: Releases crossfield against 50 and 44 fronts.
Coaching Points: He should not be deeper than five yards from the line of scrimmage. He blocks the first defender to cross his face.

Quarterback

Technique: Same as 54 counter.
Coaching Points: Same as 54 counter.

Left Halfback

Technique: Same as 54 counter.
Coaching Points: Same as 54 counter.

Fullback

Technique: Same as 54 counter.
Coaching Points: Same as 54 counter.

Right Halfback (or Wingback)

Technique: Same as 51 wham.
Coaching Points: He blocks the first man outside the 3-man.

Liz Flex 54 Counter Bootleg Slow

The traditional bootleg is designed to look as much like the counter as possible. It is a regular bootleg with the frontside end on a flag route, and the backside end on a crossing route. Liz flex 54 counter bootleg is illustrated in Figures 6-19 and 6-20. To the left, the play is Rip flex 56 counter bootleg, and the blocking assignments are reversed.

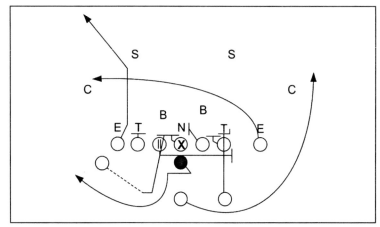

Figure 6-19. Liz flex 54 counter bootleg against 52 defense

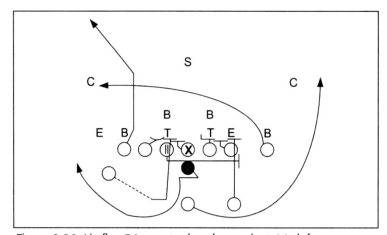

Figure 6-20. Liz flex 54 counter bootleg against 44 defense

The traditional bootleg requires the quarterback to make two fakes before gaining depth and starting his bootleg maneuver. Consequently, it takes more time to develop than any other bootleg, making it difficult for the quarterback to run by a sitting end, or to elude an end that is playing the bootleg. An innovation that will give this bootleg a much greater chance of success is to switch the routes of the two ends. The frontside end will block for three counts before releasing into the flat, and the backside end will run a deep (rather than a shallow) crossing route. Liz flex 54 counter bootleg slow is illustrated in Figures 6-21 and 6-22. To the left, the play is Rip flex 56 counter bootleg slow, and the blocking assignments are reversed. The bootleg slow is a superior play to the traditional 50 series bootleg because having the frontside end block the contain man before releasing into the flat provides the quarterback the security he needs to get outside containment with a pass/run option. (Note: All interior linemen block to the pass against all heavy fronts.)

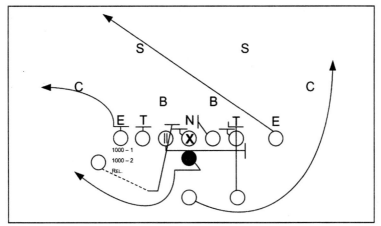

Figure 6-21. Liz flex 54 counter bootleg slow against 52 defense

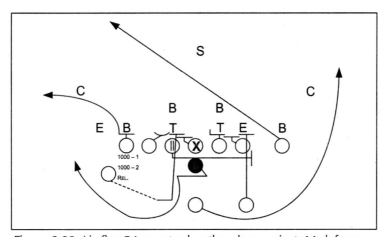

Figure 6-22. Liz flex 54 counter bootleg slow against 44 defense

BLOCKING RULES, TECHNIQUES, AND COACHING POINTS FOR LIZ FLEX 54 COUNTER BOOTLEG SLOW

2-Man

Rule: Inside releases and crosses the formation. Gains ground gradually and gets about 15 to 20 yards deep when he reaches the opposite side of the formation.
Coaching Points: As he sprints across the field, he keys the reaction of the defensive back in the frontside third of the field. If he can get behind the back, he continues to

gain depth as he crosses the field. If not, he squares his route and runs under the defensive back. If he gets man coverage, he stays on the move, makes a hump move, and runs away from his defender.

3-Man

Rule: Blocks his inside gap. Does not cross the line of scrimmage.
Coaching Points: He blocks the first hard man to his inside. He is responsible for the backside B gap. Against a 50 front, if the backer cheats up and threatens to blitz the B gap, he blocks down on the backer immediately. If not, he slams the hard man over him and slides to the backside B gap. If the backer blitzes, he blocks the backer.

4-Man

Rule: Blocks his inside gap. Does not cross the line of scrimmage.
Coaching Points: Against a 50 front, he blocks the hard man on #5. If covered by a hard man, he slams the hard man with his right shoulder and slides to the backside A gap.

5-Man

Rule: Blocks area on or backside gap. Does not cross the line of scrimmage.
Coaching Points: Against a 50 front, he drives the heel of his hands for the near number of the hard man on him, but eyeballs the backside backer. If the backside backer comes in the backside A gap, he blocks him. Against a Bear front, he blocks back on the hard man aligned on #6.

6-Man

Rule: Pulls flat across the line of scrimmage. and blocks the first man past #5. Does not cross the line of scrimmage.
Coaching Points: He gains some depth as he passes #5 to get around the wham block. He blocks the first defender outside that block.

7-Man

Rule: Blocks area on or inside. Does not cross the line of scrimmage.
Coaching Points: He uses his hands against a hard man. Against stacked fronts, he is responsible for the backside B gap. He takes a short slide step with his right foot and punches into the hard man on him. If the backer is blitzing through his gap, he blocks him. Against a 44 front, he uses a near-foot/near-shoulder block to block the 3 technique.

8-Man

Rule: Delays the flat route.

Coaching Points: He uses a high-pressure control block to block the defender over him. He keeps him on the line of scrimmage and holds his block for three counts. Then, he makes an inside or outside release—whichever is easiest—gaining four to five yards on a fan route. If the pass is to him, he catches the ball and stays outside as he runs upfield.

Quarterback

Technique: Same as on 54 counter, except fakes to the left halfback and bootlegs at the 9 hole.
Coaching Points: After he fakes the toss, he brings the ball to his pouch and moves it to the front of his left hip. He controls the ball with his left hand. He steps to the left halfback and gives him a hand fake with his right hand. After the fake, he brings both hands to the ball, bends at the waist, lowers his right shoulder, and starts his bootleg path. He looks downfield to see if #2 is open on the crossing route. If #2 is open, he throws for the touchdown. If not, he checks down to #8 in the flat. If his receivers are both covered, he shouts, "Go," and runs with the ball.

Left Halfback

Technique: Fakes 54 counter.
Coaching Points: He hits his reference point and blocks anyone in the frontside A gap.

Fullback

Technique: Fakes 51 toss.
Coaching Points: After he fakes the toss, he turns his course into a scat route and continues downfield. If no one covers his route, the quarterback can be instructed to pull up on his bootleg course and throw back to him.

Right Halfback

Technique: Loads the 5-technique area.
Coaching Points: Blocks as aggressively as he would on 51 toss. If no 5-technique player is on the line of scrimmage, he goes to the next level and blocks a backer or a defensive back.

Rip Flex 51 Quick Pitch

Before leaving the 50 series, two additional ways of getting the ball outside with pitch action will be explored. One is a pitch to the formation and the other is a pitch away from the formation. The pitch to the formation side is Rip B flex 51 quick pitch, and it is illustrated in Figures 6-23 and 6-24. To the left, the play is Liz B flex 59 quick pitch, and the blocking assignments are reversed.

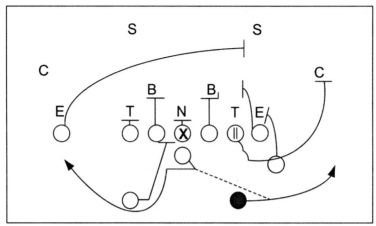

Figure 6-23. Rip B flex 51 quick pitch against 52 defense

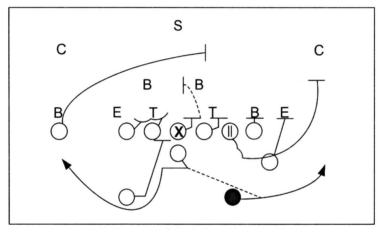

Figure 6-24. Rip B flex 51 quick pitch against 44 defense

BLOCKING RULES, TECHNIQUES, AND COACHING POINTS FOR RIP FLEX 51 QUICK PITCH

2-Man

Rule: Blocks the first backer on or to his inside.
Coaching Points: If the wing is to his side, he makes a vertical release and walls off the frontside backer. If the wing is away from him, he hooks the man on him. He aims for his outside number and drives the palms of both hands into his chest. He pushes with his outside hand to turn the defender's shoulder and positions his body between the defender and the ballcarrier.

3-Man

Rule: Pulls around the wingback/tight end's block and leads the play.

Coaching Points: He uses his arms to help him with his pull. He stays low as he gains ground on his first two steps and levels off on his third step. He swings outside the block of the last blocker on the line of scrimmage and turns upfield. He blocks the first defender to cross his path.

4-Man

Rule: Blocks man on, over, or to his frontside gap.
Coaching Points: Same as 51 easy.

5-Man

Rule: Blocks man on, over, or to his frontside gap. Steps through the frontside gap if uncovered (i.e., against a 44 defense).
Coaching Points: Same as 51 easy.

6-Man

Rule: Blocks man on, over, or to his frontside gap. Co-ops a 44 and 53 stack.
Coaching Points: Same as 51 easy.

7-Man

Rule: Blocks man on, over, or to his frontside gap. Co-ops a 44 and vertical releases against heavy fronts.
Coaching Points: Same as 51 easy.

8-Man

Rule: Releases crossfield.
Coaching Points: Same as 51 easy.

Quarterback

Technique: Reverses on 51, and opens on 59 quick pitch to the fullback or the halfback.
Coaching Points: The technique used in a quick pitch is different than the toss. The proximity of the fullback allows the quarterback to make a "dead-ball" type of a pitch without slowing the fullback down. The halfback on the quick pitch is further away from the quarterback, and a more forceful pitch is needed to get the ball to the halfback without slowing the halfback down. Therefore, the quick pitch to a halfback is an underhanded spiral. The timing of the plays works best with the dead-ball toss to the fullback, and the spiral quick pitch to the halfback. When executing 51 quick pitch, the quarterback pivots on his right foot and crosses the midline with his left foot pointing

at the pitch man. He stays low when he makes his underhanded pitch. If he rises up, the ball will also rise, which can cause a bad pitch. When executing 59 quick pitch, he opens with the left foot and takes a shuffle step toward the left halfback as he quick pitches to him. Again, he stays low to avoid a bad pitch.

Left Halfback

Technique: Fakes a 54 counter.
Coaching Points: When the quick pitch is to him (59), he open-steps with his left foot and loses some ground. He runs an arc course that will take him outside of the tight end. He keeps his shoulders as parallel to the line of scrimmage as possible. He catches the ball with his eyes and hands and follows the 7-man around the tight end. When the fullback is the pitch man, the left halfback fakes a 54 counter.

Fullback

Technique: Acts as the ballcarrier. Lines up in the left-halfback position and catches the pitch from the quarterback.
Coaching Points: When the quick pitch is to him (51), he open-steps with his right foot and loses some ground on his first couple of steps. He runs an arc course that will take him outside of the wingback. He keeps his shoulders as parallel to the line of scrimmage as possible. He catches the ball with his eyes and hands and follows the 3-man around the wingback. When the left halfback is the pitch man, the fullback fakes 56 counter. When running 59 quick pitch, he uses the same footwork as previously described for the left halfback.

Right Halfback (or Wingback)

Technique: Blocks the last man on the line of scrimmage.
Coaching Points: If the last man on the line of scrimmage is to his outside, he uses the same option-block techniques as described for a flexed end. If the defender is to his inside, he uses the same down-blocking technique as he does on a sweep. If the quick pitch is directed away from him, he releases and blocks the defender in the middle third of the field.

Liz 51 Halfback Lead

The last play to consider in the 50 series is a novel toss play to the fullback to the tight end side. It is an excellent short-yardage play, and it can be run against any defensive

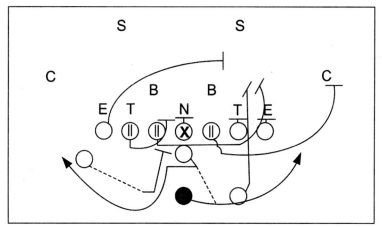

Figure 6-25. Liz 51 toss halfback lead against 52 defense

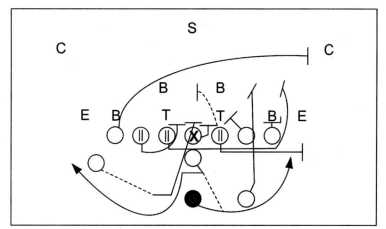

Figure 6-26. Liz 51 toss halfback lead against 44 defense

front. Liz 51 toss halfback lead is illustrated in Figures 6-25 and 6-26. To the left, the play is Rip 59 toss halfback lead, and the blocking assignments are reversed.

This play features an option block by the tight end, a lead block by the halfback through the C gap, and a block by the frontside guard on the first defender outside of the tight end. The backside guard pulls and turns up the first opening past #3 and seals inside pursuit. The fullback catches the toss and bends his course for the outside leg of the tight end. If the tight end hooks his man, he takes the ball outside. If the tight end skates outside, locked up with a defender, the fullback cuts the play back inside. This play is good against heavy and goal-line fronts, and fronts that overplay the tight-end /wingback side of the formation. It is called 59/51 halfback lead to distinguish it from 59/51 toss. The lead play is only run to the tight-end side.

BLOCKING RULES, TECHNIQUES, AND COACHING POINTS
FOR LIZ 51 HALFBACK LEAD

2-Man

Rule: Blocks the man on him.
Coaching Points: He takes a short, controlled step with his right foot and drives the palms of both hands into the chest of the man on him. He uses a high-pressure control block and tries to hook the defender. If the defender skates outside, he keeps contact and stays with the defender. The fullback will run inside or outside his block. He should not get overextended, and should not let the defender escape to the inside. He stays up and runs with the defender until the whistle blows.

3-Man

Rule: Blocks the first hard man on or inside.
Coaching Points: Against a hard man on him, he steps with his right foot and drives the palms of both hands into the hard man's chest. He keeps his hands in the framework, rises on the block, and maneuvers his body between the defender and the ballcarrier. He uses basic drive-block techniques to block a man inside of him.

4-Man

Rule: Pulls and kicks out the first defender outside #2.
Coaching Points: He pulls flat down the line of scrimmage. He must beat the right halfback to the C gap. Against an overhang front, the first defender past #2 will be aligned on the line of scrimmage. He kicks the defender out. Against seven-man fronts, the first defender outside #2's block will be a corner man. He blocks the defender in any direction he can.

5-Man

Rule: Blocks man on or over, stepping through the frontside gap.
Coaching Points: Against 61, 62, and 65 defensive fronts, he has to reach the man on #4. He uses the same reach techniques as described for 51 toss.

6-Man

Rule: Pulls and seals.
Coaching Points: Same techniques as 51 easy. He pulls close to the line of scrimmage and anticipates a defender charging through the frontside A or B gaps. He is responsible for any leakage in those gaps. He turns upfield when he gets outside of #3 and looks inside to seal any pursuit.

7-Man

Rule: Full scoops.
Coaching Points: He uses the same scoop techniques previously described for 51 wham.

8-Man

Rule: Releases crossfield.
Coaching Points: Same technique as for 51 wham.

Quarterback

Technique: Same as 51 easy.
Coaching Points: Same as 51 easy.

Left Halfback

Technique: Same as 51 easy.
Coaching Points: Same as 51 easy.

Fullback

Technique: Acts as the ballcarrier. Same as 51 easy.
Coaching Points: His arc course is similar to 51 wham. He catches the ball first, and bends his course for the outside hip of the tight end. He should be heading toward the line of scrimmage as he catches the pitch. He reads the block of the tight end and runs accordingly. If the end is hooked, he continues outside: if the end is skating outside, he cuts back inside the tight end. Against an overhang player, he turns up inside the kickout block of the frontside guard and runs off the tight end's block.

Right Halfback (or Wingback)

Technique: Leads through the C gap.
Coaching Points: He takes a short timed step with his right foot to allow the 4-man to pass in front of him. He sprints for the outside foot of #3 and blocks the first defender to cross his path in the C gap. If no resistance is encountered at the line of scrimmage, he continues to the backer level, and then to the secondary level.

7

The 60 Series and Other Play-Action Pass Plays

The 60 series is a play-action pass series. It starts out looking like the 20 series, with the fullback faking an inside trap and the halfback faking a sweep. After faking to the halfback, the quarterback retreats to a spot seven yards directly behind the 5-man, breaks on his right foot, and hops around into the throwing position. He then shuffles his feet toward the line of scrimmage as he searches for an open receiver. The progression of the quarterback in choosing receivers will be discussed later in this chapter.

Of course, the primary play-action pass off the 20 series is the waggle pass, which puts the quarterback on the perimeter with a pass/run option. In the 60 series, the quarterback sets up behind #5, and from this position he can threaten the entire width and depth of the field with a pass. It is important to remember that the 60 series is only used in running situations. The entire series is thought of as part of—and integral to—the running game. It is designed to produce big gains or touchdowns. It is not used in obvious passing situations.

This chapter will examine four 60 series passes designed against zone coverage, and six passes designed against man-to-man coverage. The zone pass plays are effective against two-, three-, and four-deep zones, and the man pass plays are effective against four-man or three-man coverage. With closed formations and an emphasis on the running game, it is unlikely that he will see five-under man coverage—especially when he is throwing the ball on running downs. He will, however, get three- and four-man coverage because many coaches think that it is the best way to get quick reads on sweeps, and to cover play-action passes against wing-T teams. For this reason, the wing-T coach needs play-action passes that are specifically designed to beat man-to-man coverage.

In addition to the 60 series, eight other play-action pass plays—designed against man coverage—will be illustrated in this chapter. These plays come off 40 series play-action, but the quarterback ends up at the same launch point as he does in the 60 series. The launch point of the quarterback in traditional wing-T play-action passes is out on the perimeter with a pass/run option. In this chapter, the play-action passes in the 60 and 40 series are thrown from the same launch point. Thus, both are included in the chapter on the 60 series. The 60 series plays are called 61 when the backfield flow is to the right, and 69 when it is to the left. These backfield-pass actions are illustrated in Figures 7-1 and 7-2. The 60 series protection is fan blocking on the backside and man blocking on the frontside. Liz 69 pass protection is illustrated in Figure 7-3 against a 44 defense, and Rip 61 pass protection is illustrated in Figure 7-4 against a 52 defense.

Sometimes a 44 defense will move its backers into the A gaps and blitz with both backers. This stunt is used on early down as a run blitz. Since the 60-series passes are also used on early downs, the wing-T coach must be able to handle this run blitz. When the quarterback sees the backers "cheat up," he makes a gap call. On a gap call, the rule for linemen is to block toward the pass, and the fullback blocks the first free rusher from the backside of the formation. If the call is 61, the line blocks to the right and the fullback blocks left. On 69, the line blocks to the left and the fullback blocks to the right. The run blitz alignment and the gap call are illustrated in Figure 7-5.

The routes in the 60 series are given names like: 61 base, 61 clear, 61 throwback, and 61 go. The end to the wingback side is the Y end, the wingback is Z, and the end away from the tight end/wingback is the X end. In a slot formation, the slot is Z, and the split end is X.

60 SERIES PASSES AGAINST ZONE COVERAGE

The following four play-action passes are called when zone coverage is anticipated. If the coverage changes to man, no adjustments are made in the patterns. The receivers run the routes called, but recognizing man coverage, they stay on the move and try to run away from defenders. They do not throttle down in open areas as they do against a zone.

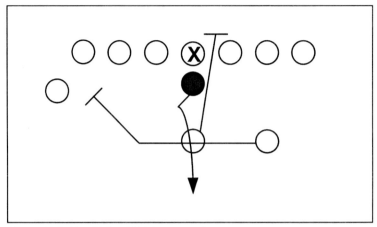

Figure 7-1. Liz 69 backfield-pass action

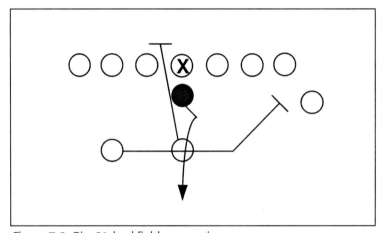

Figure 7-2. Rip 61 backfield-pass action

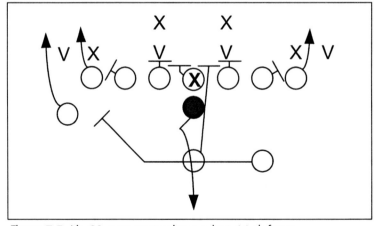

Figure 7-3. Liz 69 pass protection against 44 defense

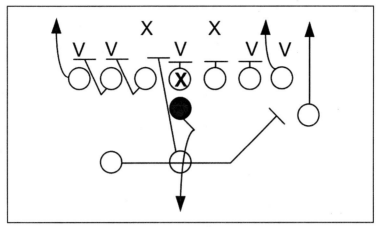

Figure 7-4. Rip 61 pass protection against 52 defense

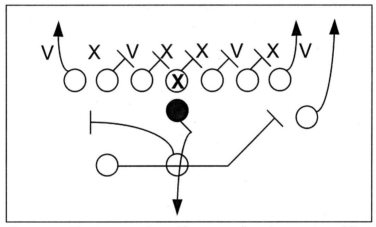

Figure 7-5. Rip 61 protection with a gap call against a 44 run blitz

Rip Split 61 Base

The base route of the 60 series—61 base—can be run from a Rip or a Rip split formation. It is illustrated as Rip split 61 base in Figures 7-6 and 7-7. To the left, the play is Liz split 69 base, and the blocking assignments are reversed.

The 61 base can also be run from a Rob or a Rob split formation. The end and wing to the formation side must know the routes of the inside and outside receivers because they can be in either position, depending on the formation call. Any combination of Rip and Rob formations can be used to execute the 60-series pass game. The backs, however, must always end up in an A set. Rip or Rob double would require motion, and jumping from one formation to another would require shifting. All these formation maneuvers can be used with the 60 series and with any of the other series mentioned in this book. Note: The blocking assignments and coaching points for linemen are the same for all plays called in the 60 series.

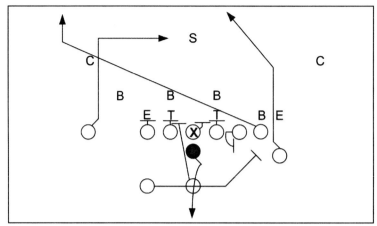

Figure 7-6. Rip split 61 base against 44 defense

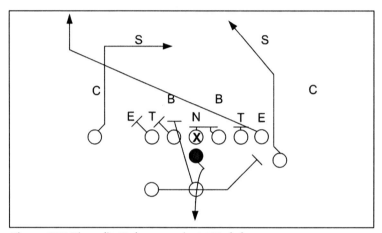

Figure 7-7. Rip split 61 base against 52 defense

BLOCKING RULES, TECHNIQUES, AND COACHING POINTS FOR RIP SPLIT 61 BASE

(Note: Against all heavy fronts, block toward the pass.)

2-Man (Y)

Rule: If he is the inside receiver (Rip formation), he runs a crossing route, gaining depth as he crosses the formation. If he is the outside receiver (Rob formation), he runs a post route.

Coaching Points: As he crosses the formation, he throttles down in an open area 15 yards deep and makes himself an easy target for the quarterback. If he doesn't get the ball, he turns upfield and gets separation from any defender trying to cover the outside quarter of the field. As he drifts upfield, he looks over his inside shoulder back to the quarterback. He is the quarterback's third choice, so he should not drift so deep that the quarterback cannot reach him with a pass.

3-Man

Rule: Blocks the hard man on or to his outside.
Coaching Points: He takes a short, controlled step into the man on him. He uses a high-pressure control block and tries to keep the defender as close to the line of scrimmage as possible. He positions his body between the defender and the quarterback. He gives ground grudgingly and does not lose the defender to the inside.

4-Man

Rule: Blocks a hard man on him. Against a backer, helps #5, but eyeballs the backer.
Coaching Points: He uses the same technique and coaching points as #3 against a hard man. Against a backer, he conceals the pass by stepping laterally and simulates a double-team with #5 on the nose man. If the backer rushes, he blocks the backer.

5-Man

Rule: Blocks a hard man on him. Against a backer (6-1 or 4-3), fans to the backside.
Coaching Points: He uses the same technique and coaching points as #3 against a hard man. Against a 61 or 43, he aggressively blocks the defender in the backside A gap. He uses a high-pressure control block and works to get his body between the quarterback and the defender. Again, he tries to keep the defender as close to the line of scrimmage as possible. Against a 44, he steps to the frontside A gap and blocks a defender that threatens that gap. If no threat is present, he comes out the back door and blocks the widest backside rusher.

6-Man

Rule: Blocks the backside B-gap defender.
Coaching Points: He aggressively blocks the defender in the backside B gap. He uses the same techniques and coaching points as #5 when #5 blocks the backside A-gap defender.

7-Man

Rule: Blocks the backside C-gap defender.
Coaching Points: He aggressively blocks the defender in the backside C gap. He uses the same techniques and coaching points as #5 when #5 blocks the backside A-gap defender.

8-Man (X)

Rule: Takes a seven-yard split and gets in a two-point stance. Drives three or four steps to the inside and then bursts upfield and makes an in move at a depth of 12 to 14 yards.
Coaching Points: From a split alignment, he takes a few steps to the inside and then

sprints perpendicular to the line of scrimmage to a depth of 12 to 14 yards downfield. He makes a sharp in cut and looks for the ball. He throttles down and makes himself an easy target. He catches the ball inside the tackle box. He is the most likely receiver to come open, so he should expect the pass. He catches the ball with his eyes and hands, puts it away, and tries to score.

Quarterback

Technique: Opens as he would on 21, but gives the fullback the entire midline. As he seats the ball, adjusts the laces to the throwing grip. Makes a quick jab fake to the fullback with both hands on the ball. As he retracts the ball back to his pocket, controls it in his right hand and fakes to the left halfback with his left hand. Continues to a depth of seven yards from the line of scrimmage and pivots around, set to pass. Getting to the launch point should take no more than six or seven steps.

Coaching Points: To get separation from rushing defenders, his retreat to the launch point should be as much like a sprint as possible. The quicker he gets there, the more time he will have to find an open receiver. He gives the midline to the fullback, and with both hands on the ball, he makes a quick jab fake to the fullback. He snaps the ball back to his pouch and continues to the left halfback. He fakes to the left halfback with his left hand as he controls and conceals the ball in his right hand. His back is to the line of scrimmage. He allows his left hand to dangle after the fake and turns his head to follow the left halfback as the halfback fakes 21. At the launch point (seven yards from the line of scrimmage), he snaps his body around to face downfield. He should be in a passing posture with his feet apart and the ball held in both hands next to his right ear. He begins to shuffle toward the line as he searches for an open receiver. Although the in route will usually be the highest percentage throw, his progression read will always be: (1) the post, (2) the in, (3) the crossing route, (4) run. Remember: the 60 series is a play-action series, and it is used when the defense is expecting a run. It is quite possible for a receiver to get behind a secondary defender who is anticipating a running play. Thus, he should look for the easy touchdown first and then follow his progression. He continues to move up into the pocket as he goes through his progression reads.

The post is a finesse pass, and he has to put some air under the ball to give his receiver a chance to catch up to it. The ball should never be underthrown. Either his receiver catches it, or the ball is over his head and falls incomplete. The in route and crossing patterns are thrown with some zip on the ball. To prevent the ball from ricocheting off the receiver's hands, he should try to hit the receiver between the numbers and the belt buckle. Remember: if no one is open, he should not force the ball, but run with it. The mark of a great quarterback is knowing what to do with the ball when all receivers are covered: run.

Left Halfback

Technique: Fakes 21 and aggressively attacks the first defender outside of #3's block.
Coaching Points: As he begins to fake 21 sweep, his eyes should go to the defender he is assigned to block. The defender's movement will determine the quality of his fake. If the defender is rushing upfield, he must block him quickly and his fake can only be a cursory one. If the defender is sitting at the line of scrimmage, he can carry out his fake for a couple of steps before curving his course toward the defender. He makes his block as close to the line of scrimmage as possible. With his momentum headed into the line, he can use a load block against the defender. He gets his right shoulder pad on the right thigh pad of the defender and tries to put the defender on the ground.

Fullback

Technique: Makes an aggressive fake into the backside A gap. Against a 6-1 or 4-3, fakes over the tail of #5 and blocks the middle backer.
Coaching Points: He recognizes the defense before the ball is snapped. Against a middle-backer front, he is responsible for the middle backer. The quarterback will give him the midline so he has a direct path to the backer. On all other fronts, he seals the backside A gap. On a gap call by the quarterback, he no longer fakes into the line. He goes directly to his left and blocks the first rusher outside #7.

Right Halfback (or Wingback) (Z)

Technique: If he is the outside receiver (Rip formation), runs a deep-post route and expects the ball. If he is the inside receiver (Rob formation), runs a 15-yard crossing route. Turns and drifts deep if he does not get the ball.
Coaching Points: On the post route (i.e., if he is the outside receiver), he should not be surprised if he is able to get behind the safety. He expects the ball to be thrown to him, so he looks for it over his inside shoulder and does not slow down unless the ball is underthrown. In that case, if he can't catch the ball, he prevents the defender from catching it. On the 15-yard crossing route (i.e., if he is the inside receiver), he controls his speed when he gets across the formation. It is easier for the quarterback to hit a target running at controlled speed than it is to hit one running at full speed. If he does not get the ball, he turns and begins to drift deeper downfield, acting as an outlet for the quarterback. He is the quarterback's third choice, so he should not drift so deep that the quarterback cannot reach him with a pass.

Rip 61 Clear

The second route in this quartet of passes against zone coverage is called Rip flex 61 clear, and it is illustrated in Figures 7-8 and 7-9. To the left, the play is Liz flex 69 clear, and the blocking assignments are reversed. This route can be run from a Rip, Rip flex, or a Rob formation. Again, the wing and end to the formation side have to know the routes of the inside and outside receiver because, depending on the formation, they will line up in both positions.

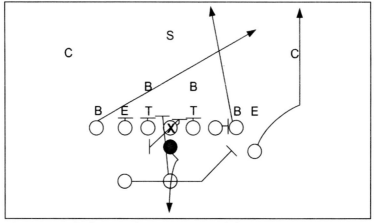

Figure 7-8. Rip flex 61 clear against 44 defense

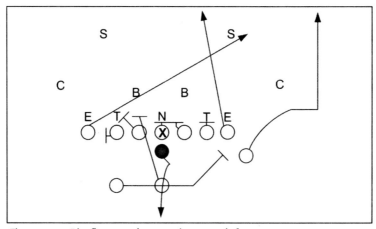

Figure 7-9. Rip flex 61 clear against 52 defense

BLOCKING RULES, TECHNIQUES, AND COACHING POINTS FOR RIP 61 CLEAR
(Note: Against all heavy fronts, blocks toward the pass.)

2-Man (Y)

Rule: When he is the inside receiver (Rip), makes an inside release and runs a post route. *Coaching Points:* He runs his post downfield and not crossfield. Against a two-deep, he must force the safety to his side to cover him since his route is more vertical, similar to a skinny post. Against a three-deep, he can aim more for the center of the crossbar as he runs his post. Again, he runs through the safety man and forces the safety to cover him. A four-deep is treated much the same as a two-deep: he runs the post so the safety to his side is forced to cover him. Refer to the base route regarding coaching points when the ball is thrown to him.

When he is the outside receiver (Rob), he runs an out-and-up route. He takes an 8- to 10-yard split, and make an out cut at a depth of six to seven yards. He takes three steps toward the sideline, pushes off his outside foot, and runs deep. He runs at controlled speed because he will be the quarterback's third choice and he does not want to outrun the quarterback's throwing range. He throttles down in an area about 18 to 20 yards downfield and slowly drifts downfield.

3-Man

Rule: Same as 61 base.
Coaching Points: Same as 61 base.

4-Man

Rule: Same as 61 base.
Coaching Points: Same as 61 base.

5-Man

Rule: Same as 61 base.
Coaching Points: Same as 61 base.

6-Man

Rule: Same as 61 base.
Coaching Points: Same as 61 base.

7-Man

Rule: Same as 61 base.
Coaching Points: Same as 61 base.

8-Man (X)

Rule: Runs a 12- to 15-yard crossing route.
Coaching Points: He sprints across the formation to get to the far third of the field. He throttles down in the open area and expects the ball. He is the receiver most likely to come open on the clear route. If he sees the corner level to protect the flat area, he adjusts his route and comes under the corner, forcing the corner to cover him in the

flat. This move will create greater separation between the corner, the wing, and the 2-man, who are running deeper patterns and who now become prime targets.

Quarterback

Technique: Same as 61 base.
Coaching Points: Again, his progression is: (1) the inside receiver on the post, (2) the crossing receiver, (3) the outside receiver on the out-and-up, and (4) run. The receiver most likely to come open on 61 clear is the 8-man (X) on his crossing route. However, he still checks the post to make sure he does not ignore a receiver running free for an easy touchdown. As he goes through his progression, he continues to shuffle toward the line of scrimmage. If the corner to the frontside levels to cover the flat, he has an excellent opportunity to throw the ball behind him to the outside receiver on the out-and-up route. The coaching points for throwing the crossing route and the deeper routes in 61 clear are exactly the same as they are in 61 base.

Left Halfback

Technique: Same as 61 base.
Coaching Points: Same as 61 base.

Fullback

Technique: Same as 61 base.
Coaching Points: Same as 61 base.

Right Halfback (or Wingback) (Z)

Rule: When he is the outside receiver (Rip), runs a quick out-and-up route.
Coaching Points: He gets width immediately six to seven yards, and bursts upfield. His job is to force the corner to his side to cover him. If the corner levels to cover the flat, he throttles down in an area about 18 to 20 yards deep and slowly drifts downfield. He stays within the passing range of the quarterback. When he is the inside receiver (Rob), he runs a post route. Refer to the coaching points emphasized for #2.

Rip Split 61 Throwback

The third route in the 60 series designed to attack zone defenses is a pass away from the flow of the backs. Rip split 61 throwback is illustrated in Figures 7-10 and 7-11. To the left, the play is Liz split 69 throwback, and the blocking assignments are reversed. As the name suggests, it is a play-action pass that is counter to the flow of backs. This typical vertical stretch route is effective against all zone defenses. The best formation for this route is Rip split.

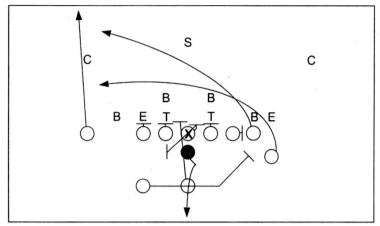

Figure 7-10. Rip split 61 throwback against 44 defense

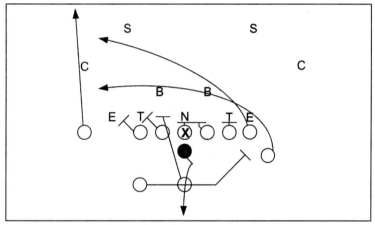

Figure 7-11. Rip split 61 throwback against 52 defense

BLOCKING RULES, TECHNIQUES, AND COACHING POINTS
FOR RIP SPLIT 61 THROWBACK

(Note: Against all heavy fronts, blocks toward the pass.)

2-Man (Y)

Rule: Runs a 15- to 17-yard crossing route
Coaching Points: He makes an inside release and sprints across the formation. He throttles down when he arrives in the opposite third of the field. He is the most likely receiver to come open, so he should expect the ball.

3-Man

Rule: Same as 61 base.
Coaching Points: Same as 61 base.

4-Man

Rule: Same as 61 base.
Coaching Points: Same as 61 base.

5-Man

Rule: Same as 61 base.
Coaching Points: Same as 61 base.

6-Man

Rule: Same as 61 base.
Coaching Points: Same as 61 base.

7-Man

Rule: Same as 61 base.
Coaching Points: Same as 61 base.

8-Man (X)

Rule: Runs a streak route at full speed.
Coaching Points: He keeps a five-yard cushion from the sideline and does not drift into the middle of the field. The coaching points for catching the deep ball are the same as they are for receivers running the post route.

Quarterback

Technique: Same as 61 base.
Coaching Points: He follows the same progression as all 60-series routes: (1) look for the deep ball, (2) look for the crossing route, (3) check down to the shallow receiver, and (4) run. Again, the receiver who will come open most of the time is the crossing receiver. The quarterback technique for throwing the deep and crossing patterns are the same as in the 61 base route.

Left Halfback

Technique: Same as 61 base.
Coaching Points: Same as 61 base.

Fullback

Technique: Same as 61 base.
Coaching Points: Same as 61 base.

Right Halfback (or Wingback) (Z)

Technique: Runs a five-yard crossing route.
Coaching Points: He avoids contact with the inside backers. He goes in front of or behind them. He runs his route at less than full speed because he is the quarterback's third choice. He does not want to get to the flat too soon. When he does arrive in the flat area, he throttles down to provide an easy target for the quarterback.

Len Double 61 Go

The last 60 series pass is designed specifically against a two-deep zone. Len double 61 go is illustrated in Figures 7-12 and 7-13. To the left, the play is Rob double 69 go, and the blocking assignments are reversed. The 61 go can be run from any combination of Rip or Rob formations. It is designed to get three-deep receivers against a two-deep secondary. The most likely receiver to come open is the tight end (Y). The wing and split end should attract the attention of the two safetymen and keep them on their respective hash marks. The middle or frontside backer has to help on the tight end by getting underneath his short post route. The play-action fake will make the backers respect the run, and this pause will give the tight end a chance to run by them and get into the soft spot of the zone: behind the backers and in front of the safetymen—about 17 to 18 yards down the field.

BLOCKING RULES, TECHNIQUES, AND COACHING POINTS
FOR LEN DOUBLE 61 GO
(Note: Against all heavy fronts, block toward the pass.)

2-Man (Y)

Rule: If he is the inside receiver, runs a 17- to 18-yard short post route. This route is 17 to 18 yards deep, directly in line with the pre-snap position of the ball.
Coaching Points: He should not drift outside the guard box. His route should split the twin safetymen and be run perpendicular to the line of scrimmage. He makes a quick inside release and hurries to get behind the backers. When he gets 15 to 17 yards deep, he throttles down and stays in the soft area (a depth of 17 to 20 yards from the line) and in the middle of the hash marks.

If he is the outside receiver, (Rob or Len formations), he runs a streak route or an out-and-up route. He should not get closer than five yards from the sideline. He needs

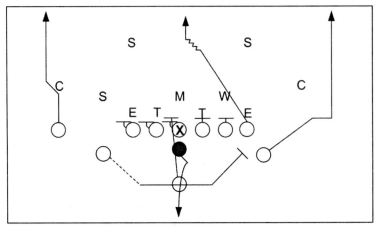

Figure 7-12. Len double 61 go against 43 two-deep defense

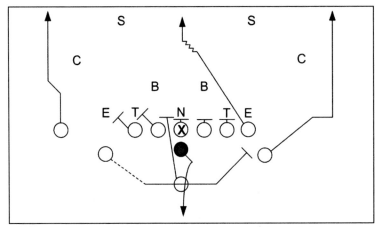

Figure 7-13. Len double 61 go against 52 two-deep defense

to give himself enough room to fade into the sideline to catch a ball to his inside. He stays far enough from the safety on his side so that the safety cannot cover him and remain on the hash mark. He gets enough width to force the safety off the hash. If the corner tries to cover him deep, he sprints and tries to beat the corner deep.

3-Man

Rule: Same as 61 base.
Coaching Points: Same as 61 base.

4-Man

Rule: Same as 61 base.
Coaching Points: Same as 61 base.

5-Man

Rule: Same as 61 base.
Coaching Points: Same as 61 base.

6-Man

Rule: Same as 61 base.
Coaching Points: Same as 61 base.

7-Man

Rule: Same as 61 base.
Coaching Points: Same as 61 base.

8-Man (X)

Rule: If he is split, runs a streak route; if he aligns as a tight end, runs an out-and-up route.
Coaching Points: He follows the same coaching points as the 2-man when #2 is the outside receiver.

Quarterback

Technique: Same as 61 base.
Coaching Points: The go route is different from the previous three passes. The progression of the quarterback is no longer to look deep first. The go-route progression is: #1 the short post route to Y, #2 the deep fade route, and #3 run. Assuming that the backers are held by the run fake, the only defenders that can cover the short post route are the safetymen. As he turns to face downfield, he looks for the short post route. If open, he throws the ball. This ball is thrown just high enough to get it over the backers' heads, and with just enough zip to get it to the receiver before either safety arrives. If the left safety takes away the short post route, he looks to the deep fade route to the left. If the right safety takes the route away, he looks to the deep fade to the right. The fade is thrown like the post, with air under the ball. He must keep the ball to the inside of the field so the receiver can catch it in bounds. Practice is needed to develop the technique for throwing the short post and the deep fade routes.

Left Halfback

Technique: Same as 61 base, except he must come in motion to be at his halfback spot when the ball is snapped.
Coaching Points: Same as 61 base.

Fullback

Technique: Same as 61 base.
Coaching Points: Same as 61 base.

Right Halfback (or Wingback) (Z)

Technique: If he is the outside receiver, runs a deep-fan route.
Coaching Points: Work for width immediately, gaining seven to eight yards in width, and then he bursts upfield. He continues to gain width to force the safety to get off the hash to cover him. If the corner tries to cover him, he turns on the speed and outruns the corner on his deep route. He allows himself enough space (five yards) to the sideline to fade in that direction to catch a deep ball thrown to his inside. If he is the inside receiver, he follows the same assignment and coaching points as the 2-man when #2 is the inside receiver.

60 SERIES PASSES AGAINST MAN-TO-MAN COVERAGE

As mentioned earlier in this chapter, some coaches believe that the best way to defend the wing-T sweeps and play-action passes is with a man-to-man defensive scheme. This strategy is credible, and every wing-T team should be prepared to combat it with patterns designed especially for man cover. Although all of the wing-T play-action passes (thrown on run downs) are good against all types of coverage, it is good to have some passes that are designed with man coverage in mind. Again, these passes are thrown in situations when the defense is expecting a run. Hopefully, the element of surprise will rest with the offense.

As previously noted, the blocking assignments and coaching points for linemen are the same for all plays called in the 60 series. The routes and coaching points will change for the wing, the 2-man, and the 8-man on the following plays. The progression reads of the quarterback are similar on all the man-coverage plays, but minor adjustments will be emphasized.

Rip Flex 61 Under

The first pass for consideration is a route by the wing coming under the tight end and crossing the formation. Rip flex 61 Z under is illustrated in Figures 7-14 and 7-15. To the left, the play is Liz flex 69 Z under and the blocking assignments are reversed. The proximity of the tight end and the wingback facilitates the crossing routes, which present problems for defenders in man-to-man coverage. The shallow route by the wingback also is problematic for man cover.

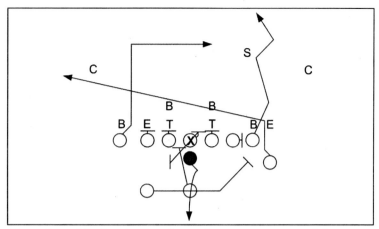
Figure 7-14. Rip flex 61 Z under against 44 man cover defense

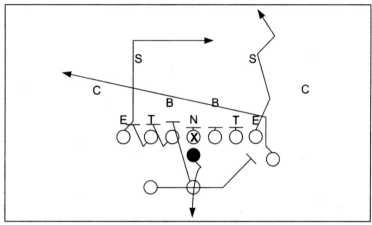
Figure 7-15. Rip flex 61 Z under against 52 man cover defense

BLOCKING RULES, TECHNIQUES, AND COACHING POINTS FOR RIP FLEX 61 UNDER

(Note: Against all heavy fronts, blocks toward the pass.)

2-Man (Y)

Rule: Makes an inside release and runs a double-post route.
Coaching Points: As he releases upfield, he bows toward the wingback and allows him to cross behind him. He makes his first post move at about seven to eight yards. He breaks to the post for three to four steps, backs to the flag for three to four steps, and then makes his final move to the post. If he beats the defender, he should expect the ball. The quarterback will look to him first in his progression. If the defender covering him gets involved with the run fake, he may be able to run by the defender. In that case, the quarterback will definitely throw the ball to him.

3-Man

Rule: Same as 61 base.
Coaching Points: Same as 61 base.

4-Man

Rule: Same as 61 base.
Coaching Points: Same as 61 base.

5-Man

Rule: Same as 61 base.
Coaching Points: Same as 61 base.

6-Man

Rule: Same as 61 base.
Coaching Points: Same as 61 base.

7-Man

Rule: Same as 61 base.
Coaching Points: Same as 61 base.

8-Man (X)

Rule: Releases upfield to a depth of 10 to 12 yards and runs an in route.
Coaching Points: He makes a good head-and-shoulder fake to the outside before running the in route. He stays on the move and tries to run away from man coverage.

Quarterback

Technique: Same footwork and technique as on 61 base.
Coaching Points: The receiver who will be open most of the time is the wingback on his crossing route. As the quarterback sets to pass, he gives the post a quick look just to make sure the tight end is not running free downfield. His progression reads are: (1) the post, (2) the crossing route, (3) the in route, and (4) the run. The techniques in throwing the post, crossing, and in routes are the same as in 61 base. However, in man-to-man coverage, he must be able to hit a receiver running at full speed, crossing from left to right or right to left. For a right-handed quarterback, throwing to a receiver crossing from right to left requires more of a lead than if the receiver were crossing left to right. Practice is needed for the quarterback to acquire a "touch" for throwing these crossing routes.

Left Halfback

Technique: Same as 61 base.
Coaching Points: Same as 61 base.

Fullback

Technique: Same as 61 base.
Coaching Points: Same as 61 base.

Right Halfback (or Wingback) (Z)

Technique: Runs a 7- to 10-yard crossing route.
Coaching Points: He releases upfield at controlled speed. He allows the tight end to start upfield and move toward him before he crosses under the tight end. He makes his cut under the tight end a few yards past the line of scrimmage and as close to the tight end as possible. As he passes under the tight end, he sprints to a spot 7 to 10 yards deep across the formation. He is the primary receiver, so he looks for the ball as he crosses the formation. If he does not receive the ball, he turns upfield and tries to outrun his defender.

Rip 61 End Cross

The second route against man-to-man coverage is another route with receivers crossing the formation and running away from man coverage. Rip 61 end cross is illustrated in Figures 7-16 and 7-17. To the left, the play is Liz 69 end cross, and the blocking assignments are reversed.

BLOCKING RULES, TECHNIQUES, AND COACHING POINTS
FOR RIP 61 END CROSS
(Note: Against all heavy fronts, blocks toward the pass.)

2-Man (Y)

Rule: Makes an inside release and runs a 7- to 10-yard crossing route.
Coaching Points: If the backers react to the run fake, he runs behind them. If they get depth, he runs in front of them. He stays on the move and tries to run away from his defender. If he does not get the ball, he takes off up the sideline.

3-Man

Rule: Same as 61 base.
Coaching Points: Same as 61 base.

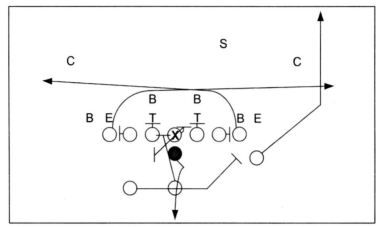
Figure 7-16. Rip 61 end cross against 44 man cover defense

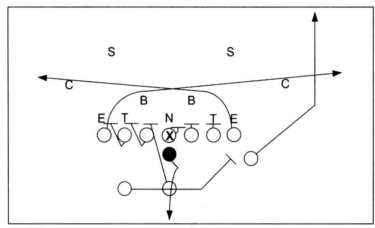
Figure 7-17. Rip 61 end cross against 52 man cover defense

4-Man

Rule: Same as 61 base.
Coaching Points: Same as 61 base.

5-Man

Rule: Same as 61 base.
Coaching Points: Same as 61 base.

6-Man

Rule: Same as 61 base.
Coaching Points: Same as 61 base.

7-Man

Rule: Same as 61 base.
Coaching Points: Same as 61 base.

8-Man (X)

Rule: Makes an inside release and runs a 7- to 10-yard crossing route.
Coaching Points: He will be the receiver to come open most of the time, so he should expect the ball and run away from his coverage. If the wingback is covered on his deep route, he will be the second choice for the quarterback.

Quarterback

Technique: Same technique as 61 base.
Coaching Points: As he sets to pass, his progression is: (1) wingback on the takeoff route, (2) the 8-man on the crossing route, (3) the 2-man on his takeoff route, and (4) the run. He gives the wingback a quick look, but he knows that the percentage pass is to the 8-man crossing from left to right. If #8 is not open, he will have time to look to the 2-man who will be breaking upfield and he will have a chance to hit #2 deep.

Left Halfback

Technique: Same as 61 base.
Coaching Points: Same as 61 base.

Fullback

Technique: Same as 61 base.
Coaching Points: Same as 61 base.

Right Halfback (or Wingback) (Z)

Technique: Runs a deep-fan route.
Coaching Points: He works immediately for width. When he gets seven to eight yards of width, he turns upfield and runs a deep route. He gives himself plenty of room to fade toward the sideline to catch a ball that is thrown to his outside. If he beats the defender covering him, the quarterback will throw him the ball. If not, his route should give the crossing end plenty of room to maneuver and beat the crossing end's defender.

Rip 61 End Cross Fullback Deep

The next route has an addition of a subtle nuance to the end's crossing route that is an excellent pass against man coverage. The nuance has the fullback sneaking through the line of scrimmage and running a deep vertical route. Rip 61 end cross fullback deep is illustrated in Figures 7-18 and 7-19. To the left, the play is Liz 69 end cross fullback deep, and the blocking assignments are reversed.

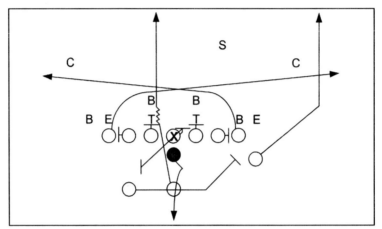

Figure 7-18. Rip 61 end cross fullback deep against 44 man cover defense

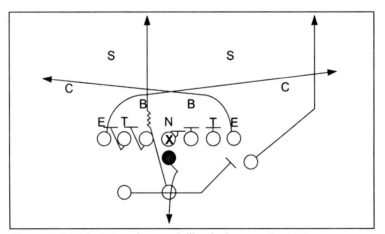

Figure 7-19. Rip 61 end cross fullback deep against 52 man cover defense

This play is a great man route, but the availability of the fullback is contingent on him not having to block a stunting backer. To compensate for the fullback not getting out in the pattern, the quarterback follows this progression: (1) the fullback deep, if he gets out in the pattern, (2) the 8-man on the crossing route, (3) the run. The blocking assignments and coaching points for the interior linemen are the same as 61 base.

BLOCKING RULES, TECHNIQUES, AND COACHING POINTS FOR RIP 61 END CROSS FULLBACK DEEP

2-Man

Rule: Same as 61 base.
Coaching Points: Same as 61 base.

3-Man

Rule: Same as 61 base.
Coaching Points: Same as 61 base.

4-Man

Rule: Same as 61 base.
Coaching Points: Same as 61 base.

5-Man

Rule: Same as 61 base.
Coaching Points: Same as 61 base.

6-Man

Rule: Same as 61 base.
Coaching Points: Same as 61 base.

7-Man

Rule: Same as 61 base.
Coaching Points: Same as 61 base.

8-Man

Rule: Same as 61 base.
Coaching Points: Same as 61 base.

Quarterback

Technique: Same as 61 base.
Coaching Points: To compensate for the fullback not getting out in the pattern, the quarterback follows this progression: (1) the fullback deep, if he gets out in the pattern, (2) the 8-man on the crossing route, (3) the run.

Left Halfback

Technique: Same as 61 base.
Coaching Points: Same as 61 base.

Fullback

Technique: Same as 61 base.
Coaching Points: If no one is there to block, he continues upfield and runs a vertical route straight towards the crossbar.

Right Halfback (or Wingback)

Technique: Same as 61 base.
Coaching Points: Same as 61 base.

Rob Double 61 Y Under

The next route is to have an end come in back of the line of scrimmage and run a fan route in the opposite flat. Hopefully, the defender assigned to the end will have a difficult time crossing the formation and covering him in the flat. The play can be run from several different formations. For the sake of variety, it will be run from a double-wing formation. Rob double 61 Y under is illustrated in Figures 7-20 and 7-21. To the left, the play is Len double 69 Y under, and the blocking assignments are reversed.

BLOCKING RULES, TECHNIQUES, AND COACHING POINTS FOR ROB DOUBLE 61 Y UNDER

(Note: Against all heavy fronts, blocks toward the pass.)

2-Man (X)

Rule: Runs a 12- to 15-yard crossing route.
Coaching Points: He makes a hump move as he gets to the center of the formation. Doing so will help to shake his cover and give the quarterback more time to find him as his third choice.

3-Man

Rule: Same as 61 base.
Coaching Points: Same as 61 base.

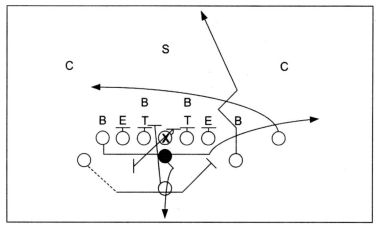

Figure 7-20. Rob double 61 Y under against 44 man cover defense

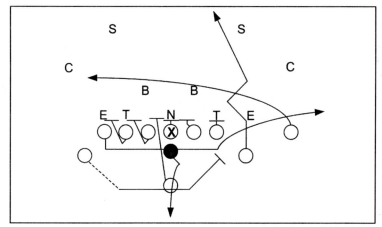

Figure 7-21. Rob double 61 Y under against 52 man cover defense

4-Man

Rule: Same as 61 base.
Coaching Points: Same as 61 base.

5-Man

Rule: Same as 61 base.
Coaching Points: Same as 61 base.

6-Man

Rule: Same as 61 base.
Coaching Points: Same as 61 base.

7-Man

Rule: Same as 61 base.
Coaching Points: Same as 61 base.

8-Man (Y)

Rule: Runs a five- to seven-yard fan route.
Coaching Points: He pulls behind the line of scrimmage, turning up the first open area past the 3-man. He runs a five- to seven-yard fan route and looks for the ball immediately. He is the primary receiver and will get the ball most of the time.

Quarterback

Technique: His technique is the same as 61 base.
Coaching Points: Although the receiver most likely to be open is the Y end, he has to give the slot a quick look on his post route. If the slot is open, he throws him the ball. If not, he hits the Y end as the Y end comes open in the flat. His progression is: (1) slot on the post, (2) Y end on flat route, (3) X end on crossing route, (4) run. The quarterback should be shuffling toward the line of scrimmage as he goes through his progression.

Left Halfback

Technique: Comes in motion and gets in his halfback spot when the ball is snapped. He has the same assignment and coaching points as in 61 base.
Coaching Points: Same as 61 base.

Fullback

Technique: Same as 61 base.
Coaching Points: Same as 61 base.

Right Halfback (or Wingback) (Z)

Technique: Runs a deep post route.
Coaching Points: He makes a double move to the post. He makes his first post move at eight yards, his second move to the flag at 12 yards, and then makes a final break to the post.

A coaching point needs to be mentioned regarding eight-man fronts that use three-man coverage and the Y-under route. If the offense lines up immediately in Rob double, the safety may align on the slot and not the tight-end/wingback side. This approach would hurt the play because the outside backer to the slot side will occupy the same flat area that the Y end is entering. Two solutions to this problem are possible.

The first is to run the play from a Liz spread formation and bring the right halfback out of the backfield on a deep vertical route. This formation will force the outside backer on the spread side to cover the halfback on his deep vertical route. The result is a big plus for the offense because it clears the flat area for the 8-man, and it forces an outside linebacker to cover the halfback on a deep vertical. The quarterback has a choice of throwing to the halfback or to the 8-man. Liz spread 61 Y under is illustrated in Figure 7-22.

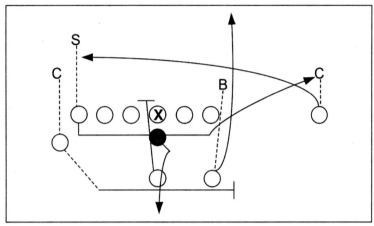

Figure 7-22. Liz spread 61 Y under against 44 three-man defense

The second solution is to line up in Liz spread and quickly shift to Rob double. The huddle call is Liz spread to Rob double 61 Y under. The shift is illustrated in Figures 7-23 and 7-24. Both of these strategies accomplish the desired goal. This shift forces an outside backer to cover the slot receiver man-to-man, and the advantage should rest with the offense. The quarterback looks to the post as his first choice on 61 Y under because the slot has a good chance of beating the outside backer to the post. If the backer is able to cover the post, the quarterback comes down to the Y-under receiver who is entering an unoccupied flat area.

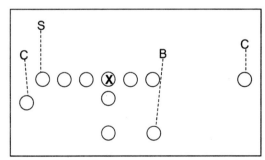

Figure 7-23. Liz spread against skeletal 44 3-man secondary

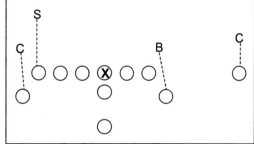

Figure 7-24. Shift from Liz spread to Rob double against 44 3-man secondary

Rob Double 61 Fullback Hide

The next route off the 60 series against man coverage is very much like Y under, except it is the fullback who comes behind the line of scrimmage. Rob double 61 fullback hide is illustrated in Figures 7-25 and 7-26. To the left, the play is Len double 69 fullback hide, and the blocking assignments are reversed. In the Y-under route a secondary defender must cover the Y end as he comes behind the line of scrimmage. In the fullback hide, it is a backer who has to cover the fullback. Since the fullback is faking into the A gap and delaying for a count, chances are the backer will ignore him long enough for the fullback to slip into the flat. This route can be run from several formations, but again, for variety, it will be run from a double-wing formation.

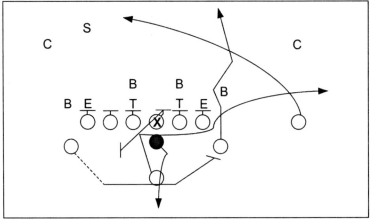

Figure 7-25. Rob double 61 fullback hide against 44 three-man secondary

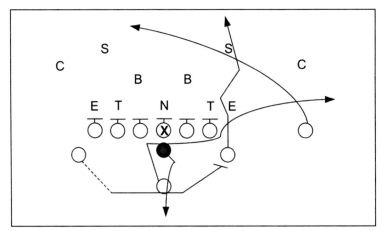

Figure 7-26. Rob double 61 fullback hide against 52 four-man secondary

BLOCKING RULES, TECHNIQUES, AND COACHING POINTS FOR ROB DOUBLE 61 FULLBACK HIDE

(Note: Against all heavy fronts, blocks toward the pass.)

2-Man (X)

Assignment: Same as 61 Y under.
Coaching Points: Same as 61 Y under.

3-Man

Rule: Same as 61 base.
Coaching Points: Same as 61 base.

4-Man

Rule: Same as 61 base.
Coaching Points: Same as 61 base.

5-Man

Rule: Same as 61 base.
Coaching Points: Same as 61 base.

6-Man

Rule: Same as 61 base.
Coaching Points: Same as 61 base.

7-Man

Rule: Same as 61 base.
Coaching Points: Same as 61 base.

8-Man

Rule: Blocks the most dangerous rusher from the backside.
Coaching Points: If he is not confronted with an overhang defender, he blocks the hard man on him. He uses a high-pressure control block. If he has an overhang defender (44 front), he hinges and blocks the most dangerous rusher. If the end and backer rush, he blocks the inside rusher.

Quarterback

Technique: Same as 61 base.
Coaching Points: His progression for fullback hide is exactly the same as it is for 61 Y under. Again, if the coverage is three-man, it is best to shift into Rob double to get the match-up he wants. As previously explained, if he gets the outside backer in a 44 front covering the wingback man-to-man, he gives the wingback a good look on his post route before looking for the fullback in the flat.

Left Halfback

Technique: Same as 61 Y under.
Coaching Points: Same as 61 Y under.

Fullback

Assignment: Runs a five- to six-yard flat route in the frontside flat area.
Coaching Points: He aims for the backside A gap and sets up about one-and-a-half yards from the line of scrimmage. He delays for a count and then comes behind the line and enters the frontside flat area. He looks for the ball immediately since he is the most likely receiver to come open on this play.

Right Halfback (or Wingback) (Z)

Technique: Same as 61 Y under.
Coaching Points: Same as 61 Y under.

Rip Double 61 Fullback Opposite

The final 60-series play against man coverage is very efficient in the score zone, especially from inside the 20-yard line. It is Rip double 61 fullback opposite, and it is illustrated in Figures 7-27 and 7-28. The blocking rules for the linemen are the same as on any 60 series pass play—the only adjustment is that the backside end stays in and blocks.

On the fullback opposite pass, the backside end (X) will stay in and block the widest rusher from the backside of the formation. The Y end and Z back, aligned to the formation side, will run crossing routes. The Y end will gain a depth of 10 to 12 yards, and the Z back will cross at a depth of 15 to 17 yards. The fullback fakes over the tail of #5 and breaks for a point five yards inside of the pylon located on the end line since he has no blocking assignment. The interior linemen and the fullback can handle as many as seven pass rushers. The quarterback is obviously looking to the fullback for the touchdown. If he is not open, or if he does not get out in the pattern, the quarterback throws the ball across the end line or runs a quarterback draw.

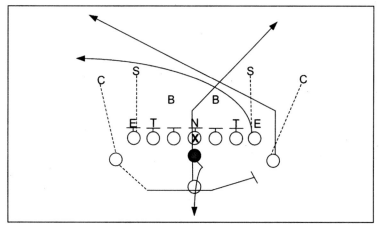

Figure 7-27. Rip double 61 fullback opposite against a 4-man secondary

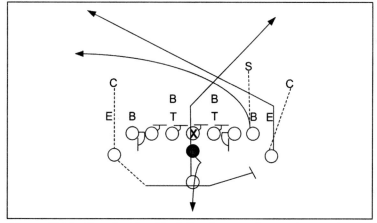

Figure 7-28. Rip double 61 fullback opposite against a 3-man secondary

BLOCKING RULES, TECHNIQUES, AND COACHING POINTS FOR RIP DOUBLE 61 FULLBACK OPPOSITE

2-Man

Rule: Same as 61 base.
Coaching Points: Same as 61 base. He stays in and blocks the widest rusher from the backside of the formation.

3-Man

Rule: Same as 61 base.
Coaching Points: Same as 61 base.

4-Man

Rule: Same as 61 base.
Coaching Points: Same as 61 base.

5-Man

Rule: Same as 61 base.
Coaching Points: Same as 61 base.

6-Man

Rule: Same as 61 base.
Coaching Points: Same as 61 base.

7-Man

Rule: Same as 61 base.
Coaching Points: Same as 61 base.

8-Man

Rule: Same as 61 base.
Coaching Points: Same as 61 base.

Quarterback

Technique: Same as 61 base.
Coaching Points: The quarterback is obviously looking to the fullback for the touchdown. If the fullback is not open, or if the fullback does not get out in the pattern, the quarterback throws the ball across the end line or runs a quarterback draw.

Left Halfback

Technique: Same as 61 base.
Coaching Points: Same as 61 base.

Fullback

Technique: Same as 61 base.
Coaching Points: He fakes over the tail of #5 and breaks for a point five yards inside of the pylon located on the end line since he has no blocking assignment.

Right Halfback (or Wingback)

Technique: Same as 61 base.
Coaching Points: Same as 61 base.

Before closing this chapter, some other novel ideas concerning passes against man coverage in other series are worthy of consideration. These passes come off plays already illustrated in chapters on the 20, 30, and 40 series.

GREEN 40 SERIES PASSES AGAINST MAN-TO-MAN COVERAGE

The next set of play-action passes against man coverage comes off 40-series action. Plays to the right are called 41 and plays to the left are called 49. The quarterback ends up in the same place as he does on the 60 series, but the backfield action is different. To eliminate confusion, the color green precedes the 40-series call to indicate that the play will fake a 40-series run, the quarterback will throw a play-action pass, and the backside end will stay in and block.

Rip B Green 41 Fullback Scat

The first route off the green 40 series is executed from a B set and is called fullback scat. This play is excellent against man coverage and can very likely result in a big play or a touchdown. The play is Rip B green 41 fullback scat, and it is illustrated in Figures 7-29 and 7-30. To the left, the play is Liz B green 49 fullback scat, and the blocking assignments are reversed.

**BLOCKING RULES, TECHNIQUES, AND COACHING POINTS
FOR RIP B GREEN 41 FULLBACK SCAT**
(Note: Against all heavy fronts, blocks toward the pass.)

2-Man (Y)

Rule: Runs a crossing route.
Coaching Points: As he releases inside, he forces the frontside backer to alter his course by going inside, rather than outside him. Against a 50 front, the playside backer is assigned to the fullback. The 2-man gets his head and shoulders past the backer as he runs his crossing route. He lets the backer initiate any contact that may occur. Against a 44 front, the backer on him is assigned to the fullback. He gets his head and shoulders past the backer and lets the backer fight through him to get to the fullback. After forcing the backer to his inside, he continues on his crossing route.

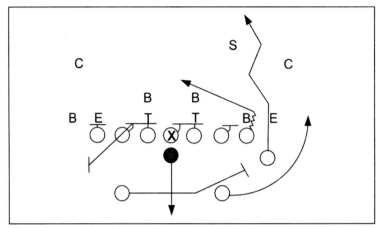

Figure 7-29. Rip B green 41 fullback scat against 44 three-man secondary

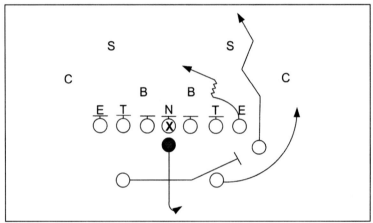

Figure 7-30. Rip B green 41 fullback scat against 52 four-man secondary

3-Man

Rule: Blocks the man on him or in his inside gap.
Coaching Points: Against a hard man, he uses a high-pressure control block. He keeps the defender as close to the line as possible, and gets his body between the defender and the quarterback. Against a backer, he blocks the man to his inside. He and #4 will combo block the tackle and the frontside backer in a 44 front.

4-Man

Rule: Same as the 3-man.
Coaching Points: Same as the 3-man.

5-Man

Rule: Blocks the man on him or in the backside A gap.
Coaching Points: Against a hard man, he uses a high-pressure control block. If he is open, he hinges and protects the backside A gap.

6-Man

Rule: Same as the 5-man.
Coaching Points: Same as the 5-man, except if he is open, he hinges and protects the backside B gap.

7-Man

Rule: Same as the 5-man.
Coaching Points: Same as the 5-man, except if he is open, he hinges and protects the backside C gap. If that gap is not threatened, he comes out the back door and blocks the widest backside rusher.

8-Man

Rule: Blocks the last rusher on the line of scrimmage.
Coaching Points: If no overlap player is present, he blocks the man on him. If an overlap player is present, he hinges and blocks the inside rusher.

Quarterback

Technique: Opens back to the hole and seats the ball. Stays on the midline and makes a fake to the left halfback with his left hand as he secures the ball in his right hand. Takes two more steps on the midline and pivots into the throwing position.
Coaching Points: His progression is: (1) scat, (2) post, and (3) run. The scat is a touch pass, and the throw should allow the fullback to catch the ball in stride about 7 to 10 yards upfield. He keeps the ball to the fullback's inside and hits the fullback in stride.

Left Halfback

Technique: Same as 60 series.
Coaching Points: Same as 60 series.

Fullback

Technique: Lines up in the right-halfback position and runs a scat route.
Coaching Points: He works for width immediately as he runs his scat route. He sprints until his momentum is headed downfield. Then, he throttles a bit to be an easier target for the

quarterback to hit. He adjusts his speed to the flight of the ball. He catches it with his eyes and hands, and he stays on the perimeter after the catch. He is the primary receiver.

Right Halfback (or Wingback) (Z)

Technique: Runs a post route.
Coaching Points: He makes a double move to the post when he is covered man-to-man. The fullback is the primary receiver on this route, but if the fullback is not open, the quarterback will come to him. He runs his route like he will get the ball.

Rip Green 41 Fullback Fan

The second pass in the 40 green series is from A or B backs, with the fullback running a fan route from his regular position. With the exception of the fullback and the quarterback, all players have identical assignments and coaching points as they do on the fullback scat route. This call is excellent on a third-and-short situation when the defense is expecting a run. The huddle call is Rip green 41 fullback fan, and it is illustrated in Figure 7-31. To the left, the play is Liz green 49 fullback fan, and the blocking assignments are reversed.

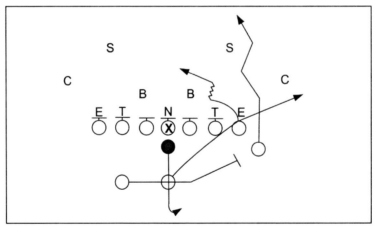

Figure 7-31. Rip green 41 fullback fan against 52 4-man secondary

Again, a subtle coaching point to keep in mind regarding the fullback scat and fan routes is that if he is playing against an eight-man front with three-man coverage, he must get the safety and corner to align away from the tight-end/wingback formation. Doing so will force the frontside outside backer to cover the Y end and the inside backer to cover the fullback. If the offense lines up in a Rip formation, the safety and corner will align to that side. That alignment is not what the offense wants when it is running Rip green 41 fullback fan. Once again, a shift is necessary to get the match-ups that give the offense the best chance of success. By lining up in a Liz and shifting to a Liz double, the desired match-ups are realized. The huddle call is Liz to Liz double green

41 fullback fan. This shift is illustrated in Figures 7-32 and 7-33. To the left, the play is Rip to Rip double green 49 fullback fan, and the blocking assignments are reversed.

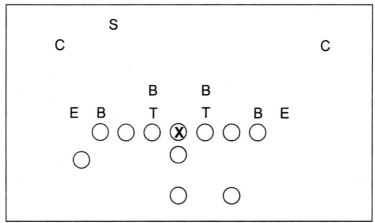

Figure 7-32. Liz formation before shifting to Liz double against 44 three-man secondary fullback fan

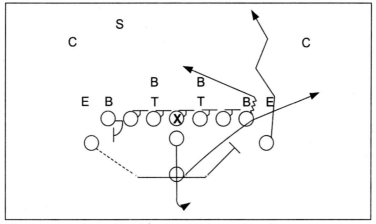

Figure 7-33. Liz double after the shift from Liz against 44 three-man secondary fullback fan

BLOCKING RULES, TECHNIQUES AND COACHING POINTS FOR RIP GREEN 41 FULLBACK FAN

2-Man

Rule: Same as 41 fullback scat.
Coaching Points: Same as 41 fullback scat.

3-Man

Rule: Same as 41 fullback scat.
Coaching Points: Same as 41 fullback scat.

4-Man

Rule: Same as 41 fullback scat.
Coaching Points: Same as 41 fullback scat.

5-Man

Rule: Same as 41 fullback scat.
Coaching Points: Same as 41 fullback scat.

6-Man

Rule: Same as 41 fullback scat.
Coaching Points: Same as 41 fullback scat.

7-Man

Rule: Same as 41 fullback scat.
Coaching Points: Same as 41 fullback scat.

8-Man

Rule: Same as 41 fullback scat.
Coaching Points: Same as 41 fullback scat.

Quarterback

Technique: Same as 41 fullback scat.
Coaching Points: The fullback is running a fan route. The quarterback should not lead the fullback too much. He should try to keep the ball between the fullback's numbers and belt line. Unlike the scat route, this ball is thrown with some zip on it. His progression is (1) fan, (2) post, and (3) run.

Left Halfback

Technique: Same as 41 fullback scat.
Coaching Points: Same as 41 fullback scat.

Fullback

Technique: Aims for the tail of #2 and runs a five- to six-yard fan route.
Coaching Points: He sprints past #2, then throttles a bit to be an easy target for the quarterback to hit. He stays on the perimeter after the catch and gets as much yardage as he can.

Right Halfback (or Wingback)

Technique: Same as 41 fullback scat.
Coaching Points: Same as 41 fullback scat.

Rip Green 49 Quarterback Throwback

No discussion of pass plays against man coverage would be complete without a pass to the quarterback. This play is done in the 40 green series with B backs and a closed or open formation. The line blocking is the same as all other green 40 series pass plays. What is needed is a back who is able to throw a decent pass. The huddle call is Rip B green 49 quarterback throwback, and it is illustrated in Figures 7-34 and 7-35. To the left, the play is Liz B green 41 quarterback throwback, and the blocking assignments are reversed. Assignments and coaching points for linemen are identical on all green 40 series plays. (Note: Against all heavy fronts, blocks toward the pass.)

BLOCKING RULES, TECHNIQUES, AND COACHING POINTS FOR RIP B GREEN 49 QUARTERBACK THROWBACK

2-Man

Rule: Runs a crossing route at about 8 to 10 yards deep.
Coaching Points: Same as 41 fullback scat.

3-Man

Rule: Same as 41 fullback scat.
Coaching Points: Same as 41 fullback scat.

4-Man

Rule: Same as 41 fullback scat.
Coaching Points: Same as 41 fullback scat.

5-Man

Rule: Same as 41 fullback scat.
Coaching Points: Same as 41 fullback scat.

6-Man

Rule: Same as 41 fullback scat.
Coaching Points: Same as 41 fullback scat.

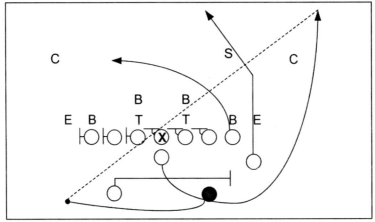

Figure 7-34. Rip B green 49 quarterback throwback against 44 three-man secondary

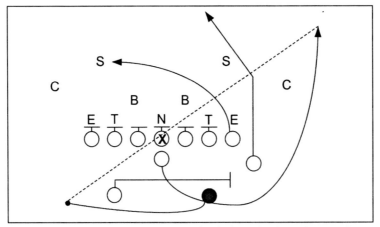

Figure 7-35. Rip B green 49 quarterback throwback against 52 four-man secondary

7-Man

Rule: Same as 41 fullback scat.
Coaching Points: Same as 41 fullback scat.

8-Man

Rule: Blocks the most dangerous rusher from the backside.
Coaching Points: Same as 41 fullback scat.

Quarterback

Technique: Hands the ball to the right halfback and turns bootleg course into a deep circle route.
Coaching Points: After the snap, he seats the ball. He opens back to the hole and steps under the midline toward the right halfback. He hands the right halfback the ball with his right hand, fakes a bootleg for a few steps, and then turns upfield and quickly gains width and depth. He looks for the ball over his inside shoulder and catches it with his eyes and hands. He stays on the perimeter after the catch and gets as much yardage as possible.

Left Halfback

Technique: Starts with his inside foot and takes two short steps for the tail of the 7-man. On his second step, pushes off his outside foot and comes parallel to the line of scrimmage toward the formation side. Blocks the first defender to show from the outside in.
Coaching Points: Same as 41 fullback scat.

Fullback

Technique: In B backs, lines up at the right halfback position.
Coaching Points: He lines up in the right-halfback position. He comes across the backfield as he would on 49. He receives the ball from the quarterback and begins to position it so his fingers are on the laces. As he passes the fullback position, he throttles and bows his course as he would on 49 wham. He sets up inside the 8-man and looks for the quarterback. If the quarterback is open, he puts some air under the ball so the quarterback can catch it on the run. If the quarterback is not open, he converts the play into 49 sweep.

Right Halfback

Technique: Runs a quick post route.
Coaching Points: Same as 41 fullback scat.

OTHER PASSES AGAINST MAN-TO-MAN COVERAGE

The passes in this section are part of the regular wing-T repertoire and have been discussed previously in the book. They are good when used in running situations against any type of coverage. The assignments and coaching points for linemen and backs have already been explained in previous chapters. However, a few coaching points for the quarterback are in order when executing these passes against man-to-man coverage. Also, some minor nuances added to these base plays are helpful against man coverage.

Rip B Flex 42 Keep

The first play is Rip B flex 42 keep. It is illustrated in Figures 7-36 and 7-37. To the left, the play is Liz B flex 48 keep, and the blocking assignments are reversed.

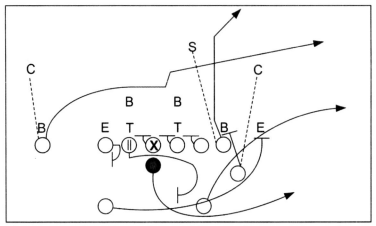

Figure 7-36. Rip B flex 42 keep against 44 three-man secondary

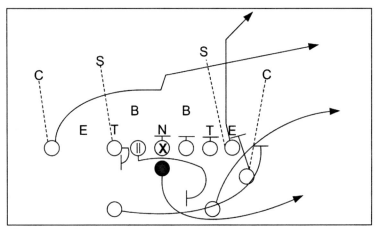

Figure 7-37. Rip B flex 42 keep against 52 four-man secondary

Against four-man coverage, the receiver most likely to come open is the fullback in the flat. The quarterback, after faking to the left halfback, gets his eyes on the safety covering #2. If he ignores #2, the quarterback throws deep for the touchdown. If #2 is wide open, he should not overthrow him. The quarterback must be taught when to put air under the ball and when to just get the ball to the receiver if the receiver has to slow down to catch the ball.

If #2 is covered, the quarterback eyes the corner who is assigned to the wingback. If he reads the down block by the wing as a run and moves toward the line of scrimmage, the fullback will have some room to operate in the flat. The fullback will be covered by the inside frontside backer. The backer will be occupied by the play fake, and the fullback should gain a few steps on him. The left halfback will block the corner, and the quarterback will have time to dump the ball to the fullback. A right-handed quarterback should not lead a receiver who is moving in the same direction as he is. The ball is thrown at the fullback's outside shoulder, so the momentum of the quarterback will automatically cause the ball to drift to the right. The opposite is true when a right-handed quarterback is moving to his left. In this case, he should lead the receiver. If the fullback is not open, the quarterback continues to move on the perimeter, and he will either run the ball or throw late to #8 on the crossing route.

Against three-man coverage, the situation is a bit different. First, the force man is aligned on the line of scrimmage and is more of a threat to the quarterback than is the corner in four-man coverage. Because the quarterback is moving toward him, the force man can quickly put pressure on the quarterback—unless the left halfback knocks him down. The quarterback may have to pull up and stay inside the block of the left halfback to complete the pass. The wingback blocks down on the frontside backer who is assigned to the fullback. The frontside corner, assigned to the wingback, will sit in the flat when he sees this. From this position, he can cover the fullback, or get depth and cover the crossing receiver. Therefore, the progression of the quarterback against three-man coverage is: (1) Y end deep, (2) X end crossing, (3) fullback in the flat, and (4) run.

Rip B flex 42 keep X Throwback

An innovative route off the 40 series is Rip B flex 42 keep X throwback. It is illustrated in Figures 7-38 and 7-39. To the left, the play is Liz B flex 48 keep X throwback, and the blocking assignments are reversed. Everyone has the same assignments as 42 keep, except the backside end (X). He starts on his crossing route to get his defender moving in that direction, then he quickly breaks for a spot five yards inside the backside pylon. His break can be in front of or behind the defender. Since the backside end runs so many crossing routes, the sudden break away from the flow of the play gives him a good chance to beat the defender to the pylon. This one-on-one challenge is an excellent call in the score zone. The quarterback should pull up behind the 3-man and look to throw the ball back to X. If X is covered, the quarterback checks the two frontside receivers. If they too are covered, he shouts, "Go," and runs with the ball.

Rip 28 Counter Bootleg Special

This pass adds a little nuance to an established wing-T play. Rip 28 counter bootleg special is illustrated in Figures 7-40 and 7-41. To the left, the play is Liz 22 counter bootleg special, and the blocking assignments are reversed. The assignments and coaching points for linemen and backs are explained in Chapter 2. However, a change is made for the frontside guard and the wingback. Because the fullback is in the

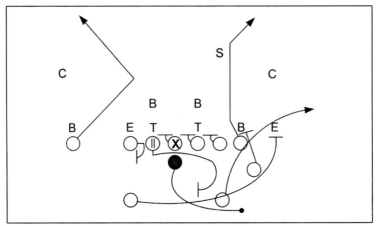

Figure 7-38. Rip B flex 42 keep X throwback against 44 three-man secondary

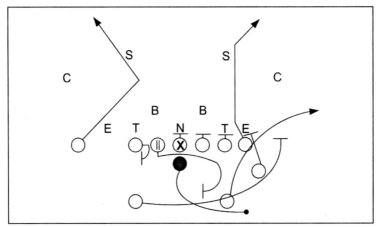

Figure 7-39. Rip B flex 42 keep X throwback against 52 four-man secondary

pattern, the frontside guard does not pull to block the backside end. The wingback blocks the backside end as he fakes the counter; the frontside guard blocks the backer if he rushes. Doing so frees the fullback of his assignment and allows him to release into the pattern. The basic counter bootleg has the frontside end on a flag, the backside end on a crossing route, and the fullback blocking at the line of scrimmage. Adding the word "special" alerts the receivers of the changes in the pattern. It tells the frontside end (Y) to run a crossing route instead of a flag, the backside end (X) to stay with his crossing route, and the fullback to run a deep pattern. The fullback, who will be covered by an inside backer, is the primary receiver. He will still fake into the line, but he continues past the backers and into the secondary, heading for a spot halfway between the near upright and the pylon. If he runs past the backer and is open in the secondary, he should throttle down and become an easy target for the quarterback to hit. He looks for the ball over his outside shoulder. Again, the quarterback should never overthrow an open receiver. If the fullback is wide open, it is better that he has to slow down, or even stop to catch the ball, rather than to have it sail over his head.

Against four-man coverage, the fullback is again the primary receiver and the offense is looking for an easy touchdown. After faking to the wingback, the quarterback starts his bootleg course and looks deep for the fullback. If the fullback is open, the quarterback throws him the ball. If not, he sprints to break contain and looks for the crossing receiver. The frontside corner, assigned to the wingback, may chase the wing across the formation, or he may sit in the flat. If he chases the wing, the quarterback looks to hit the X as he crosses into the flat: if not, he runs the ball.

Against three-man coverage, the force man is on the line of scrimmage, and it may be more difficult to break contain. As he completes his fake to the wingback, he starts on his bootleg and looks to the fullback. If the fullback is open, he throws him the ball.

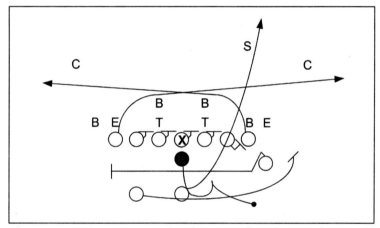

Figure 7-40. Rip 28 counter bootleg special against 44 three-man secondary

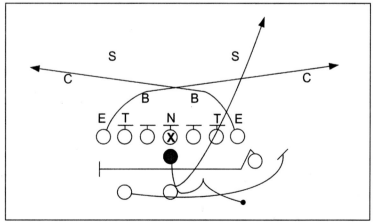

Figure 7-41. Rip 28 counter bootleg special against 52 four-man secondary

If not, he sprints to break contain and reads the corner as he does in four-man coverage. If the corner chases the wing, he looks for the crossing receiver; if not, he runs the ball.

Rip Double 29 Waggle Wingback Block

This short-yardage call is excellent, especially in the critical zone. It is illustrated in Figure 7-42. To the left, the play is Liz double 21 waggle wingback block, and the blocking assignments are reversed. Many wing-T coaches have used this variation off the regular waggle pass with great success. The word "block" tells the wingback—who usually fakes a sweep—to block down on the defender to his inside. It also tells the backside end to block. The backside wing runs a deep route, and the frontside end runs his normal flag route. The wing's block is key because the quarterback must get outside containment to execute his pass/run option. Assignments and coaching points for the waggle pass are explained in Chapter 2.

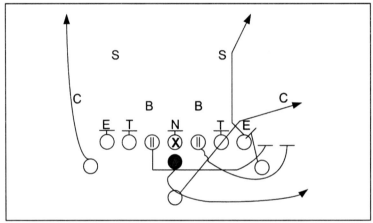

Figure 7-42. Rip double 29 waggle wingback block against 52 four-man secondary

Against four-man coverage, the corner to the side of the play has the wingback man-to-man. The quarterback executes his waggle course without faking and sprints to break contain. With the wing blocking down, the corner may come up to contain the play, or he may zone off into the flat. If he comes up to support the corner, the quarterback dumps the ball to the fullback; if he zones off into the flat, the quarterback shouts, "Go," and the guards lead him upfield. The guards must be disciplined not to cross the line of scrimmage until the quarterback shouts, "Go!" He cannot have a better outside running play than one that has the secondary players retreating to cover receivers and the ball outside containment. A coaching point for the guards on this play is for the frontside guard to block the flat defender, and the backside guard to seal the first defender outside of the wings block.

Against three-man coverage—as in a 44 front—it is important to get the safety man aligned away from the side of the pass. It is also important to force an alignment to the frontside that will put the contain man inside the wingback. To accomplish these two objectives, a shift is needed at the line of scrimmage. The huddle call is Liz to Rob double 29 waggle block. It is illustrated in Figures 7-43 and 7-44. To the left, the play is Rip to Len double 21 waggle block, and the blocking assignments are reversed.

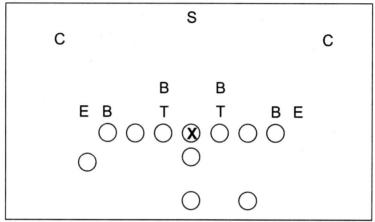

Figure 7-43. Liz formation before the shift to Rob double against 44 three-man

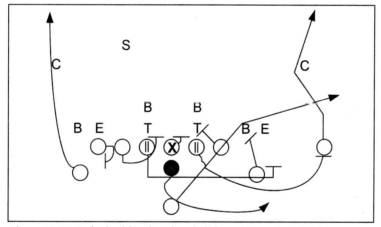

Figure 7-44. Rob double after the shift from Liz against 44 three-man

The offense aligns in a Liz formation. To the tight end/wingback side, the safety covers the tight end and the corner covers the wingback. Away from the formation, to the tight-end side, the corner covers the tight end. On the quarterback's "now" call, the right halfback moves into a slot position and the 2-man (Y) splits seven yards. This shift forces the outside backer to cover the slot (Z) and the corner to cover the tight end (Y).

The split end (X) runs the flag route, and the fullback runs a fan route in the flat. The outside backer can cover the fullback in the flat, or he can contain the quarterback.

If he covers the fullback, the quarterback shouts, "Go," and runs the ball; if the backer comes up to contain the quarterback, the ball is thrown to the fullback.

Rip C 33 Keep Solid

This play is a variation of the 30-series keep pass. It is run with C backs and is a flood route. Rip C 33 keep solid is illustrated in Figure 7-45. To the left, the play is Liz C 37 keep solid, and the blocking assignments are reversed. The solid call tells the backside end to stay in and block. Assignments and coaching points for the keep pass are explained in Chapter 3.

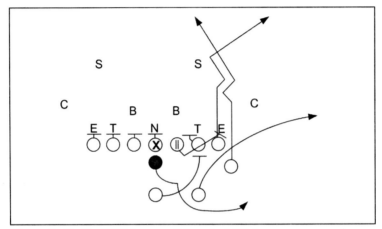

Figure 7-45. Rip C 33 keep solid against 52 four-man secondary

The formation is contingent upon the secondary coverage. Against four-man coverage, the formation should be Rip C. As the inside receiver, the tight end (Y) runs a flag route, making a double move to the flag, and as the outside receiver, the left halfback (Z) runs a double post. The right halfback runs a quick fan route into the flat area. The quarterback reverses back to the hole and makes a quick hand fake with his left hand to the fullback. The ball is moved to the right hip and controlled with the right hand. After the fake, the quarterback runs through the right-halfback area, bowing slightly and starting toward the line of scrimmage. The primary receiver is the halfback on the fan route. The quarterback uses the same throwing mechanics previously explained when running to the right.

Against three-man coverage, the objective is to go for the touchdown by forcing the outside backer to cover a back. To achieve this objective, a formation shift is needed at the line of scrimmage. It is done with the huddle call Liz to Rob double 31 keep solid Z flag. This shift is illustrated in Figures 7-46 and 7-47.

The outside receiver runs the fan route, and the inside receiver run the flag route. The primary receiver is the Z on the flag route. The quarterback comes off the fake to the fullback and looks immediately for Z on the flag pattern. He should put some air under the ball and allow the Z to run under it. The second option for the quarterback is to run the ball. The quarterback is obviously looking to the fullback for the touchdown. If the fullback is not open, or does not get out in the pattern, the quarterback throws the ball across the end line or runs a quarterback draw.

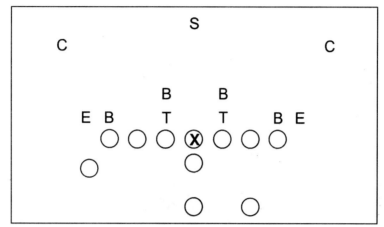

Figure 7-46. Liz formation before the shift to Rob double against 44 three-man

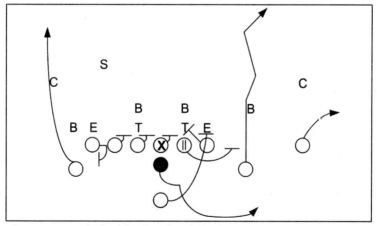

Figure 7-47. Rob double after the shift from Liz against 44 three-man

8

Attacking Heavy Fronts

Sooner or later, every wing-T team—especially ones featuring closed formations—will face defensive fronts that will put all 11 defenders within five yards of the line of scrimmage. Defenses that use this tactic to stop the running game are similar to teams that blitz open formations to stop the pass game. Both strategies are a gamble. If the blitz gets to the quarterback before he can pass, the defense wins; if not, the offense may get a big play. Similarly, with defenses that try to stop the wing-T running game by crowding the line of scrimmage, if the defense can prevent the ballcarrier from breaking past the first line of defense, or can keep a receiver from getting behind a shallow secondary, the defense wins; if not, the offense gets a big play. In both cases, the defense is rolling the dice. For a defense to be sound and to minimize the threat of a big play or an easy touchdown, it must defend in depth. Those defenses that do not defend in depth will eventually give up a big play or an easy touchdown.

Some coaches try to combat heavy fronts by opening up their formations and by adding new plays. But opening the formation emasculates the wing-T offense, and teaching new plays consumes precious practice time that should be spent on perfecting wing-T plays. Frank Broyles, the legendary former University of Arkansas football coach, said in a speech about defense at a clinic in the 1960s, "When you strengthen here, you weaken there," and it is as true today as it was then. If you look at heavy fronts, you will see that six defenders are inside the tackle box, which is why the defense is strong in that area. Running plays inside the tackles, with the exception of an occasional fullback trap, is futile.

The most important precept of offensive football is to find the strength of the defense and to run or pass away from it. Getting the ball outside, featuring play-action passes, and getting the quarterback on the perimeter with a pass/run option are good ideas against defenses that crowd the line of scrimmage. These strategies attack the defense away from its strength, and they will produce big plays. The key is to be patient and not to panic when you see a heavy front. Having (and practicing) a plan against eight- and nine-man fronts will give your team the confidence and poise that it needs to defeat them.

Heavy fronts have the potential to pressure the run game by stunting through every gap along the line of scrimmage. If successful, this tactic can inflict big losses on a wing-T offense. Consequently, plays selected against these fronts must be designed to handle gap-8-type defenses. When confronted by heavy fronts, the wing-T coach must get the ball on the perimeter, exploiting both the running and the passing games. The plays he selects should come from his wing-T repertoire. Remember the words of Frank Broyles: "When you strengthen here, you weaken there." Heed these words by finding the strength of the defense, and run or pass away from it. The heavy fronts include the 53 stack, the 62 stack, the 52 chase, the 44 stack, and the 65 goal-line defenses. These defenses are illustrated in Figures 8-1 through 8-5.

The chase front is one way 52 teams try to stop the wing-T. They put the strong safety behind the nose man about five yards from the line of scrimmage. From that alignment, he is in good position to team up with the backers, and he can stunt into either the A or B gap, or he can just chase the plays from behind. Like the other heavy fronts, the chase defense has the potential to end up in a gap-8 after the snap of the ball. Consequently, the interior linemen step to their gap responsibility before going up to the backer level. If their gap is threatened, they block the threat.

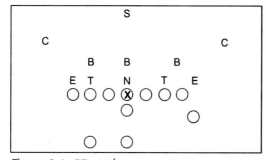

Figure 8-1. 53 stack

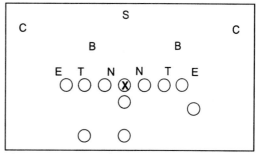

Figure 8-2. 62 stack

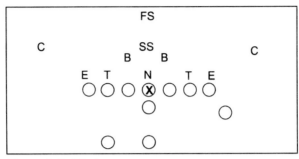

Figure 8-3. 52 chase

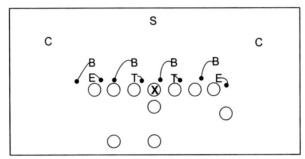

Figure 8-4. 44 stack

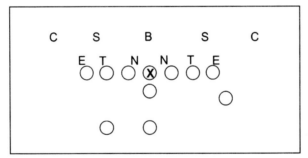

Figure 8-5. 65 goal line

Most teams that line up in a 44 stack against wing-T teams will stunt the entire front and end up in a gap-8, or they will stunt segments of the defense. The figures that follow assume that the defense will stunt all defenders and end up in the gap-8. If no stunt occurs, the linemen simply revert to their gap read-up rule.

This chapter will look at plays that have the best chance of success against heavy fronts. It will examine five or six plays from each series, starting with the teen series and ending with the 50 series, and diagram them against the heavy fronts. Each play will not be illustrated against each front, although all plays diagrammed are effective against all heavy fronts. Coaching points and techniques have already been explained in previous chapters, and they will not be repeated here.

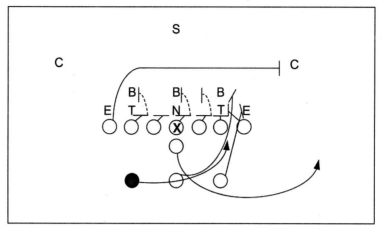

Figure 8-6. T 13 J against 53 stack

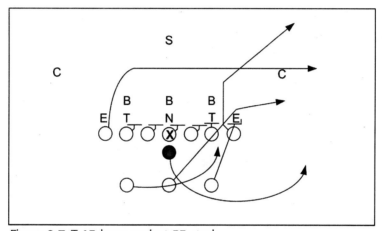

Figure 8-7. T 13 keep against 53 stack

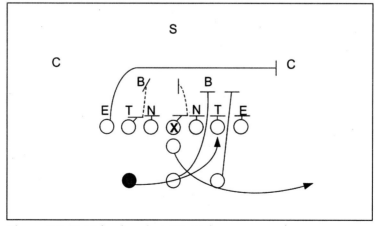

Figure 8-8. T 13 lead against 62 stack

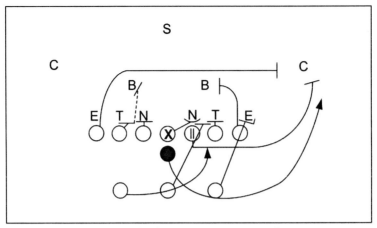

Figure 8-9. T 13 quarterback @ 1 against 62 stack

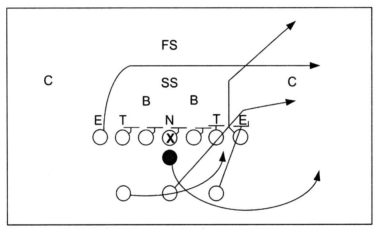

Figure 8-10. T 13 keep against 52 chase

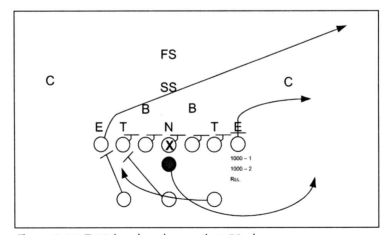

Figure 8-11. T 17 bootleg slow against 52 chase

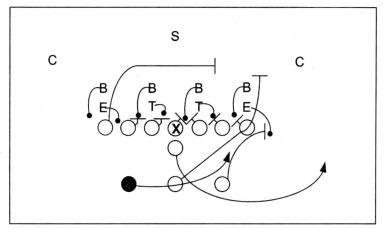

Figure 8-12. T 13 J against 44 stack

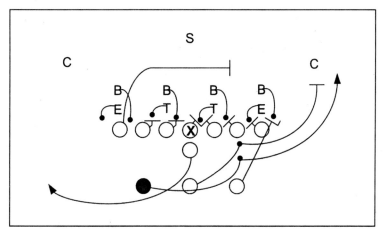

Figure 8-13. T 13 bounce against 44 stack

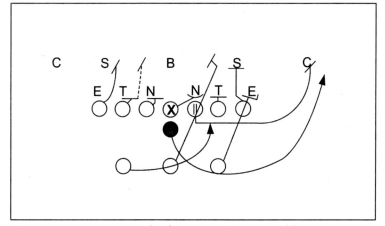

Figure 8-14. T 13 quarterback @ 1 against 65 goal line

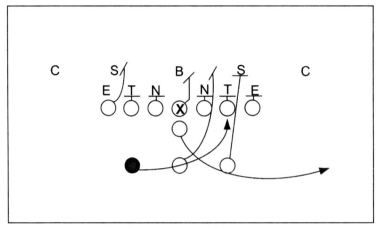

Figure 8-15. T 13 lead against 65 goal line

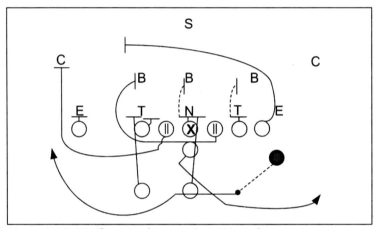

Figure 8-16. Rip flex 29 wham against 53 stack

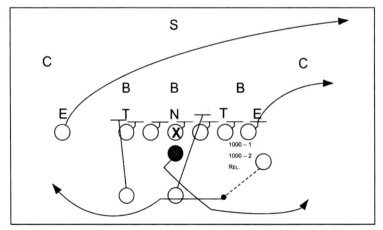

Figure 8-17. Rip flex 29 wham bootleg slow against 53 stack

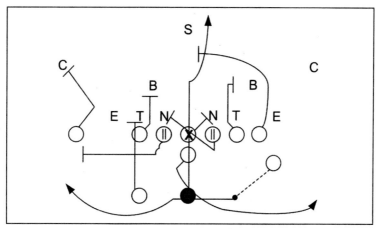

Figure 8-18. Rip flex 26 trap against 62 stack

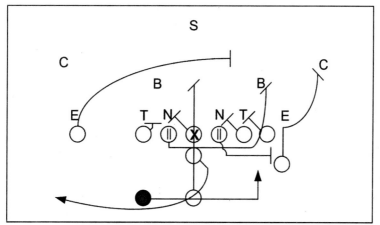

Figure 8-19. Rip flex 22 cut against 62 stack

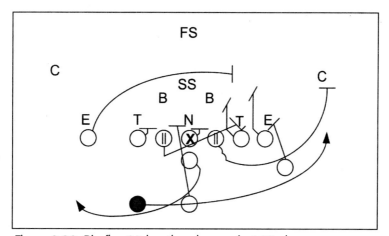

Figure 8-20. Rip flex 21 bootleg slow against 52 chase

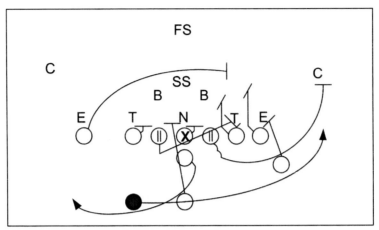

Figure 8-21. Rip flex 21 Iowa against 52 chase

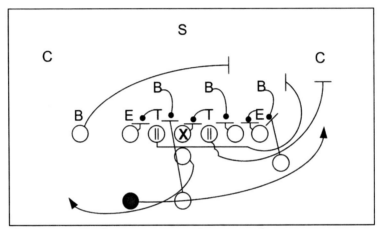

Figure 8-22. Rip flex 21 sweep against 44 stack

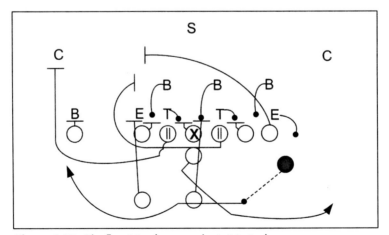

Figure 8-23. Rip flex 29 wham against 44 stack

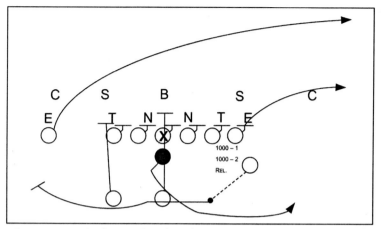

Figure 8-24. Rip flex 29 bootleg slow against 65 goal line

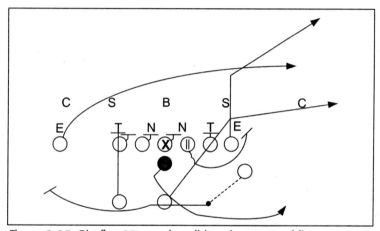

Figure 8-25. Rip flex 29 waggle solid against 65 goal line

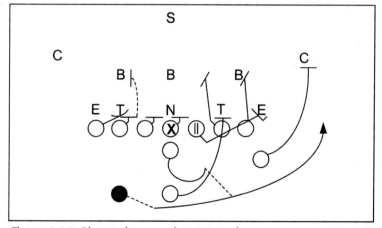

Figure 8-26. Rip 31 down against 53 stack

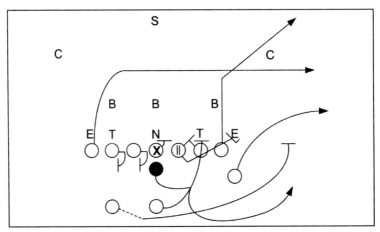

Figure 8-27. Rip 33 down keep against 53 stack

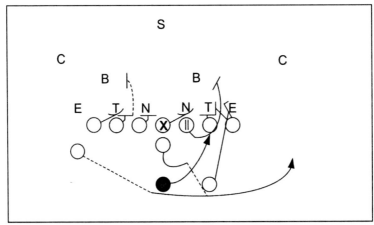

Figure 8-28. Liz 33 H against 62 stack

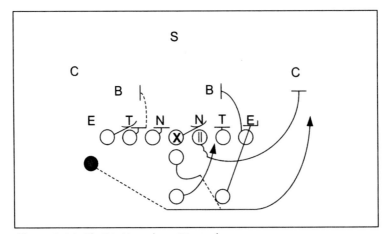

Figure 8-29. Liz 31 H against 62 stack

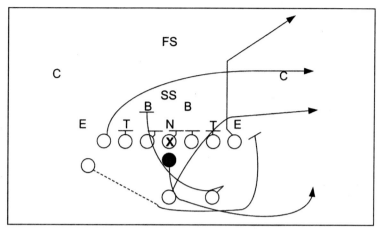

Figure 8-30. Liz 36 counter bootleg against 52 chase

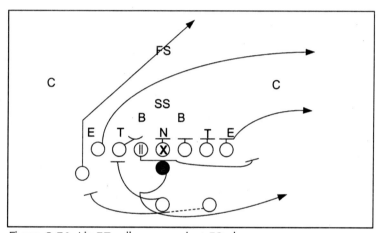

Figure 8-31. Liz 37 roll-away against 52 chase

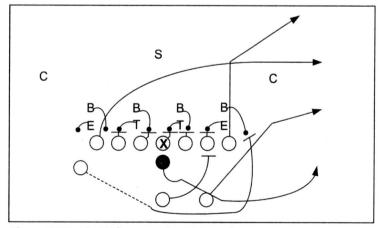

Figure 8-32. Liz 33 keep against 44 stack

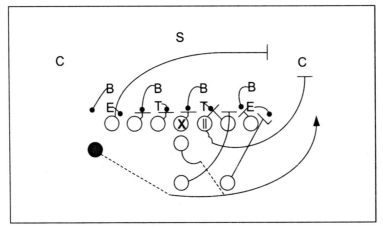

Figure 8-33. Liz 31 H against 44 stack

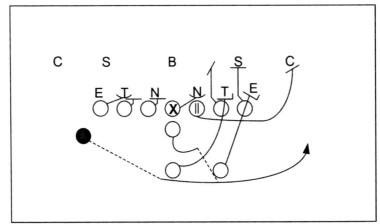

Figure 8-34. Liz 31 H against 65 goal line

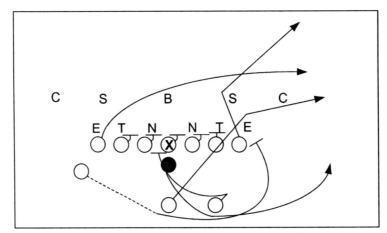

Figure 8-35. Liz 36 counter bootleg against 65 goal line

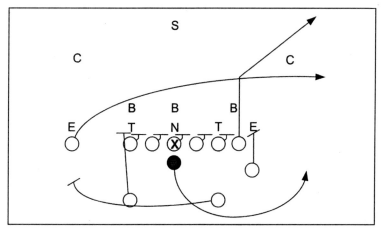

Figure 8-36. Rip B flex 49 wham boot and block against 53 stack

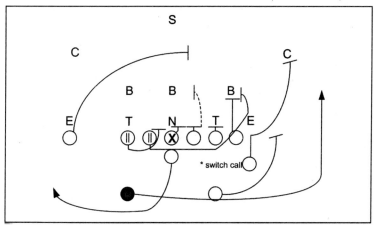

Figure 8-37. Rip B flex 41 arc against 53 stack

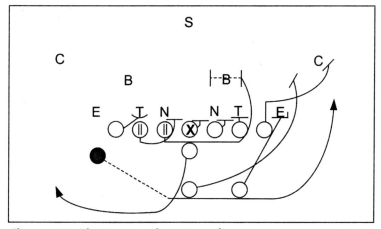

Figure 8-38. Liz 41 arc against 62 stack

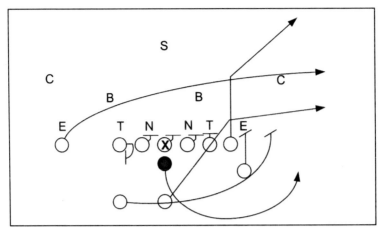

Figure 8-39. Rip flex 42 keep against 62 stack

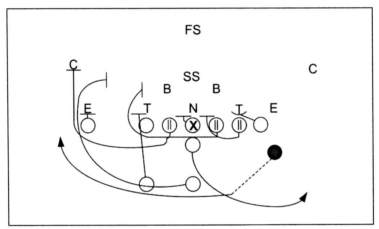

Figure 8-40. Rip flex 49 wham against 52 chase

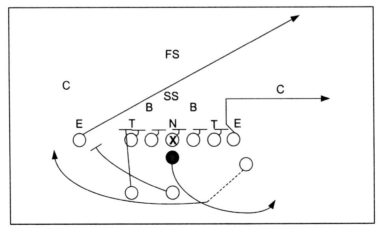

Figure 8-41. Rip flex 49 wham bootleg quick against 52 chase

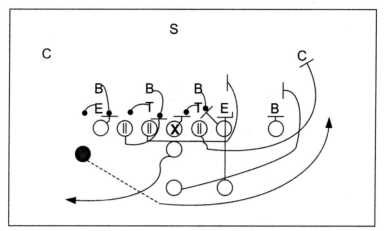

Figure 8-42. Liz flex 41 wham against 44 stack

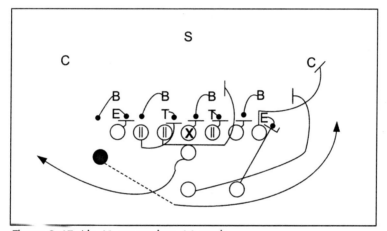

Figure 8-43. Liz 41 arc against 44 stack

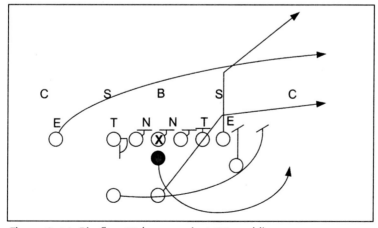

Figure 8-44. Rip flex 42 keep against 65 goal line

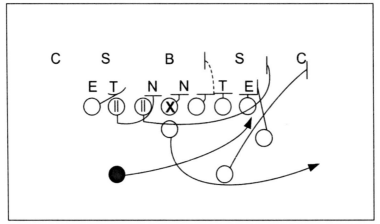

Figure 8-45. Rip B 42 power against 65 goal line

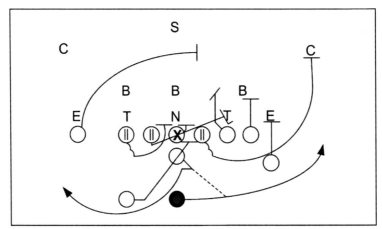

Figure 8-46. Rip flex 51 toss Iowa against 53 stack

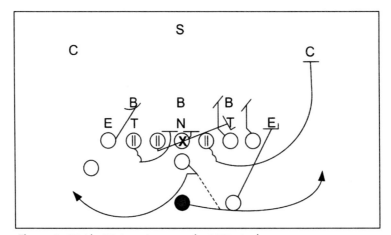

Figure 8-47. Liz 51 toss Iowa against 53 stack

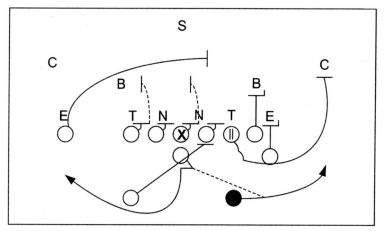

Figure 8-48. Rip B flex 51 quick pitch against 62 stack

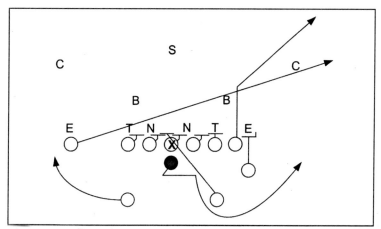

Figure 8-49. Rip B flex 59 quick pitch boot and block against 62 stack

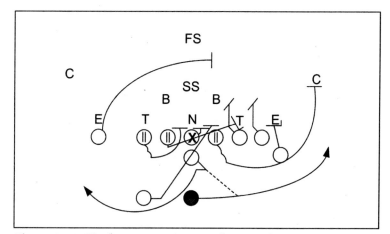

Figure 8-50. Rip flex 51 toss Iowa against 52 chase

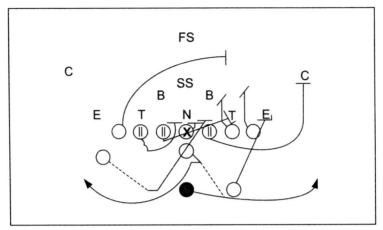

Figure 8-51. Liz 51 toss Iowa against 52 chase

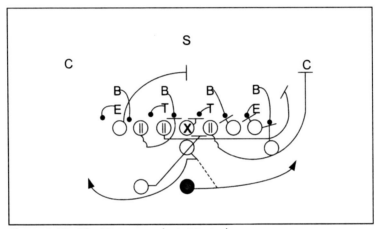

Figure 8-52. Rip 51 toss against 44 stack

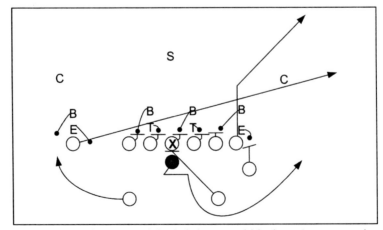

Figure 8-53. Rip B 59 quick pitch boot and block against 44-stack

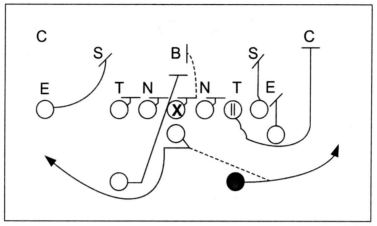

Figure 8-54. Rip B flex 51 quick pitch against 65 goal line

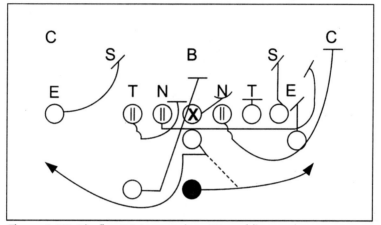

Figure 8-55. Rip flex 51 toss against 65 goal line

9

The 80 Series

The 80 series is a five-step dropback, or show-pass, series. It is used when the tactical situation definitely calls for a pass play. In these situations, play-action passes lose much of their effectiveness because the element of surprise no longer exists. Not everyone will agree when a dropback pass should be used in place of a play-action pass. This decision will depend on a number of factors: how many yards are needed for a first down, if you are in three- or four-down territory, the strength and weaknesses of a particular team, and the philosophy of the individual coach.

However, most coaches will agree that in some situations a dropback pass is in order. For instance, if you get a holding penalty on first down and are confronted with a first-and-20 situation, you need a big play to get back to a tactical situation that will allow he to run his normal offense. The first-and-20 situation dictates a pass play—and the defense knows it. On second down, with eight or more yards to go for a first down, most coaches would agree that a dropback pass is in order. A play-action pass on second-and-eight would not be nearly as productive as it would be in a second-and-short situation. A third down and six or more yards to go for a first down is another obvious passing down. All of these long-yardage situations are examples of when the dropback pass should take precedence over the play-action pass.

The chapter on the 80 series is approached by separating long-yardage situations into second-and-long, with two downs to make a first down, and third-and-long, with only one down to make a first down. The first example will feature short and delayed routes that allow a receiver to catch the ball close to the line of scrimmage and run for the first down. A correlation exists between the distance a pass travels and the completion percentage. The shorter the pass, the higher the completion rate. If a receiver catches a five-yard pass and run for five more yards, the net gain is 10 yards. If successful, you make the first down. If unsuccessful, you still have another down to make a first down. The patterns that follow will reflect this philosophy.

The second example will deal with long-yardage situations with only one down left to make a first down. Here the routes have to be deep enough to make a first down even if the receiver is tackled immediately after he catches the ball. With only one down left, he cannot rely on a receiver catching a short pass and running for a first down. Of course, the exact numbers of yards needed for a first down would affect the call. If it is third and 20 yards to go for a first down, he would consider throwing shorter passes that would allow the receiver to catch the ball and run for as much yardage as he can get. Screen passes and draw plays are also considerations in this situation.

As has been the pattern of this book, formations and pass plays will be diagrammed from a right formation. The reader simply needs to flop the formation to see what the play would look like from a left formation. The reads for the quarterback will be the same from either a left or right formation. The plays will be diagrammed against a 52 and 44 defense, and the quarterback reads will include zone coverage, man coverage, and five-under man coverage.

The base pattern in the 80 series is a vertical stretch route. It features a deep, medium, and short receiver all in the middle of the field and in the quarterback's cone of vision. It is designed to attack the vulnerable areas in a zone defense. The soft spots in zone coverage—whether it is a four-under three-deep or a five-under two-deep—are the areas in front of and in back of the backers. A pass thrown four to five yards past the line of scrimmage is too short for backers to get to, and a pass that is thrown 15 to 17 yards beyond the line of scrimmage is too long for the backers to get to. The base route is designed to exploit these weaknesses. It is good against zone and man coverage, and it is applicable on second or third down in long-yardage situations. It should be mastered before any of the companion plays are added.

The 80-series pass protection has the frontside blockers blocking man-on-man, and the backside blockers using a fan protection. The frontside will be the tight-end/wingback side, and the backside will be the spread end side. The frontside is to the right on pro 81, and it is to the left on con 89. The fullback blocks to the man-protection side, and the halfback blocks to the fan-protection side. The receivers are designated as X (the spread end), Y (the tight end), and Z (the flanker or the wingback). When Z is a flanker, he takes a five- to seven-yard split from the Y end.

SECOND-AND-LONG SITUATION

Pro 81 Base Y Under

The first play is pro 81 base Y under. It is illustrated in Figures 9-1 and 9-2. To the left, the play is con 89 base Y under, and the blocking assignments are reversed. The base route is a vertical stretch pattern, and it is a good route against both zone and man coverage. All pass plays in this chapter will stem from the base route. The idea is to complete a five- to six-yard pass and let the receiver run after the catch and gain as much yardage as possible. The primary receiver in Y under is the tight end.

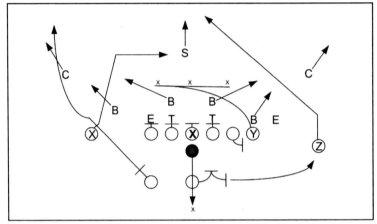

Figure 9-1. Pro 81 base Y under against a 44 zone defense

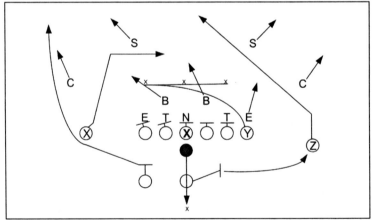

Figure 9-2. Pro 81 base Y under against a 52 zone defense

BLOCKING RULES, TECHNIQUES, AND COACHING POINTS FOR PRO 81 BASE Y UNDER

2-Man (Y)

Rule: Runs a four- to five-yard drag route.
Coaching Points: He is the primary receiver on this route, so he should expect the ball. Against zone coverage, he makes an inside release and drags under the backers at a depth of four to five yards. He runs at a controlled speed and becomes an easy target for the quarterback. If he does not get the ball when he arrives in the backside-tackle area, he begins to work back to his original position. He faces the quarterback and stays at four to five yards of depth from the line of scrimmage. When he does get the ball, he secures it and turns upfield. He runs north and south and get as much yardage as possible. He looks for the backers and tries to split them as they converge to tackle him. He stays low, protects the ball with two hands, and drives into and through the backers. He gets low enough so that he will fall forward when he is tackled. Against three-man or four-man coverage, he runs the same route but stays on the move. He should not work back. He tries to run away from the coverage. Against five-under man, he converts his route to a zoom out. In five-under man, the backer will take an inside alignment on him. He releases outside of the backer and starts on the drag route, gaining five to seven yards of depth. When he gets to the center of the formation—the backer will be to his inside—he fakes with his hands and eyes, pretending the ball is on its way. This fake will get the backer to look for the ball. At that moment, he pivots on his inside foot, makes a 180-degree turn away from the backer, and sprints back to the formation side. He gains ground as he runs away from coverage. The quarterback will throw him the ball as soon as he breaks away from the defender. He should be 8 to 10 yards deep when he catches it.

3-Man

Rule: Blocks the man on him.
Coaching Points: Against a backer, he pass sets and checks the backer. If the backer rushes, he blocks the backer; if not, he hinges and blocks the first rusher to show from the outside. Against a hard man, he steps with his right foot and jolts the defender by driving the palms of both hands into the defender's chest. He does not allow the defender to escape to the inside. He gives ground grudgingly and keeps the defender as close to the line of scrimmage as possible. He keeps his body between the defender and the quarterback, and blocks until the whistle blows.

4-Man

Rule: Blocks the man on him.
Coaching Points: Against a backer, he pass sets and checks the backer. If the backer rushes, he blocks the backer; if not, he helps #5 block the nose man.

5-Man

Rule: Blocks the man on or to his left.
Coaching Points: Against a nose man, he takes a short, controlled step and jolts the nose man on the line of scrimmage. He recoils quickly into a good pass posture. If the frontside guard's backer does not blitz, the frontside guard will help him with the nose man. He tries to force the nose man to rush to the frontside guard's side so he can get help from the frontside guard.

6-Man

Rule: Same as the 7-man.
Coaching Points: Same as the 7-man.

7-Man

Rule: From a two-point stance, blocks the man on or to his outside.
Coaching Points: He takes a short controlled step with his outside foot and jolts the defender on the line of scrimmage. He hits up and not out, and should not get overextended. He recoils quickly into a good pass posture: head up, knees bent, feet moving, and arms ready to strike the numbers of the defender. As he strikes the defender, he keeps a bend in his knees, his head up, and his back straight. He tries to force the defender to the outside. He does not allow the defender to escape to the inside. He gives ground grudgingly and tries to keep the defender as close to the line of scrimmage as possible. He keeps his body between the defender and the quarterback, and blocks the defender until the whistle blows.

8-Man (X)

Rule: Splits 8 to 10 yards and runs an in route.
Coaching Points: He drives upfield and makes an in move at a depth of 12 to 14 yards. He stays on the move against man coverage, but throttles in the open area against zone coverage. The quarterback will look to him if the Y end is not open.

Quarterback

Technique: Completes his five-step drop and places the ball with both hands next to his right ear. Finds a passing lane to the tight end.
Coaching Points: Remember: all dropback passes are thrown on the number, when the linemen are in a two-point stance. On a second-and-long-yardage situation, his primary receiver is the Y end on his drag route. On a third-and-long situation, his primary receiver is X on the in route, and he checks down to the Y end as an outlet receiver. Before the snap, he tries to determine the type of coverage the defense is

using. If the free safety is in the middle of the field, it is likely to be a zone defense; if he aligns over the Y end, it is probably a man-type coverage. If he sees a two-deep and a backer on the Y end, he should be alive for five-under man coverage. As he receives the ball, he begins his five-step drop. On his very first step, his head and eyes should be looking downfield. On each of his five steps, he should assess and reassess the reaction of the secondary. By the time he gets to the launching point, he should know if the coverage is man or zone, and the receiver that he plans to throw to.

Following is the technique for the quarterback against a three-deep or two-deep zone coverage: on his first step or two, he should confirm that the safety man has retreated to cover the post. Next, he looks at the inside backers and makes a decision to throw the ball in front of or behind them. If the backers get good width and depth on their drops, he works up into the pocket and finds a throwing lane to pass the ball to the Y end. The Y end will be working in the tackle box under the backers with the freedom to move left or right to get open (Figure 9-3). The Y end will be close to the line of scrimmage, so the quarterback should not throw the ball too hard. If the backers do not get good drops, his attention shifts to X on the in route (Figure 9-4).

He passes the ball over the backers and in front of the safety man. He should put some zip on this pass since it should be no higher than the receiver's numbers, and it should be above the receiver's knees. If the safety aligns over the Y end, the quarterback should expect man-to-man coverage. Against four-man, Y will stay on the move and he will have to lead Y with the ball (Figure 9-5). The inside backers will vacate the middle of the field by covering the remaining backs, or by coming on a blitz. Against three-man, the last man on the line of scrimmage to his right will be free, and he will have to dump the ball to the Y end quickly (Figure 9-6). If the quarterback sees five-under man coverage, the Y will try to shake his defender by starting on the crossing route and then quickly breaking back to the outside (Figure 9-7). The quarterback slides up into the pocket to give the Y time to execute his route, and throws the ball as the Y breaks away from his defender. The quarterback's last option is to run the ball.

Left Halfback

Technique: Checks or releases.
Coaching Points: If the 5-man is covered by a nose man, he is responsible to block the backside backer if the backer rushes. If the backer does not rush, he runs a takeoff route. If the 5-man is covered by a backer, he is responsible for the widest rusher from the outside in. The rusher can be a backer or a secondary player. If no rusher appears, he can run his takeoff route.

Fullback

Technique: Checks or releases.

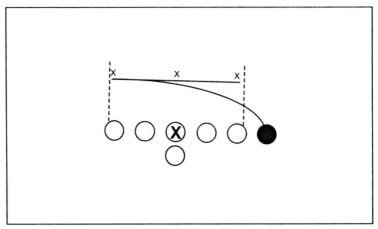

Figure 9-3. Y end working under the backers inside the tackle box

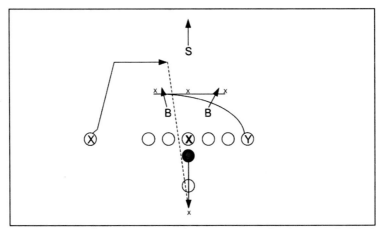

Figure 9-4. Backers cover Y, and X is open on the in route behind the backers and in front of the safety man

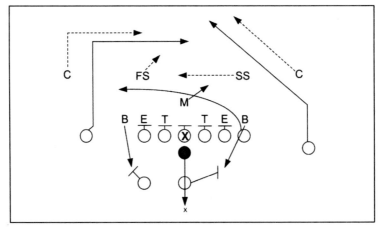

Figure 9-5. Safety aligns over the Y end in four-man coverage from a seven-man front

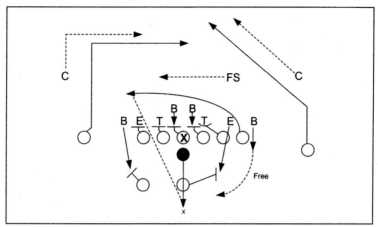

Figure 9-6. Safety aligns over the Y end in three-man coverage from an eight-man front

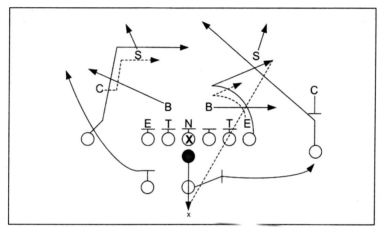

Figure 9-7. Y end converts under route to a zoom-out route against five-under man coverage

Coaching Points: Against a seven-man front, he blocks the first rusher outside the 3-man. If no one rushes, he runs a scat route to the frontside. Against an eight-man front, he has dual responsibility: he blocks the inside backer if the backer rushes, or the outside backer if that backer rushes. If they both rush, he blocks the inside backer. If neither rushes, he runs his scat route.

Right Halfback (Z)

Technique: Runs a post route.
Coaching Points: Against zone coverage, he runs a standard post. It is important to force the safety man deep to open up the in route by X. Against man coverage, he makes a double move to the post.

Pro 81 Base Left Halfback Delay

Pro 81 base left halfback delay is illustrated in Figures 9-8 and 9-9. To the left, the play is con 81 base right halfback delay, and the blocking assignments are reversed. This play is an excellent and a safe call. However, a plan is needed to compensate for a blitz that will force the left halfback to remain in the backfield and block the blitzing backer. For this contingency, the Y end—running a shallow crossing route—is the hot receiver. The Y end will get the ball when the backer assigned to the left halfback comes on a blitz. The X and Z receivers will stay with their routes. The left halfback blocks the blitz, the fullback runs a flare route, and the Y end is hot and runs a shallow crossing route. This hot-receiver contingency is illustrated in Figures 9-10 and 9-11.

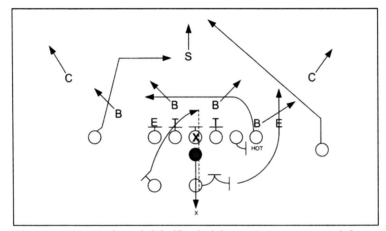

Figure 9-8. Pro 81 base left halfback delay against a 44 zone defense

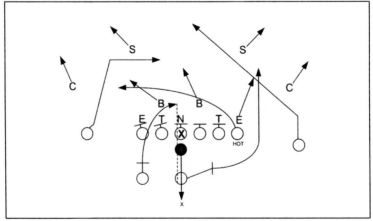

Figure 9-9. Pro 81 base left halfback delay against a 52 zone defense

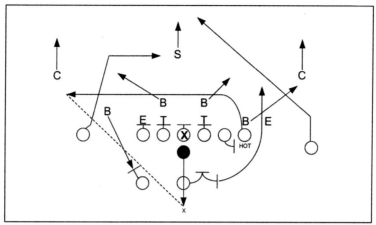

Figure 9-10. Pro 81 base left halfback delay against a 44 backer blitz, Y hot

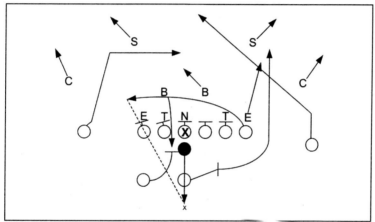

Figure 9-11. Pro 81 base left halfback delay against a 52 backer blitz, Y hot

BLOCKING RULES, TECHNIQUES, AND COACHING POINTS FOR PRO 81 BASE LEFT HALFBACK DELAY

All five interior linemen have the same assignments and coaching points on all the 80-series plays, with the exception of screens and draw plays.

2-Man (Y)

Rule: Runs a five- to seven-yard crossing route.
Coaching Points: He tries to get a pre-snap read on what type of coverage he is facing. He checks to see if the safety is lined up on him or in the middle of the formation. He is the hot receiver if the backside backer comes on a blitz. The location of the safety man will give him some indication whether the coverage is zone or man. In either case, as he crosses the formation, he checks the backside backer. If the backer is on a blitz,

he should expect the ball. He stays on the move and gets separation between himself and the defender covering him. If the coverage is five-under man, he does not convert to a zoom route as he normally would. He hustles across the formation, and the backer covering him will follow. This move will vacate the area the left halfback will occupy and give the left halfback more room to maneuver and separate from the backer covering the left halfback.

3-Man

Rule: Same as pro 81 base Y under.
Coaching Points: Same as pro 81 base Y under.

4-Man

Rule: Same as pro 81 base Y under.
Coaching Points: Same as pro 81 base Y under.

5-Man

Rule: Same as pro 81 base Y under.
Coaching Points: Same as pro 81 base Y under.

6-Man

Rule: Same as pro 81 base Y under.
Coaching Points: Same as pro 81 base Y under.

7-Man

Rule: Same as pro 81 base Y under.
Coaching Points: Same as pro 81 base Y under.

8-Man (X)

Rule: Same as pro 81 base Y under.
Coaching Points: Same as pro 81 base Y under.

Quarterback

Technique: Completes his five-step drop and places the ball with both hands just outside his right ear. Finds a passing lane and gets the ball to the left halfback.
Coaching Points: As he takes his five-step drop, he checks the backside backer to see if the backer drops into coverage or comes on a blitz. He sees him with peripheral vision,

with his head and eyes looking down the center of the field. If the backer drops into coverage, he completes his five-step drop and assumes the passing posture. He gives the pattern time to develop by bouncing at the launch point before shuffling toward the line of scrimmage. He keeps the backside backer in his vision to determine if the backer is in a zone or a man assignment. If the backer is in a zone assignment, the left halfback will turn to face him as the left halfback slips through the line of scrimmage. If the backer is waiting for the left halfback, the left halfback will sift through the line and stay on the move by breaking to the formation side at a depth of five to seven yards. In both situations, he finds a passing lane to throw the ball to the left halfback. When the left halfback is on the move, he will have to lead the left halfback to the ball. If the backer comes on a blitz, the left halfback is no longer in the pattern. Now his primary receiver is the Y end. Against a four-man cover scheme, he will have time to allow the Y end to cross the formation and separate from Y's defender. Against a three-man cover scheme, if both inside backers come on a blitz, he will have to dump the ball to Y as soon as possible. With both backers coming, the widest rusher to his right will not be blocked (Figure 9-12).

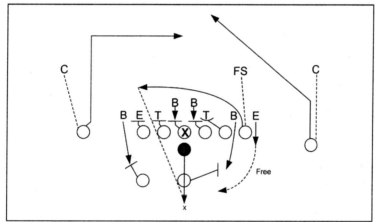

Figure 9-12. Three-man coverage, full blitz, widest rusher to quarterback's right is unblocked

Left Halfback

Technique: Checks or releases. Same blocking assignment on all 80-series passes, except for delays, screens, and draws.

Coaching Points: He is the primary receiver on this play. He checks the backer assigned to him. He has to know if the backer is dropping into coverage, waiting for him to come through the line, or blitzing. If the backer drops into coverage, he delays for two counts and then sifts through the line of scrimmage. He gains a depth of four to five yards and turns to face the quarterback. If necessary, he moves laterally to open a passing lane between himself and the quarterback. If the backer is waiting for him, he sifts through the line and runs at him. He gives him a head-and-shoulder fake to the left, and breaks right to separate from the backer. He should not be any deeper than seven to eight yards when he catches the ball. If the backer comes on a blitz, he must stay in the backfield and block the backer. He is no longer involved in the pattern.

Fullback

Technique: Same blocking assignment on all 80-series pass plays.
Coaching Points: If he does not have to pick up a blitz, he runs a flare route. He tries to attract the backer to his side and takes the backer as deep and wide as possible. Doing so will allow the left halfback to have running more room after the left halfback catches the ball.

Right Halfback (Z)

Technique: Same as pro 81 base Y under.
Coaching Points: Same as pro 81 base Y under.

Pro 81 Base Y Delay

The delay to Y is similar to the halfback delay pass. It is an easier delay route because Y is not involved in blocking backers and will always be able to release from the line of scrimmage. Pro 81 base Y delay is illustrated in Figures 9-13 and 9-14. To the left, the play is con 89 base Y delay, and the blocking assignments are reversed.

BLOCKING RULES, TECHNIQUES, AND COACHING POINTS FOR PRO 81 BASE Y DELAY

All interior linemen have the same assignments and coaching points on all 80 series plays, except for screens and draw plays.

2-Man (Y)

Rule: Runs a delay route.
Coaching Points: He pass sets on the line of scrimmage for three counts. He should not lose more than one yard of depth as he pass blocks. After three counts, he releases to a spot directly over the ball at a depth of four to five yards from the line of scrimmage. After he catches the ball, he turns upfield and runs north and south, looking to split the backers. As the backers close on him, he protects the ball with both arms, lowers his shoulders, and tries to split the backers. He should be low enough to fall forward after contact.

3-Man

Rule: Same as pro 81 base Y under.
Coaching Points: Same as pro 81 base Y under.

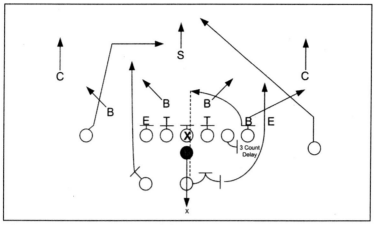

Figure 9-13. Pro 81 base Y delay against a 44 zone defense

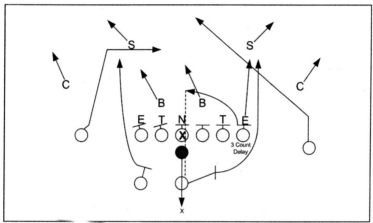

Figure 9-14. Pro 81 base Y delay against a 52 zone defense

4-Man

Rule: Same as pro 81 base Y under.
Coaching Points: Same as pro 81 base Y under.

5-Man

Rule: Same as pro 81 base Y under.
Coaching Points: Same as pro 81 base Y under.

6-Man

Rule: Same as pro 81 base Y under.
Coaching Points: Same as pro 81 base Y under.

7-Man

Rule: Same as pro 81 base Y under.
Coaching Points: Same as pro 81 base Y under.

8-Man (X)

Rule: Runs a 12- to 14-yard in route.
Coaching Points: If he sees three-man coverage, he converts to a seven-yard slant route. He is the hot receiver against three-man coverage.

Quarterback

Technique: Completes his five-step drop and places the ball with both hands just outside his right ear. Finds a passing lane to the tight end.
Coaching Points: His execution of the Y-delay route is basically the same as it is on the halfback-delay route. The major difference is against three-man coverage. In this situation, an eight-man rush is possible, and he will not have the time needed to complete the pass. The X receiver will convert his route to a seven-yard slant when he sees three-man coverage. X now becomes the hot receiver. The quarterback will take five short steps and throw the ball to the X receiver on his fifth step. He throws the ball into the open area and lets the receiver run to it.

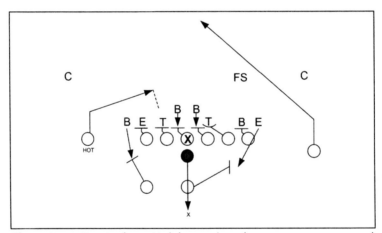

Figure 9-15. Pro 81 base Y delay against three-man coverage and full blitz

Left Halfback

Technique: Checks or releases.
Coaching Points: His blocking assignment is the same on all 80-series pass plays. If his backer does not blitz, the route he runs on Y delay is a flare route through the backside

hook zone to his side of the formation. He tries to get the backer's attention and drive the backer as deep and wide as the backer will go. Doing so will give the Y end more room to work in.

Fullback

Technique: Checks or releases.
Coaching Points: If his backer does not blitz, he runs a flare through the frontside hook zone and drives the backer as deep and as wide as the backer will go. The flare route by both backs will give the Y end more room to operate.

Right Halfback (Z)

Technique: Runs a deep post route.
Coaching Points: He drives the safety as deep as possible.

Pro 81 Base Crack Screen Left

The crack screen is an excellent call on second-and-long yardage. It is illustrated in Figures 9-16 and 9-17. To the left, the play is con 89 base crack screen right, and the blocking assignments are reversed. The crack screen is a play with great utility because it is good against zone or any type of man coverage. It is also a great play in the score zone because of the probability of getting man coverage. The quarterback does not have to read the defense; he just has to execute the play. Another plus for this play is that, because the ball is thrown behind the line of scrimmage, the split end can crack back on a backer and legally block as the pass is completed to the left halfback. A minor blocking adjustment—from the basic 80-series protection—with the crack screen has the linemen on both sides of the ball blocking man protection.

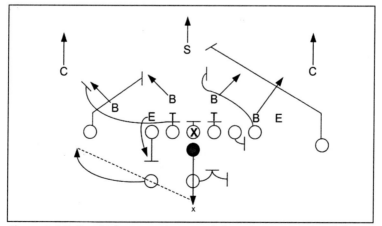

Figure 9-16. Pro 81 base crack screen left against a 44 zone defense

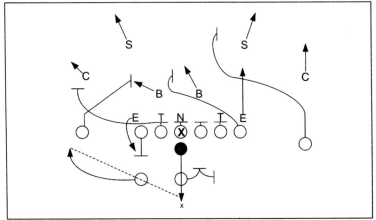

Figure 9-17. Pro 81 base crack screen left against a 52 zone defense

BLOCKING RULES, TECHNIQUES, AND COACHING POINTS
FOR PRO 81 BASE CRACK SCREEN LEFT

2-Man

Rule: Blocks the defender in the deep middle third of the field.
Coaching Points: He gets his body between the defender and the left halfback, and uses a high-pressure control block to wall him off.

3-Man

Rule: Same as #5.
Coaching Points: Same as #5.

4-Man

Rule: Same as #5.
Coaching Points: Same as #5.

5-Man

Rule: Blocks the man on him.
Coaching Points: Against a hard man, he shows pass and invites the hard man to rush away from the direction of the pass. Against a backer, he shows pass for a second and sprints for a position that will put him between the backer and the left halfback. He walls off the backer with a high-pressure control block.

6-Man

Rule: Pulls and blocks the frontside corner.
Coaching Points: If he has a hard man on him, he jolts the hard man to break the hard man's charge, and then he sprints left down the line of scrimmage. He is responsible for blocking the first threat on the corner—usually the force man. If he has a backer on him, he shows pass for a second and then sprints down the line to block at the corner.

7-Man

Rule: Blocks the man on him.
Coaching Points: He gets depth immediately and comes straight back off the line of scrimmage. He draws his defender deep into the backfield so #6 can come under him to block at the corner.

8-Man (X)

Rule: Cracks the first backer to his inside.
Coaching Points: He starts with his inside foot and takes two steps upfield. He pushes off his second step and cracks the backer. He blocks above the waist and gets under control as he approach the backer. His block is more like a wall-off block: he just gets his body between the backer and the left halfback and walls him off.

Quarterback

Technique: Completes his five-step drop and throws to the left halfback.
Coaching Points: After receiving the snap, he begins his drop with his head and eyes looking downfield. He takes five quick steps to the launch point. As soon as his fifth step hits the ground, he throws the ball to the left halfback. A perfect pass is about one foot in front of the numbers so the left halfback can catch it with his momentum headed downfield.

Left Halfback

Technique: Runs a crack screen route.
Coaching Points: At the snap of the ball, he loses some ground and runs a bowed course toward the line of scrimmage. He runs at a controlled speed and makes himself an easy target for the quarterback to hit. After the catch, he stays on the perimeter and runs away from pursuit.

Fullback

Technique: Blocks first rusher outside the 3-man.

Coaching Points: He hustles to a point three yards behind #3. He assumes a good hitting posture and blocks the first defender to show outside #3.

Right Halfback (Z)

Technique: Stalk blocks the defender in his deep third zone.
Coaching Points: As he drives upfield, he positions himself between the safety man and the left halfback. He uses a stalk block to wall off the safety.

Pro 81 Base Left Halfback Slow Screen Left

The slow screen to the left halfback is another good call on second-and-long yardage. It has big potential and is quite capable of picking up the first down. Again, if he falls short of the mark, he still has another down to make a first down. Pro 81 base left halfback slow screen left is illustrated in Figures 9-18 and 9-19. To the left, the play is con 89 base right halfback slow screen right, and the blocking assignments are reversed.

BLOCKING RULES, TECHNIQUES, AND COACHING POINTS
FOR PRO 81 LEFT HALFBACK SLOW SCREEN LEFT

2-Man

Rule: Blocks the defensive back in the middle of the field.
Coaching Points: Same as the 8-man.

3-Man

Rule: Steps and hinges.
Coaching Points: He kicks back with his inside foot and gets inside position on the defender. He keeps his outside foot between the defender's feet and forces the defender wide and deep.

4-Man

Rule: Same as the 6-man.
Coaching Points: As he releases down the line of scrimmage and reaches the end of the line, he peels back on the line of scrimmage and blocks any pursuing defender who threatens the play from behind. If no threat is present, he pivots on his right foot and continues downfield. He looks inside for a defender to block.

5-Man

Rule: Same as the 6-man.

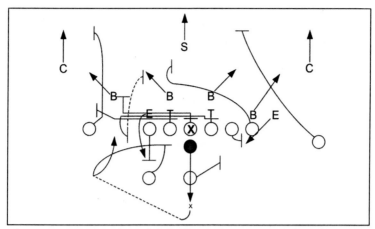

Figure 9-18. Pro 81 base left halfback slow screen left against a 44 zone defense

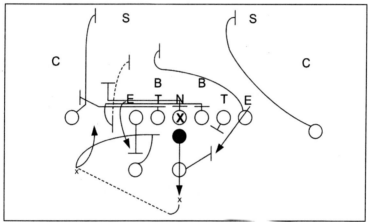

Figure 9-19. Pro 81 base left halfback slow screen left against a 52 zone defense

Coaching Points: As he releases down the line of scrimmage, he turns upfield inside the 6-man's block and blocks the most dangerous defender in the area.

6-Man

Rule: Sets for three counts on the line of scrimmage and gets into screen.

Coaching Points: He assumes pass-protection posture and sets as close to the line of scrimmage as possible. His set should take one second, then he punches into the defender to break his charge, and releases flat down the line of scrimmage. He should not get any deeper than one yard from the line. He has the key block on the screen play. As he approaches the corner defender, he gets into a good hitting position and explodes through the defender. He keeps his feet and blocks until the whistle blows.

7-Man

Rule: Hinges.
Coaching Points: He is responsible for blocking the widest rusher to his side. He kicks straight back for two to three yards and gets inside position on the defender on him. He blocks the defender if the defender is the widest rusher. If not, he lets the defender go and blocks the next defender from the outside. He tries to retreat straight back as he blocks his defender, and he gives ground grudgingly.

8-Man (X)

Rule: Releases and blocks the frontside deep-third defender.
Coaching Points: He releases straight upfield and forces the defensive back out of his backpedal. When the back reacts to the screen, he breaks down and stalk blocks the back. He tries to get his body between the defensive back and the runner.

Quarterback

Technique: Completes his drop and places the ball with both hands just outside his right ear. Finds a passing lane to the left halfback.
Coaching Points: He takes five big steps to get to the launch point. As he retreats, he tries to look off the backers by turning his head and eyes away from the direction of the screen pass. At the launch point, he hesitates for a second, and then uses short steps to retreat back and toward the back receiving the screen pass. He finds a passing lane and gets the ball to the left halfback. His pass should be aimed at the left halfback's downfield shoulder. He keeps the ball above the waist and below the shoulders of the left halfback.

Left Halfback

Technique: Sets up for the screen.
Coaching Points: As the ball is snapped, he sets up in a pass-protection posture for one count. Then, he moves to a position between the 6-man and the 7-man two yards from the line of scrimmage. As he approaches the line of scrimmage, he looks to see if the 7-man is blocking the man on him. If so, he does not have a blocking assignment. If #7 is blocking a wide rusher, he must jolt the unblocked defender before he releases. If he does not have a man to block, he releases when the guard in front of him releases. He releases under the tackle's block, aiming for a spot five yards outside the tackle's alignment and five yards deep in the backfield. He turns to face the quarterback and shouts, "Go" when the catch is made. He turns to the inside and follows his blockers.

Fullback

Technique: Blocks the first defender outside of the 3-man's block.

Coaching Points: He sets up between the 4-man and the 3-man and uses good pass-blocking techniques to block any rusher outside of #3.

Right Halfback (Z)

Technique: Same assignment as X.
Coaching Points: Same as X.

Pro 81 Base Fullback Draw Left

The lead draw play is most effective when run to the split end side. Pro 81 base fullback draw left is illustrated in Figures 9-20 and 9-21. To the left, the play is con 89 base fullback draw right, and the blocking assignments are reversed. The draw play is a good second-and-long call, especially when you are backed up deep in your own territory. When run from B backs, the fullback must slide to his regular position as the ball is snapped.

BLOCKING RULES, TECHNIQUES, AND COACHING POINTS FOR THE FULLBACK DRAW

2-Man (Y)

Rule: Releases to deep third.
Coaching Points: He sprints at the safety man and gets the safety out of his backpedal. When the safety recognizes the draw, he collects himself, gets into a good hitting position, and stalk blocks the safety.

3-Man

Rule: Steps and hinges.
Coaching Points: Same as #7.

4-Man

Rule: Steps and hinges.
Coaching Points: Same as #7.

5-Man

Rule: Blocks man on or a backside backer.
Coaching Points: Against a hard man, he sets on the line of scrimmage and allows the hard man to pick a side. He takes the hard man in the direction the hard man chooses to go. The fullback will run off his block. He keeps his feet and blocks until the whistle blows. Against a backer, he sets for a count at the line of scrimmage and allows the

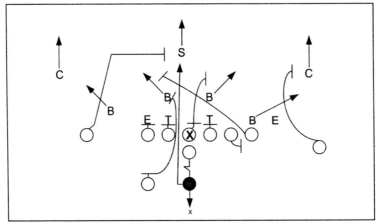

Figure 9-20. Pro 81 base fullback draw left against a 44 zone defense

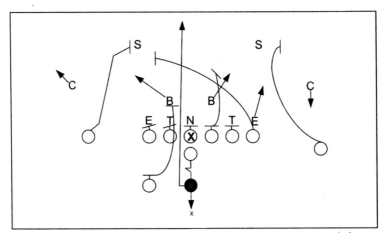

Figure 9-21. Pro 81 base fullback draw left against a 52 zone defense

backer to start his drop. Then, he attacks him with a high-pressure control block. He keeps his body between the backer and the fullback, keeps his feet moving, and maintains the block until the whistle blows.

6-Man

Rule: Steps and hinges.
Coaching Points: Same as #7.

7-Man

Rule: Steps and hinges.
Coaching Points: He takes a position step with his right foot to get inside position on the man he is blocking. He drives the palms of both hands into the numbers of the man he is blocking and assumes a good pass posture: head up, back arched, knees

bent, and feet apart. He keeps his outside foot between the defender's feet and invites the defender to the outside. He takes the defender as deep as the defender wants to go, but do not allow the defender to get inside him.

8-Man (X)

Rule: Releases and blocks the defensive back in the frontside third of the field.
Coaching Points: He sprints downfield and gets the defensive back out of his backpedal. When the back recognizes the run, he breaks down and stalk blocks the defensive back. He tries to get inside-out position and keep the defensive back from getting to the middle of the field.

Quarterback

Technique: Completes his drop and hands the ball to the fullback.
Coaching Points: He starts his dropback technique and makes a one-handed handoff to the fullback between his second and third steps. After the handoff, he brings both hands to his pouch and continues to the launch point to set up and fake a pass.

Left Halfback

Technique: Blocks the frontside backer.
Coaching Points: He takes a short, lateral step inside and shows pass. He should be between the tackle and guard on his side. Then, he sprints through the line of scrimmage and blocks the frontside backer. He gathers himself before the block. He should have a wide base, a bend in the knees, and he should explode up and into the backer. He stays on his feet and blocks until the whistle blows.

Fullback

Technique: Acts as the ballcarrier on the draw.
Coaching Points: As the ball is snapped, he takes a short, lateral step with his left foot to the frontside. He should be in a good pass-protection posture and form a pocket with his right arm up. If the center is covered by a hard man, he reads the center's block and decides where he will run as the quarterback hands him the ball. He heads for the tail of the 5-man and runs to daylight.

Right Halfback (Z)

Technique: Same as X.
Coaching Points: Same as X.

Pro 81 Base Fullback Scat

The fullback scat pass is executed from either an A or B backfield set. Pro 81 base fullback scat is illustrated in Figures 9-22 and 9-23. To the left, the play is con 89 base fullback scat, and the blocking assignments are reversed. The scat pass is a quicker play from B backs than it is from A backs. The pass is a good second-and-long play, and it is also good as a "kill the clock" play. After the fullback catches the ball, and gets as much yardage as possible, the fullback can easily step out of bounds.

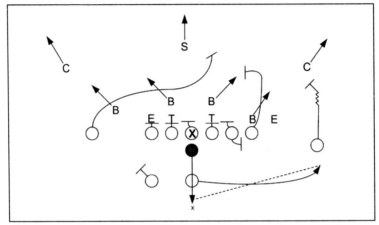

Figure 9-22. Pro 81 base fullback scat against a 44 zone defense

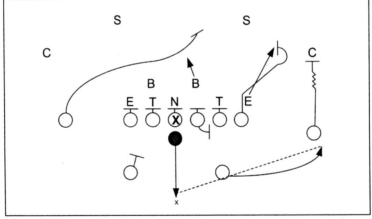

Figure 9-23. Pro B 81 base fullback scat against a 52 zone defense

BLOCKING RULES, TECHNIQUES, AND COACHING POINTS FOR PRO 81 BASE FULLBACK SCAT

2-Man (Y)

Rule: Runs a 10-yard curl route.

Coaching Points: He makes an outside release and eyeballs the frontside backer. He keeps the backer inside his route, positioning himself between the backer and the fullback. When the backer reacts to the pass, he uses a high-pressure control block and walls off the backer. Against four-short zone defenders, he blocks the defender in the hook zone. Against five-short zone defenders, he blocks the defender in the curl zone. He stays high on his block and stays on his feet.

3-Man

Rule: Dual responsibility. Same as #4.
Coaching Points: Same as #4.

4-Man

Rule: Dual responsibility.
Coaching Points: Because the fullback has a free release on this play—no blocking assignment—the 4-man (the uncovered frontside lineman) assumes the fullback's dual responsibility. He will block the backer if the backer comes, or, block the first rusher outside the frontside tackle's block. If he has a backer over him, he drop-steps with his inside foot, pivots on that foot, and ends up one yard behind the line, with his shoulders at a 45-degree angle to it. His head and eyes should be on the backer as he assumes this posture. If the backer does not rush, he gets width and depth to the outside and blocks the widest rusher. If the backer rushes, he squares up and blocks him. Against a hard man, he reverts to 80-series techniques.

5-Man

Rule: Same as pro 81 base Y under.
Coaching Points: Same as pro 81 base Y under.

6-Man

Rule: Same as pro 81 base Y under.
Coaching Points: Same as pro 81 base Y under.

7-Man

Rule: Same as pro 81 base Y under.
Coaching Points: Same as pro 81 base Y under.

8-Man (X)

Rule: Blocks the defender in the middle third of the field.

Coaching Points: He runs a shallow crossing route, trying to get inside-out position on the safety man, and uses a wall-off block to prevent the safety from getting to the fullback.

Quarterback

Technique: Completes his drop and gets the ball to the fullback.
Coaching Points: On this play, he takes five quick steps and passes the ball to the fullback as the fullback is moving toward the line of scrimmage. If the frontside backer rushes, the last man on the line of scrimmage will not be blocked, which means that he must get the ball to the fullback before that rusher gets to him. He may have to throw the ball on his third or fourth step. In a 50 defense, the backer to watch is over the frontside guard; in a 40 defense, the backer is over the frontside tackle. He looks downfield as he retreats from the line of scrimmage, forcing the underneath defenders to gain some depth on their drops. He completes his five steps as quickly as possible and puts enough zip on the pass so the fullback does not have to wait for it. The ball should be firm enough so the fullback can catch it in stride, and soft enough to facilitate the catch. The fullback should catch the ball as he is moving toward the line of scrimmage, and it should be about one foot in front of the fullback's numbers.

Left Halfback

Technique: Same as pro 81 base Y under.
Coaching Points: Same as pro 81 base Y under.

Fullback

Technique: Runs a scat route.
Coaching Points: He has no blocking responsibilities on the scat route. He makes a slight bow as he begins his route, gaining width and depth. He catches the ball a yard behind or right on the line of scrimmage. After the reception, he stays on the perimeter. He uses the sideline to his advantage, forcing the defenders to attack him from one direction only. He should not attempt to cut back unless an obvious opening is present. On the sideline, he stays low and gives the tacklers the hard parts of his body. He has good body lean and always falls forward as he is tackled.

Right Halfback

Technique: Releases downfield and blocks the underneath defender in the outside quarter or fifth of the field.
Coaching Points: Against four-short zone defenders, he blocks the defender in the outside quarter of the field. Against five-short zone defenders, he blocks the defender in the outside fifth of the field. He uses a high-pressure control block. He stays high on the block and stays on his feet.

THIRD-AND-LONG SITUATION

The next tactical situation is a third-and-long call in which the offense has one down to gain 7 to 12 yards for a first down. As stated earlier in this chapter, with just one down left to gain a first down, the ball should be thrown to a receiver who is one or two yards deeper than the yardage needed for the first down. If the pass is completed, you have a first down—even if the receiver is tackled immediately after the catch. Conversely, if you complete a five-yard pass and the receiver runs for another five yards before being tackled, you still come up two yards short of a first down.

Pro 81 Base X In

The first pass play for a third-and-long situation is an in route run by the outside receivers: X or Z. Pro 81 X in is illustrated in Figures 9-24 and 9-25. To the left, the play is con 89 X in, and the blocking assignments are reversed. If X is called on the in route, Z runs the post route. If Z is called on the in route, X runs the post route. Again, Pro 81 X in/Z in should be perfected before any additional third-and-long plays are added to the third and long category.

BLOCKING RULES, TECHNIQUES, AND COACHING POINTS FOR PRO 81 BASE X IN

2-Man (Y)

Rule: Runs an under route.
Coaching Points: He will be a checkdown receiver if the X receiver is not open on his in route. Against zone coverage, he runs his under route. He should be five to six yards deep, but under the frontside or middle backer. He should not go any further across the formation than the backside tackle's alignment. When he gets to that position and the quarterback still has the ball, he continues to face the quarterback and works back to his original position. He opens a passing lane between himself and the quarterback. Against four- or three-man coverage, he stays on the move as he crosses the formation and tries to run away from coverage. Against five-under man, he converts his route to a zoom-out pattern.

3-Man

Rule: Same as pro 81 base Y under.
Coaching Points: Same as pro 81 base Y under.

4-Man

Rule: Same as pro 81 base Y under.
Coaching Points: Same as pro 81 base Y under.

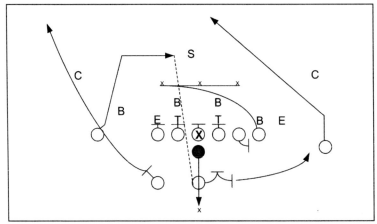

Figure 9-24. Pro 81 base X in against a 44 zone defense

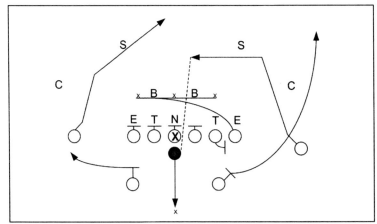

Figure 9-25. Pro B 81 base Z in against a 52 zone defense

5-Man

Rule: Same as pro 81 base Y under.
Coaching Points: Same as pro 81 base Y under.

6-Man

Rule: Same as pro 81 base Y under.
Coaching Points: Same as pro 81 base Y under.

7-Man

Rule: Same as pro 81 base Y under.
Coaching Points: Same as pro 81 base Y under.

8-Man (X)

Rule: Runs a 12- to 14-yard in route. He is the primary receiver.

Coaching Points: He knows how many yards are needed for the first down. He should be one or two yards deeper than what is needed. Against zone coverage, he cruises across the formation at controlled speed. He tries to get between the backers to open a passing lane for the quarterback. Against any kind of man coverage, he sprints through the defender to get the defender out of his backpedal. Then, he makes a fake to the outside before breaking into his in route. He stays on the move and runs away from coverage. If the defensive back aligns inside of him, he releases on an inside angle so he will be head on the defender as he sprints upfield. This technique will negate his inside leverage and give him a better chance to beat the defender inside.

Against five-under man coverage, the defender will crowd him and try to deny him an inside release. He makes a good head-and-shoulder fake to the outside and simultaneously clubs the defender with his inside arm. He uses a swim move with his outside arm to release inside of the defender. He drives straight up the field for six to seven yards and bends his route outside three to four steps, looking back for the ball. This move will make the defender cut under him to get between him and the ball. As soon as this move occurs, he quickly breaks back into the middle of the field and runs away from his coverage. Again, his final break should not put him any deeper than 15 yards from the line of scrimmage.

Quarterback

Technique: Completes his drop and places the ball with both hands just outside his right ear. Finds an open passing lane to the X receiver.

Coaching Points: His primary receiver is X on the in route. He tries to get a pre-snap read of what the coverage is by locating the position of the free safety. Doing so will help him to anticipate minor adjustments the receivers will make against man coverage. As he begins his retreat to the launch point, he keeps his head and eyes looking directly down the center of the field. Against zone coverage, he looks first to the post route. If Z gets behind the safety man, he throws to Z on the post. Next, he checks the drop of the backers and begins to decide to throw the ball over the backers or in front of them. On each of his five steps, he should be assessing and reassessing his chances of getting the ball to the primary receiver.

As he reaches the launch point on his fifth step, he should know if he can throw to X or check down to Y. The depth and location of the backers will determine which receiver will get the ball. If his judgment is to throw to X on the in route, he throws the ball over and between the backers. The X receiver will run at controlled speed, so he should throw the ball into an open area and let X run to it. The pass is thrown on a line and should be between the receiver's shoulders and waist. If he is not sure he can get the ball to X, he checks down to Y. He should never force the ball to X. An interception is far worse than not making a first down. Against four-man coverage, and a five- or six-man rush, the left halfback will not get out into his route. The free safety will zone off, and the X receiver will be double-teamed by the corner and the free safety. His most secure pass is to the Y end on his crossing route (Figure 9-26).

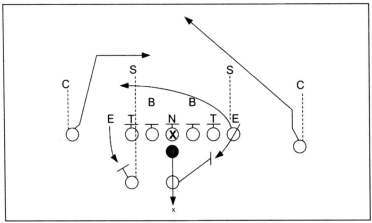

Figure 9-26. Pro 81 base X in against a 52 blitz four-man coverage

He moves up into the pocket and anticipates X's break. When he sees X lower his center of gravity just before X's break, he begins the throwing motion and allows X to run to the ball. Against three-man coverage, the widest rusher to his right will not be blocked (Figure 9-27). He will recognize this coverage when he sees the safety man in an eight-man front aligned on the Y end. His best choice in this situation is go to Y on the crossing route. Against five-under man, the percentage play is to go to Y on the zoom-out route.

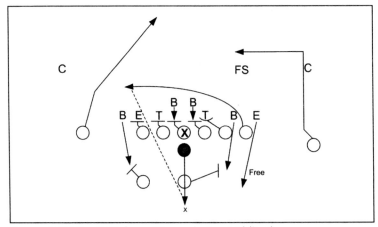

Figure 9-27. Pro B 81 base Z in against a 44 blitz three-man coverage

Left Halfback

Technique: Checks or releases.
Coaching Points: His release on 81 base X in is a takeoff route.

Fullback

Technique: Checks or releases.
Coaching Points: His release on 81 base X in is a scat route.

Right Halfback (Z)

Technique: Runs a post route.
Coaching Points: He takes the top off the coverage. Against zone coverage, he forces the safety man to cover him deep. Doing so will open the middle for X on the in route. He makes a double move to the post against any kind of man coverage.

Pro 81 Y Choice

The second route is pro base 81 Y choice. It is illustrated in Figures 9-28 and 9-29. To the left, the play is con 89 Y choice, and the blocking assignments are reversed. This route is excellent on second-and-long when 7 to 10 yards are needed to make a first down. The Y end is the primary receiver. On Y choice, the Y end can choose to run an out or to hook up to the inside. Against a deployment of four backers, the Y end will run the out route; against five backers, he will hook up to the inside. Against five-under man, he will convert his route to zoom out. On the zoom-out route, the Y end will bend to the inside for three to four steps. The backer will follow, staying between Y and the quarterback. The Y end will then pivot on his inside foot and break to the outside, gaining a depth of 10 to 12 yards. The quarterback will deliver the ball as the Y end makes his pivot and moves to the outside.

BLOCKING RULES, TECHNIQUES, AND COACHING POINTS FOR PRO 81 Y CHOICE

2-Man

Rule: Runs a choice route.
Coaching Points: He releases outside, if possible. He runs the out or hook route one yard deeper than the yardage needed for a first down. Against four-short zone coverage, he runs the out route. He has to beat the inside backer. No fakes are necessary; he just sprints upfield and breaks to the outside. He should catch the ball in between the hook and the curl defender. He expects the ball to be in the air as he makes his break. He snaps his head around quickly to pick up the ball and catch it on his third or fourth step. Against

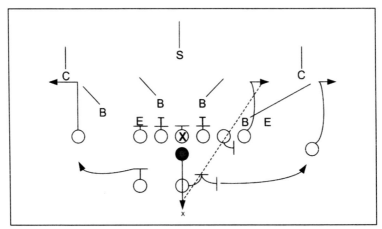

Figure 9-28. Pro 81 base Y choice against a 44 zone defense

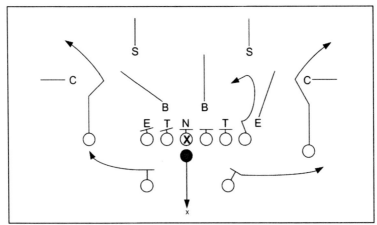

Figure 9-29. Pro B 81 base Y choice against a 52 zone defense

five-short zone coverage, he hooks up to the inside. He should catch the ball in between the backer covering the middle fifth of the field and the defender in the curl area.

Against three- or four-man coverage, the safety will cover him. It is best to have a prearranged route in mind against man coverage so that the timing of the play is good. The quarterback should know if the tight end is going to break to the inside or the outside so he can anticipate the break and deliver the ball on time. A head-and-shoulder fake would be helpful just before he makes his final break. Again, he expects the ball to be in the air as he makes his break. Against five-under man, he converts his route to a zoom out. If he runs the out or the hook, the backer will streak under him and be in good position to defend the pass. Therefore, he releases upfield for five to six yards and then breaks inside for three to four yards. He raises his hands and looks back, pretending the ball is on its way. This move will cause the defender to turn and look for the ball. He quickly turns away from the defender and sprints for the sideline, gaining depth as he goes. The quarterback will throw the ball as he breaks away from the man coverage.

3-Man

Rule: Same as pro 81 base Y under.
Coaching Points: Same as pro 81 base Y under.

4-Man

Rule: Same as pro 81 base Y under.
Coaching Points: Same as pro 81 base Y under.

5-Man

Rule: Same as pro 81 base Y under.
Coaching Points: Same as pro 81 base Y under.

6-Man

Rule: Same as pro 81 base Y under.
Coaching Points: Same as pro 81 base Y under.

7-Man

Rule: Same as pro 81 base Y under.
Coaching Points: Same as pro 81 base Y under.

8-Man (X)

Rule: Runs an out route.
Coaching Points: He runs his out route one yard deeper than the yardage needed for a first down.

Quarterback

Technique: Completes his drop and places the ball with both hands just outside his right ear. Finds an open passing lane to the Y end.
Coaching Points: His primary receiver is the Y end. He tries to get a pre-snap read of the coverage as he approaches the line of scrimmage. It helps to know if the coverage is zone, three- or four-man, or man under. The alignment of the safety, and a backer aligned on the Y end, will tip off the coverage. As he begins his five-step drop, he looks down the center of the field. If the coverage is a four-short zone, he gets the ball to the Y end outside the inside backer and inside the outside backer. Just before the Y end breaks out, the Y end will lower his center of gravity (i.e., his butt). As he sees this happen, he begins the throwing motion. He throws the ball to a spot where only the Y end can get to it. He does not wait to see the end open; rather, he anticipates Y's

break and gets Y the ball between the backers. This ball is thrown with some zip on it. He keeps it above the waist and below the shoulders of the Y end. If the coverage is five-short zone, the Y end will hook up to the inside. He gets Y the ball between the middle and the curl backer. Again, he anticipates Y's break and puts some zip on the ball.

If the coverage is five-under man, the Y end will convert his route to a zoom out. Give the Y end time to run the route by bouncing at the launch point and then shuffling toward the line. The Y end will bend to the inside before breaking back outside. He anticipates the break and gets the ball in the air as the Y end breaks outside. This throw is a little softer, and he needs to lead the receiver to the ball. His second choice, if Y is not open, is to dump the ball to the fullback on his scat route. This touch pass requires him to put the ball a foot in front of the fullback's numbers. His last option is to run the ball.

Left Halfback

Technique: Checks or releases.
Coaching Points: His release route is a scat on Y out.

Fullback

Technique: Checks or releases.
Coaching Points: His release route is a scat.

Right Halfback (Z)

Technique: Runs an out route.
Coaching Points: He runs his out route one yard deeper than what is needed for a first down.

Pro 81 Curl

The third route is pro 81 base curl is illustrated in Figures 9-30 and 9-31. To the left, the play is con 89 base curl, and the blocking assignments are reversed. For this route, the X, Y, and Z receivers run curl routes a yard deeper than the yardage needed for a first down. The route will not exceed 14 yards, and it will not be shorter than eight yards. No receiver is singled out as being primary; the ball can go to X, Y, or Z. The quarterback decides who will get the ball, and his decision is based on the position of the linebackers.

BLOCKING RULES, TECHNIQUES, AND COACHING POINTS FOR PRO 81 CURL

2-Man (Y)

Rule: Runs an 8- to 14-yard curl route.

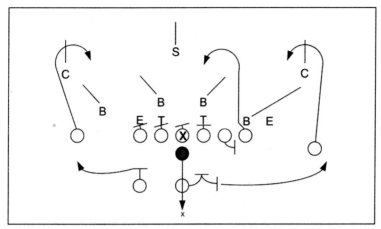

Figure 9-30. Pro 81 base curl against a 44 zone defense

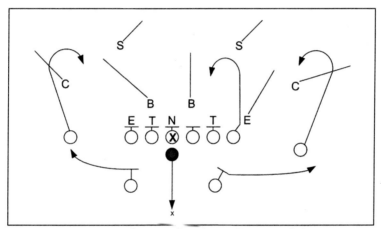

Figure 9-31. Pro B 81 base curl against a 52 zone defense

Coaching Points: He takes the easiest release the defender gives him. He sprints to a depth one yard deeper than needed for a first down. He hooks up at an equal distance between the frontside and backside backers. He moves laterally if necessary to open the passing lane between himself and the quarterback. If the ball is thrown to him, he moves forward to meet it. He catches the ball with his hands, secures it, and turns upfield. As the backers approach him, he bends at the waist, lowers his shoulders, covers the ball with both hands, and drives through the backers. He hits with enough power to fall forward after he is tackled.

3-Man

Rule: Same as pro 81 base Y under.
Coaching Points: Same as pro 81 base Y under.

4-Man

Rule: Same as pro 81 base Y under.
Coaching Points: Same as pro 81 base Y under.

5-Man

Rule: Same as pro 81 base Y under.
Coaching Points: Same as pro 81 base Y under.

6-Man

Rule: Same as pro 81 base Y under.
Coaching Points: Same as pro 81 base Y under.

7-Man

Rule: Same as pro 81 base Y under.
Coaching Points: Same as pro 81 base Y under.

8-Man (X)

Technique: Runs an 8- to 14-yard curl route.
Coaching Points: He sprints through the outside shoulder of the defensive back and makes him think he is going deep. He forces the back out of his backpedal before he runs his curl route. He lowers his center of gravity and turns to the inside. He moves laterally to open up a passing lane between himself and the quarterback. If the ball is thrown to him, he moves back toward the line of scrimmage to meet it. He does not wait for the ball to come to him. He catches the ball with his hands, secures it, then turns upfield and makes as much yardage as possible.

Quarterback

Technique: Uses the same technique to execute his five-step drop as he does on all other 80-series passes.
Coaching Points: Against zone coverage, his progression on the curl pass is to work the frontside, looking for the Y end first, the Z back second, and the fullback third. However, he first must make sure the backside backer drops to the backside hook zone—not to the middle of the field. If both backers drop to their respective sides of the formation, the offense has an advantage to the frontside: three receivers against two defenders (Figure 9-32). If he drops to the frontside of the formation, the offense has a two to one advantage to the backside of the formation (Figure 9-33).

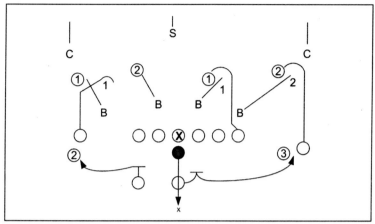

Figure 9-32. Pro 81 base curl: three receivers against two defenders to formation side against 44 defense

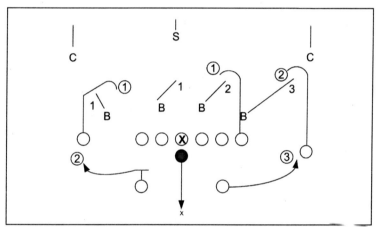

Figure 9-33. Pro B 81 base curl: two receivers against one defender away from formation against 52 defense

In the latter situation, the progression would be to work the X receiver first, and the left halfback second. The balls thrown to the X, Y, or Z receivers are thrown with great velocity. The ball should be between the receiver's shoulders and belt buckle. They also should be thrown into open areas and away from defenders. If the curl route does not look good to him, he dumps the ball to the fullback (when going frontside) or the left halfback (when going backside) and let the backs run for a first down. The pass to either back on scat routes is a touch pass, and it should be caught a foot in front of the numbers. The backs should not have to wait to catch the ball. They should catch it as they are going downfield. He should never force the ball downfield when defenders are in good position to defend the pass. He should dump it off to a back.

Left Halfback

Technique: Checks or releases.
Coaching Points: His route on the curl pass is a scat.

Fullback

Technique: Checks or releases.
Coaching Points: His route on the curl pass is a scat.

Right Halfback (Z)

Technique: Run a 7- to 12-yard curl.
Coaching Points: Same as X receiver.

Pro 81 Out

The third route is pro base 81 out, and it is illustrated in Figure 9-34. To the left, it is con base 89 out, and the blocking assignments are reversed. This route is excellent on third down when 7 to 10 yards are needed for a first down. However, it should be noted that the out route is, paradoxically, the safest and the most dangerous pass in all of football. It is the safest pass when no underneath defender is sitting in the flat, and when it is thrown on time. It is the most dangerous pass when it is not thrown on time, or when an underneath defender is sitting in the flat, It is good against zone or man coverage. The only adjustment needed would be against five-under zone or five-under man. In this instance, with an underneath defender sitting in the flat, all receivers would convert their routes to a predetermined conversion route. It could be a fade, a bench, or an out-and-up route. The conversion route should be predetermined, and the receivers and the quarterback should automatically convert to it. The bench adjustment is illustrated in Figure 9-35.

BLOCKING RULES, TECHNIQUES, AND COACHING POINTS FOR PRO 81 OUT

2-Man (Y)

Rule: Runs a curl route.
Coaching Points: He makes an inside release and curls to the inside. He establishes a position that is equidistant between the inside backers. He turns and faces the quarterback at a depth of one to two yards deeper than first-down yardage. It is his responsibility to open up a passing lane by sliding laterally.

3-Man

Rule: Same as pro 81 base Y under.
Coaching Points: Same as pro 81 base Y under.

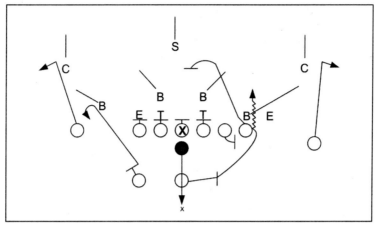

Figure 9-34. Pro base 81 out against 44 zone defense

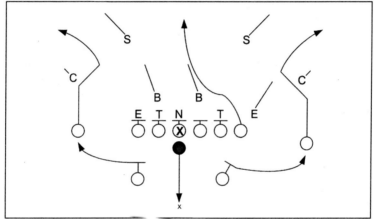

Figure 9-35. Pro B 81 base out against 52 five-under zone defense

4-Man

Rule: Same as pro 81 base Y under.
Coaching Points: Same as pro 81 base Y under.

5-Man

Rule: Same as pro 81 base Y under.
Coaching Points: Same as pro 81 base Y under.

6-Man

Rule: Same as pro 81 base Y under.
Coaching Points: Same as pro 81 base Y under.

7-Man

Rule: Same as pro 81 base Y under.
Coaching Points: Same as pro 81 base Y under.

8-Man (X)

Rule: Runs an out route one to two yards deeper than what is needed for a first down. The range of the out route is 7 to 12 yards.
Coaching Points: If the defender aligns outside of him, he takes away the defender's outside leverage by driving for the defender's outside shoulder on his release. He gets the defender out of his backpedal by sprinting full speed downfield. It is more difficult for a defender to cover an out route when the defender is in a crossover run than when the defender is in a backpedal. As he reaches his break point, he lowers his center of gravity and breaks sharply toward the sideline. His head should turn toward the quarterback to pick up the ball, which should be in the air as he begins the out cut. He runs his route as square to the line of scrimmage as he can. Doing so will establish a buffer zone between himself and the defender. If necessary, he goes back toward the line to meet the ball. After the reception, he turns upfield and gains as much yardage as possible. He protects the ball and falls forward after being tackled. Against five-under man or zone, he converts to a bench route.

Quarterback

Technique: Uses the same technique to execute his five-step drop as he does on all other 80-series passes.
Coaching Points: This pass is available because of the alignment of the defensive personnel. The pass must be thrown on time and with plenty of zip on it. It should be thrown to a spot where only the receiver can reach it, and it should be between the shoulders and waist of the receiver. He gets a pre-snap read to determine the coverage and to decide which receiver he intends to throw the ball to. Throwing the ball toward the near sideline is a safer pass than throwing it to the far sideline. On his retreat to the launch point, he keeps his eyes looking down the center of the field. He should not tip off his intentions by looking at the intended receiver as he starts his drop. Usually, a right-handed quarterback is less likely to tip off the direction of his pass if he throws the ball to his left. If he makes that pre-snap decision, he veers slightly to the right as he start his drop. When he reaches the launch point, he will be slightly outside the right foot of the 5-man. This technique will help a right-handed quarterback open his hips and facilitate a throw to the left. He anticipates the break and begins the throwing motion as the receiver lowers his center of gravity. Throw the ball to a spot where the defensive back would have to run through the receiver to get to the ball. The best way to evaluate the timing of the quarterback is to look at the out route on

tape and stop the picture when the distance between the receiver and the defender is at its apogee. If the ball is in the hands of the receiver, the timing is perfect. If not, the efficiency of the pass will suffer with each tenth of a second it takes for the ball to find its mark. If neither side looks good to him, he can check down to the left halfback on a hook route, or the fullback on a rim route. The Y end is running a curl pattern to the inside and is his third choice. Again, this ball is thrown between the receiver's shoulders and belt buckle. It needs to be thrown with some zip on it. His last option is to run the ball.

If the coverage is five-under zone or man, the out route is cancelled and the conversion route (pre-game decision) is run. Whether it is the fade, bench, or the out-and-up route, all receivers must be on the same page. In the following example, the bench route will be used as the conversion route. If he decides to throw to the outside receiver, the ball must be thrown swiftly and travel no less than 17 and no more than 20 yards downfield. He has to drill it into the open area before the safety on the hash can get over to defend it. If he decides to throw to the Y end on his short post route, it has to be a touch pass: long enough to get over the head of the backer, and in the 17- to 20-yard area to prevent the safeties from getting to it.

Left Halfback

Technique: Checks or releases.
Coaching Points: His release on the out route is a hook route. He runs to a spot three yards outside the 7-man and six yards deep. He turns and faces the quarterback. If the quarterback throws him the ball, he turns upfield and looks for the backers. He tries to split the backers as they converge to tackle him. He should have good body lean, give the tacklers the hard parts of his body, and fall forward as he is being tackled.

Fullback

Technique: Checks or releases.
Coaching Points: His release on the out route is a rim route. He releases outside the Y end and delays at the line of scrimmage. He stays underneath the backers. If the quarterback throws him the ball, he should catch it no deeper than four yards downfield. He tries to split the backers as they converge to tackle him. He should have good body lean, give the tacklers the hard parts of his body, and fall forward as he is being tackled.

Right Halfback (Z)

Technique: Runs an out route a couple of yards deeper than what is needed for first-down yardage.
Coaching Points: Same coaching points as the X receiver.

Pro 81 X Seam

The last route on third-and-long is a deeper route designed to convert situations when 12 or more yards are needed for a first down. It is a weakside flood route designed to hit in the seam between the safety man and the corner. Some coaches refer to this route as a skinny post. Pro 81 base X seam is illustrated in Figures 9-36 and 9-37. To the left, the play is con 89 base X seam, and the blocking assignments are reversed.

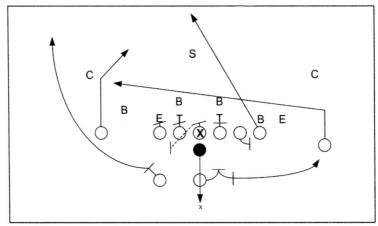

Figure 9-36. Pro 81 base X seam against 44 zone defense

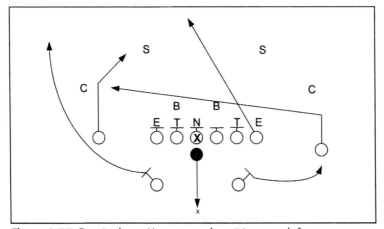

Figure 9-37. Pro 81 base X seam against 52 zone defense

BLOCKING RULES, TECHNIQUES, AND COACHING POINTS FOR PRO 81 X SEAM

2-Man (Y)

Rule: Runs a deep post.
Coaching Points: He releases inside and runs a vertical route directly up the field. He

takes the top off the coverage by sprinting past the safety man. Although he is not the primary receiver, the quarterback will throw him the ball if the safety man bites on the seam route. Against two-deep, man or zone, he remains equidistant between the twin safety men and runs downfield (and not crossfield). He tries to get separation between himself and the backer covering him. The quarterback will try to get the ball over the head of the backer, and he should catch it at a depth of 17 to 20 yards downfield. Against man coverage, he makes a double move to the post and expects the ball.

3-Man

Rule: Same as pro 81 base Y under.
Coaching Points: Same as pro 81 base Y under.

4-Man

Rule: Same as pro 81 base Y under.
Coaching Points: Same as pro 81 base Y under.

5-Man

Rule: Same as pro 81 base Y under.
Coaching Points: Same as pro 81 base Y under.

6-Man

Rule: Same as pro 81 base Y under.
Coaching Points: Same as pro 81 base Y under.

7-Man

Rule: Same as pro 81 base Y under.
Coaching Points: Same as pro 81 base Y under.

8-Man (X)

Rule: Runs a seam route. He is the primary receiver.
Coaching Points: He takes a split of 10 to 12 yards and sprints straight ahead to his break point 12 yards downfield. He gains depth on the break and positions himself equidistant from the corner and safety man. He should be on a vertical route, running with controlled speed straight down the field. Against zone coverage, he throttles in the open area and stays in the seam between the safety and the corner man. The quarterback will throw the ball into the open area, and he will have to adjust his course to catch the ball. The ball should be caught no deeper than 15 to 17 yards from the line

of scrimmage. Against man coverage, he fakes to the outside before he executes the inside move. He stays on the move and tries to run away from man coverage. Against five-under man, he converts his route to a bench route or as dictated by the game plan.

Quarterback

Technique: Uses the same technique to execute his five-step drop as he does on all other 80-series passes.

Coaching Points: He gets a pre-snap read to distinguish a three-deep, two-deep, or man defensive scheme. On the X seam, he takes five big steps to reach the launch point. His primary receiver is X. Against a three-deep zone, he checks the safety man to make sure the safety is covering the deep middle of the field. If not, he throws the ball to the Y on the post route. If the safety man is covering Y, he throws the ball to X. The ball should be thrown between the safety man and the corner, no deeper than 15 to 17 yards downfield. It is thrown on a line and into an open area. He should let the receiver run to the ball. He keeps the pass between the shoulders and belt buckle of the receiver. Against a two-deep zone, X runs the vertical route between the corner and the safety man on the near hash mark. If the left halfback releases, his takeoff route should keep the twin safeties on the hash marks, and the Y end should also force the safety men to stay on the hash marks. If the safety comes off the hash and covers X, he lays the ball out to the left halfback and lets the halfback run under it. Against three- or four-man coverage, the percentage pass would be to the Y end on a double-post move. Against five-under man, all receivers will convert to either a bench or fade route as the game plan dictates. He should be aware that Z is the hot receiver. Three-deep schemes can rush four defenders to the frontside, and this play can only block three of them. If this situation occurs, Y is the receiver he goes to as his fifth step hits the ground (see Figure 9-27).

Left Halfback

Technique: Checks or releases.

Coaching Points: His route on X seam is a takeoff. If the backside backer does not blitz, he releases and runs his route. He gives himself a five-yard cushion as he runs down the sideline, and begins to throttle down at a depth of 15 to 17 yards. He runs at controlled speed to stay in range of the quarterback. If the backside safety chases the X receiver, the quarterback will throw him the ball. The five-yard cushion will allow him to fade to the sideline to catch a ball thrown behind him.

Fullback

Technique: Same as pro 81 base Y under.
Coaching Points: Same as pro 81 base Y under.

Right Halfback (Z)

Technique: Runs a crossing route.

Coaching Points: He is the hot receiver. He sprints across the formation at a depth of five to seven yards. If both of the frontside backers blitz, he stays on the move and expects the ball. He catches it and runs for as much yardage as he can get. If no blitz occurs, he slows down and stays underneath the backers.

10

Coming From Behind and Stopping the Clock

Chapter 9 dealt with the use of the 80 series as a means to solve two problems: one was to convert a second-and-long situation, and the other was to convert a third-and-long situation. The 80 series will be of help to the wing-T coach in two other game situations. The first one is when a team has to come from behind to win the game—not a pleasant thought, but a possibility that the wing-T coach must prepare for. For such a predicament, a coach has to rely on a system of pass plays that will gain yardage in large chunks. The goal is to move the ball down the field quickly and score. The come-from-behind offense is used late in the game, and the 80 series gives the wing-T coach his greatest chance to make big plays, score quickly, and get his team back into the game. It will be discussed first.

The only thing worse than being behind late in the game is being behind and not having any time-outs left to stop the clock. Therefore, the second objective is to have the ability to kill the clock and conserve time. To achieve this end, a "hurry-up" offense (called "clutch offense") is used in the final minutes of the half or of the game. It is particularly important to have such a plan if you are out of time-outs and cannot stop the clock. The quarterback initiates the transition from a normal pace to a hurry-up pace. He does it by calling a play in the huddle, but before breaking the team to the line of scrimmage, he adds the phrase "followed by clutch." Clutch tells the team not to huddle, but to line up in a pro formation immediately after the whistle blows to end a play. It also tells the team that the ball will be snapped to the quarterback on the first sound. The quarterback usually starts his cadence by calling a three-digit number. But in clutch offense, as soon as his team is set, he simply shouts the number two—and the center snaps him the ball. So, the quarterback shouts, "Two," the ball is snapped to him, and he spikes it to stop the clock. After he spikes the ball, the quarterback will huddle the team and call a play and add the alert phrase: "followed by clutch." The team breaks the huddle and runs the play called. When the whistle blows to end the play, the quarterback calls clutch, and the team hustles to the line of scrimmage and aligns in a pro formation. The ball is snapped to the quarterback and he spikes it to kill the clock. The team then huddles and the procedure is repeated.

Note: The blocking rules and coaching points for linemen in 80 series protection have already been explained in Chapter 9. They will not be repeated in this chapter.

COMING FROM BEHIND

Pro 81 Out-and-Up

In a come-from-behind situation, the ball has to be moved down the field using as little time as possible. Plays with big play potential are good calls in this situation. The first play suggested is pro 81 out-and-up. It is illustrated in Figures 10-1 and 10-2. To the left, the play is con 89 out-and-up, and the blocking assignments are reversed. The out route is fully discussed in Chapter 8. The out-and-up route has to be set up by completing the basic out route. Once a defensive back has a few out routes completed in front of him, he is likely to overplay it and leave himself vulnerable to the out-and-up. Both wide receivers run the same pattern and the tight end runs a post route. The release pattern for both backs is a scat route. The quarterback can decide at the line of scrimmage which receiver he will throw to, or this can be predetermined by the game plan.

BLOCKING RULES, TECHNIQUES, AND COACHING POINTS
FOR PRO 81 OUT-AND-UP

X Receiver

Technique: Runs an out-and-up route.
Coaching Points: He drives upfield to a depth of seven yards. He lowers his center of gravity as he breaks on his inside foot. He pushes off the inside foot and takes three steps toward the sideline. He turns his head back to the quarterback and raises his

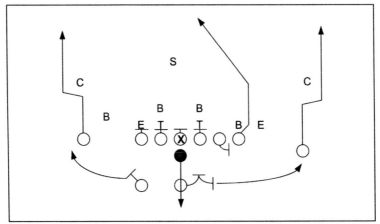

Figure 10-1. Pro 81 out-and-up against 44 zone defense

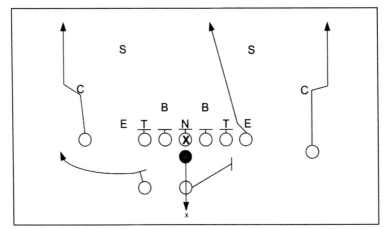

Figure 10-2. Pro 81 out-and-up against 52 zone defense

hands in an effort to sell the out route. He pushes off on his third step and sprints up the field. He keeps a five-yard cushion from the sideline and looks over the inside shoulder for the ball. If the pass is to his outside, he fades into the sideline to allow the ball to pass over his inside shoulder, which is the reason for keeping the five-yard cushion from the sideline. On all deep routes, he pumps his arms as he would if he were running a 40-yard sprint. He should not run downfield with his arms in position to catch the ball—since it will slow him down. His hands reach for the ball when it is in position to be caught.

Y End

Technique: Runs a post route.
Coaching Points: He runs a deep post route and occupies the safety man. His route is important because it will keep the safety man in the middle of the field and not allow the safety to help out on the long pass up the sideline.

Z Receiver

Technique: Same as X receiver.
Coaching Points: Same as X receiver.

Quarterback

Technique: Completes his five-step drop and places the ball with both hands next to his right ear.
Coaching Points: As he reaches the launch point, he makes a pump fake on the out move, and releases the ball as the receiver starts his sprint up the sidelines. He should not wait for the receiver to be open before releasing the ball. By then, the receiver may be out of his throwing range. The trajectory of the ball should allow the receiver to run under it and catch it in stride. It is important to keep the ball on the receiver's inside shoulder, and equally important not to underthrow it. All deep passes should either be caught by the receiver, or overthrown. The outlet route for the backs is a scat route.

Pro 81 Squirrel

The second route is pro 81 squirrel, and it is illustrated in Figures 10-3 and 10-4. To the left, the play is con 89 squirrel, and the blocking assignments are reversed. The squirrel route starts out looking like the out-and-up route. The outside receiver fakes the out, then sprints up the field and makes a second out move at about 17 yards downfield.

BLOCKING RULES, TECHNIQUES, AND COACHING POINTS FOR PRO 81 SQUIRREL

X Receiver

Technique: Runs a squirrel route.
Coaching Points: He starts the squirrel route exactly as he runs the out-and-up route. He fakes the out route and goes deep. When he gets to a depth of 17 yards, he plants his outside foot and pivots to the inside of the field. His chest is facing the quarterback. He begins to move back to the quarterback and the sideline. The ball will be thrown close to the sideline so if he does not catch it, the ball will go out of bounds. He positions his body between the ball and the defensive back. He catches the ball, gains as much yardage as possible, and gets out of bounds.

Y End

Technique: Runs a 12-yard in route.
Coaching Points: Against a blitz, he is the hot receiver. He will recognize the blitz when

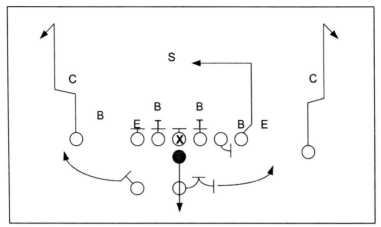

Figure 10-3. Pro 81 squirrel against 44 zone defense

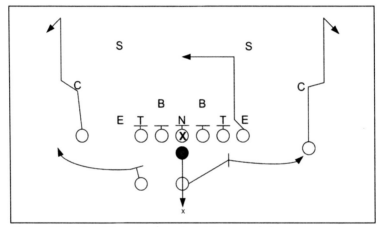

Figure 10-4. Pro 81 squirrel against 52 zone defense

the safety covers him man-to-man. He gives the safety a good outside fake and separates from the safety on his in route. Against man coverage, he cuts his route to a six- to seven-yard in route.

Z Receiver

Technique: Same as X receiver.
Coaching Points: Same as X receiver.

Quarterback

Technique: Completes his five-step drop and places the ball with both hands next to his right ear.
Coaching Points: He starts the squirrel route just like the out-and-up route. After he makes his pump fake, he takes a step or two backward to allow the pattern to develop. As the receiver drives up the field, the quarterback starts to slide toward the line of

scrimmage and throws the ball as the receiver breaks and comes back toward him. He should not wait to see the receiver open before he throws him the ball. He starts the throwing motion when the receiver breaks and is about to make the squirrel move. He throws the ball to a spot where it would go across the sideline if no one touched it. He brings the receiver to the ball and throws it hard and low. Against a blitz, the Y end is hot. The Y end will cut an in route to six to seven yards. He gets the Y end the ball as Y runs away from the safety man. The outlet route for the backs is a scat route.

Pro 81 Streak

The next route with big gain potential is the streak route. Pro 81 streak is illustrated in Figures 10-5 and 10-6. To the left, the play is con 89 streak, and the blocking assignments are reversed. The streak route is another attempt to complete a long pass and either score an easy touchdown or make a big gain. The coaching points for the receivers and the quarterback are similar to the out-and-up route. Again, the quarterback can choose the primary receiver at the line of scrimmage, or it can be predetermined by the game plan.

BLOCKING RULES, TECHNIQUES, AND COACHING POINTS FOR PRO 81 STREAK

X Receiver

Technique: Runs a deep streak route.
Coaching Points: He has two methods of running his streak route: he can simply sprint up the sideline and try to run by the defender, or he can sprint up the field and at about seven to eight yards deep, take a few stutter steps, head fake inside or outside, and then burst up the field. The stutter steps are meant to draw the defensive back toward the receiver in anticipation of a short route. This technique will give the receiver a better chance of running by the defensive back. As in the out-and-up route, the streak receiver should maintain a five-yard cushion from the sideline, and the ball should pass over his inside shoulder. As in all deep routes, he should not raise his hands until the ball is in position to be caught.

Y End

Technique: Runs a deep post route and occupies the safety man.
Coaching Points: His route is important because it will keep the safety man in the middle of the field and not allow him to help out on the long pass up the sideline.

Z Receiver

Technique: Same as X receiver.
Coaching Points: Same as X receiver.

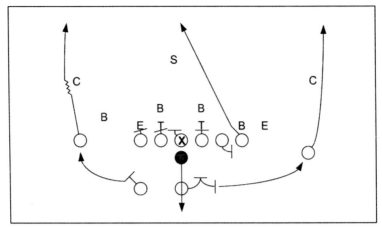

Figure 10-5. Pro 81 streak against 44 zone defense

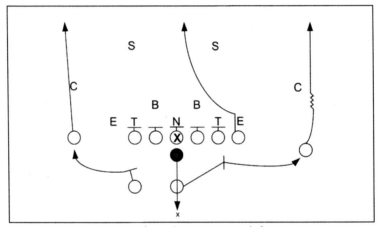

Figure 10-6. Pro 81 streak against 52 zone defense

Quarterback

Technique: Completes his five-step drop and places the ball with both hands next to his right ear.

Coaching Points: If the receiver is using a stutter step on the streak route, the quarterback makes a pump fake as he does on the out-and-up route. Again, he should not wait to see the receiver open before he throws the ball. The trajectory of the ball should allow the receiver to run under it and catch it in stride. It is important to keep the ball on the receiver's inside shoulder, and equally important not to underthrow it. All deep passes should either be caught by the receiver or overthrown. The outlet route for the backs is a scat route.

Pro 81 Flag

The final pass with big-play potential is particularly good in the score zone. Pro 81 flag is illustrated in Figures 10-7 and 10-8. To the left, the play is con 89 flag, and the blocking assignments are reversed. The flag route is a great pattern to throw in the score zone. It is an effective pass play up to about the 10-yard line. Inside the 10, you begin to run out of space, and the post fake has to be shortened for the receiver to stay in bounds. Again, the quarterback can choose the primary receiver at the line of scrimmage, or it can be predetermined by the game plan.

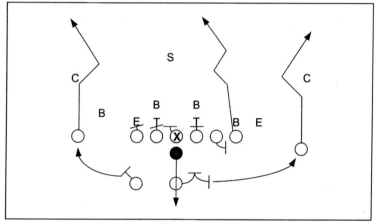

Figure 10-7. Pro 81 flag against 44 zone defense

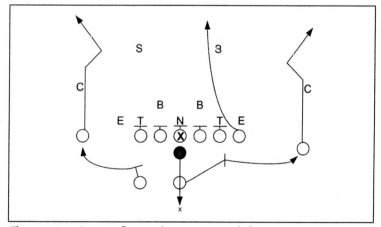

Figure 10-8. Pro 81 flag against 52 zone defense

BLOCKING RULES, TECHNIQUES, AND COACHING POINTS FOR PRO 81 FLAG

X Receiver

Technique: Runs his flag route.

Coaching Points: He sprints off the line of scrimmage and gets the defensive back out of the backpedal. Then, he makes a sharp enough move to the post to force the defensive back to turn his hips to the inside. Once the defensive back turns to the inside, he is beat. The receiver now breaks to the flag (cutting in front of or behind the defensive back), aiming for a point five yards inside the pylon. The receiver should be running on an angle that would take him across the end line, not the sideline. Too often, the flag route is caught out of bounds because the receiver breaks the flag route on too sharp of an angle toward the sideline. Aiming for a spot five yards inside the flag will give enough of a cushion to keep the receiver in bounds. The ball should be thrown over the receiver's outside shoulder.

Y End

Technique: Runs a double-post route and occupies the safety man.
Coaching Points: Although the quarterback will be looking to throw the ball to an outside receiver, the double post is another excellent route from inside the score zone. On the huddle call, the two outside receivers run the flag route, but the quarterback looks to the Y end on his double-post route for the touchdown. When the flag route is called, the quarterback looks to complete his pass to either the X or Z receiver.

Z Receiver

Technique: Same as X receiver.
Coaching Points: Same as X receiver.

Quarterback

Technique: Completes his five-step drop and places the ball with both hands next to his right ear.
Coaching Points: The flag route is thrown more to a spot on the field than to a receiver, and it must be thrown on time. Again, the quarterback cannot wait for the receiver to break open before throwing the ball. The receiver will set up the flag route by faking to the post. Just before the receiver breaks to the flag, he will lower his center of gravity. At that point, the quarterback starts the throwing motion. He should aim the ball for a spot five yards inside the flag and allow the receiver to run to it. The pass should be over the receiver's outside shoulder.

The Y end, on his double-post route, is another excellent play from inside the score zone. If he were singled out in the huddle, the quarterback would throw the ball to the Y end. The ball is thrown just before Y makes his final move to the post. The outlet route for the backs is a scat route.

STOPPING THE CLOCK

The next objective for the wing-T coach is to find patterns to stop the clock when his team is out of time-outs. The pattern that immediately comes to mind is the out route. It is fully discussed in Chapter 8, and it is an excellent choice for stopping the clock. Many of the wing-T play-action and bootleg passes are good in this situation because receivers are moving toward the sideline and can get out of bounds after making the catch. These routes, along with the fullback scat route and other routes that have receivers stationed on or moving toward the sideline, are good choices. The next two routes to be discussed are 80-series passes that put receivers in position to step out of bounds after a reception and stop the clock.

Pro 81 Long

Two routes used in the "clutch" offensive mode are pro 81 long (flood left) and pro 81 ride (flood right). Both routes are designed to clear out an area and get the ball to a receiver headed toward the sideline. If the ball were on or near the left hash mark, pro 81 long is a good choice. It is illustrated in Figures 10-9 and 10-10. To the left, the play is con 89 ride, and the blocking assignments are reversed.

BLOCKING RULES, TECHNIQUES, AND COACHING POINTS FOR PRO 81 LONG

X Receiver

Technique: Runs a deep streak route.
Coaching Points: He should not use a stutter step on his streak route. He takes the defender in his third of the field as deep as he can and as fast as he can.

Y End

Technique: Runs a deep crossing route
Coaching Points: He runs diagonally across the formation, gaining ground as he heads for the opposite sideline. His depth should be about 17 to 20 yards from the line of scrimmage. If the ball is thrown to him, he catches it and gains as much yardage as possible before stepping out of bounds.

Z Receiver

Technique: Closes his split to five yards. Runs a crossing route.
Coaching Points: His crossing route should put him 12 to 14 yards deep on the opposite sideline. If the ball is thrown to him, he catches it, gains as much yardage as possible, and steps out of bounds.

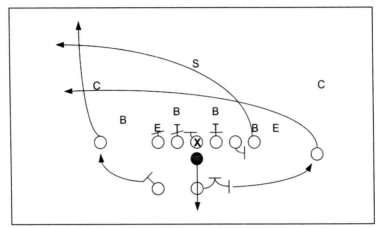

Figure 10-9. Pro 81 long against 44 zone defense

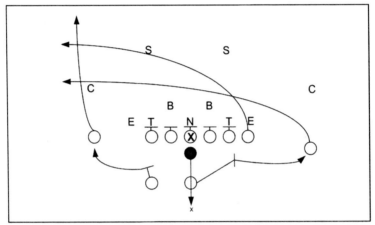

Figure 10-10. Pro 81 long against 52 zone defense

Quarterback

Technique: Completes his five-step drop and places the ball with both hands next to his right ear.

Coaching Points: He looks to see if X is covered on the streak route. If X is open, he throws X the ball. If not, he checks down to the Y end, the Z back, and the left halfback, in that order. The velocity of his pass will depend on the depth of the receiver. The deeper throws will require more velocity than the shorter throws. The outlet route for the backs is a scat route.

Pro 81 Ride

If the ball is on or near the right hash mark, pro 81 ride is the call. It is illustrated in Figures 10-11 and 10-12. To the left, the play is con 89 ride, and the blocking assignments are reversed.

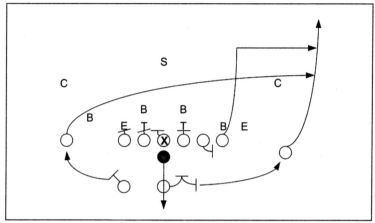

Figure 10-11. Pro 81 ride against 44 zone defense

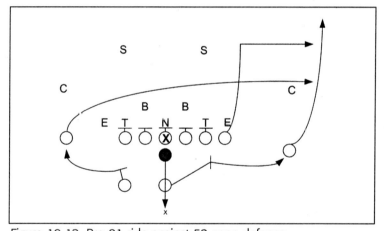

Figure 10-12. Pro 81 ride against 52 zone defense

BLOCKING RULES, TECHNIQUES, AND COACHING POINTS FOR PRO 81 RIDE

X Receiver

Technique: Closes his split to five yards. Runs a crossing route.
Coaching Points: His crossing route should put him 12 to 14 yards deep on the opposite sideline. If the ball is thrown to him, he catches it, gains as much yardage as possible, and steps out of bounds.

Y End

Technique: Runs a 17- to 20-yard out route.
Coaching Points: If the ball is thrown to him, he catches it, gains as much yardage as possible, and steps out of bounds.

Z Receiver

Technique: Runs a deep streak route.
Coaching Points: He should not use a stutter step on his streak route. He takes the defender in his third of the field as deep as he can and as fast as he can.

Quarterback

Technique: Completes his five-step drop and places the ball with both hands next to his right ear.
Coaching Points: He looks to see if Z is covered on the streak route. If Z is open, he throws Z the ball. If not, he checks down to the Y end, the X receiver, and the fullback, in that order. The velocity of his pass will depend on the depth of the receiver. The deeper throws will require more velocity than the shorter throws. The outlet route for the backs is a scat route.

Conclusion

This book contains a great deal of technical information regarding the wing-T offense. A lot more information than any coach can use. However, if a wing-T coach can utilize some of the innovations illustrated in this book, my purpose for writing it will be achieved. What would be especially exciting and rewarding for me is if wing-T coaches who read this book become self-motivated and begin to search for innovative ways to update and revitalize traditional wing-T plays.

At the end of World War II, many coaches returned to their colleges and universities with new ideas about offensive football. The most popular idea was to change from a single-wing system to a T-formation system. Several variations of the T formation sprung up after 1945, one of which was the wing-T. Many reasons justified putting the quarterback under the center and going to a balanced line, and these reasons are fully discussed in Chapter 1.

Defensive coaches throughout the country had their hands full trying to keep up with the new offensive trends. The contrast in styles ranged from the finesse system of Bud Wilkinson's split-T at the University of Oklahoma to the power and misdirection attack of Forrest Evashevski's wing-T at Iowa University. In this era, the running game was emphasized and formations were selected with it in mind. As for the pass, the conventional wisdom at that time was that three things could happen when you passed the ball—and two of them were bad.

Football has changed a great deal since the early days of the wing-T. Today, a dropback pass game is an indispensable dimension of any offensive system. To that end, this book offers the wing-T coach a simple dropback passing attack that will meet every contingency that may occur in a football game. It covers second-and-long, and third-and-long-yardage situations, and it suggest the types of passes that are suitable when two downs are available and when only one down is available to convert a long-yardage situation into a first down. The book covers two other situations when a dropback pass is warranted. One is when a coach is behind late in the game and needs to score quickly. The other situation is when a coach is out of time-outs and needs to kill the clock. Both of these examples are indicative of the importance of having a dropback passing game as an integral part of the wing-T offense.

The wing-T play-action passes (its strongest suit) are still effective pass plays. However, some changes are necessary to counter the defensive strategies that are being used today to defend those passes. For example, crossing routes off play-action have always been big gainers for wing-T teams. But, as defenses have become more familiar with the wing-T, they recognize the play-action passes more quickly and do a better job of covering crossing receivers with linebackers. The minor innovations of play-action patterns suggested in this book will keep the play-action passes productive. Changing the routes of traditional wing-T play-action passes will present new problems for the defense, and it will force teams to search for new methods to defend the play-action pass.

Wing-T power plays off tackle, and off the edge, were at one time very effective running plays. Again, through film study and recognition, defensives are taking those plays away by coaching the contain man to wrong-arm the kickout blocker and to bounce the plays to the outside. This technique causes the running back to slow down and bow his course to get around the collision between the kickout blocker and the contain man. By the time the back can get started again, the pursuit catches up with him, and the play results in either a short gain or a loss of yardage. The wing-T coach needs a solution to the problems that the defense presents by coaching the contain man to wrong-arm the kickout blocker. This book offers such a solution, and this solution can be applied to the power and sweep plays in four of the series that are featured in this book.

One of the selling points of the early wing-T was that plays were mirrored and could be run—with equal facility—to either side of the formation. The sweep play, for example, had to be run to both sides of the formation to keep the defense from overplaying the tight end and wingback side. However, as explained earlier in this book, an eight-man front with overhang players limited the wing-T attack away from the formation. The traditional sweep was especially difficult to run to the overhang defender's side. Therefore, something had to be done to neutralize the overhang player. The innovative idea of flexing the end away from the formation forced him to align on the flexed end. This adjustment allows the wing-T coach to run a conventional sweep to the wingback formation side and a pro-type sweep to the flexed end side. This major innovation in updating the wing-T offense is an answer to all the troublesome eight-man fronts and overshifted defenses that have plagued the wing-T in the past. It also gives the wing-T coach the confidence of knowing that he can run an effective sweep play to or away from the formation side.

Three different bootlegs are illustrated in this book. Two of them are traditional bootleg plays and are used by many wing-T teams. However, one is a major innovation to the traditional bootleg passes that were used in the early days of the wing-T. When a bootleg play is called, the wing-T coach cannot always predict the play of the defensive end to the side of the bootleg. He may have been chasing plays from behind during the entire game, and just when a bootleg is called he charges upfield and tackles the quarterback for a loss of yardage. The play called "bootleg slow" can solve the problem of not being able to predict the play of an erratic and unpredictable defensive end. This bootleg provides the quarterback with the assurance that he will get outside containment because the end to the side of the bootleg blocks the contain man before he releases into his route. This innovation gives the wing-T coach the confidence to run the bootleg often, and to not have to worry about the contain man coming upfield and tackling the quarterback for a loss. This advantage is not present in the traditional bootleg passes.

Although many wing-T coaches use finesse schemes in their blocking patterns, some new schemes are illustrated and discussed in this book. One scheme offers an innovative idea on how to seal the frontside backer on a sweep, and others suggest new ways to keep the internal trap plays alive. This book also deals with the use of several types of motion, and examples are suggested as to how they can be implemented. The use of motion to augment the wing-T began with the inception of the offense and has continued to evolve throughout the years. Some examples of motion in this book have the wingback trapping interior linemen, leading up a hole, and changing the force on the corner by motioning to a flanker position. Motion can be used in the wing-T in various ways; the variations are limited only by the imagination of the wing-T coach.

The belly series is mirrored and can be run to and away from the formation. It is approached from a different perspective than the traditional wing-T belly series. The traditional fullback down-blocking scheme has the wingback sealing the inside backer, and uses an option as the companion play to the fullback belly. The down scheme introduced in this book has the wingback arc blocking the corner instead of sealing the inside backer. This technique sets up a pitch off the inside fake to the fullback instead of an option play. The time a wing-T coach would have to spend to perfect the option would be better spent on perfecting the play-action pass game. Proficiency in the play-action pass game—not the option game—will determine the success or failure of the wing-T offense. The option plays are best executed from open formations, and they fit in nicely with finesse offensive schemes. The wing-T does not feature open formations, and it is not a finesse offense.

Another innovation in the belly series is running it to a tight-end side. A hallmark of the wing-T is double-team blocking or angle blocking at the point of attack. The belly play to the tight-end side is blocked with a double-team, or a cross block, with the halfback leading through the hole. The defensive spacing will dictate which blocking scheme will be used, and the play is called at the line of scrimmage, which is quite a departure from the traditional wing-T philosophy. Like the down scheme, it is mirrored and has a pitch play to get the ball to the outside. These two schemes are truly novel ideas that can easily be incorporated into a wing-T system.

The importance of excelling in the play-action pass game has been emphasized throughout this book. For a wing-T team to be successful, the one aspect of its game that it must perfect is the play-action pass. It's another answer to heavy fronts and other defensive ploys used to stop the wing-T running game. The play-action pass is integral to—and has to be considered as part of—the running game. It should be used in running situations and from anywhere on the field. The only time it loses its effectiveness is in obvious passing situations, which is when the wing-T coach relies on the dropback pass game. The play-action pass game is to the wing-T coach what the pocket pass is to the shotgun coach.

Today, the trend is toward open formations and a vertical and lateral passing game. To be successful with this attack, two things are essential: receivers who can beat a man-to-man defense, and a quarterback who can read defensive coverage and has the arm strength to threaten the entire length and width of the field. This type of personnel cannot always be counted on in a high school or small college setting. The wing-T coach has to understand and believe that a well-executed play-action pass game can be just as effective as one from an open formation. The point is that the play-action passes in the wing-T have to be called as often as passes thrown from a wide-open formation—and the wing-T coach must be willing to use them from anywhere on the field.

The wing-T quarterback has some advantages over the pocket passer when it comes to play-action passes. With a play-action pass, the wing-T quarterback, in most cases, ends up on the perimeter with a pass/run option. Several advantages result from passing from the perimeter. First, it gets the quarterback away from the pass rush. Secondly, it puts the quarterback closer to his receivers. Throwing to a receiver running toward the sideline is more easily done from the perimeter than it is from the pocket. And, thirdly, it gives the quarterback the option of running with the ball if his receivers are covered. Another bonus for the wing-T quarterback is that he does not have to read secondary coverage when executing play-action passes. He simply follows his progression of receiver #1, #2, #3, or run.

Finally, it would be grossly naive for any coach to think that illustrations and ideas alone will bring success to a football team. Without the proper execution of the fundamentals associated with the wing-T, success will never be attained. All plays look good on paper, but the success or failure of any team is contingent upon how well its players are able to execute the fundamentals of the game. No coach has emphasized the importance of mastering fundamentals more incisively and succinctly that the legendary basketball coach at UCLA, John Wooden. After winning his 10th national championship in basketball—an unprecedented achievement—he was asked for the secret to his success. Without missing a beat, he replied that three essentials are necessary for success in athletics: a team must be in superior physical condition, a team must have a perfect grasp of the fundamentals of the game, and a team must have great esprit de corps. Coach Wooden was also honest enough to follow up with the caveat that if you have these three essentials, and personnel as good as or better than your opponents, you have the potential to win a championship. Good luck, and keep the wing-T flying.

Glossary

2i technique: A defender aligned on the inside half of either guard

2 technique: A defender aligned head on either guard

3 technique: A defender aligned on the outside half of either guard

4i technique: A defender aligned on the inside half of either tackle

4 technique: A defender aligned head on either tackle

5 technique: A defender aligned on the outside half of either tackle

6i technique: A defender aligned on the inside half of a tight end

6 technique: A defender aligned head on a tight end

7 technique: A defender aligned on the outside half of a tight end

8i technique: A defender aligned on the inside half of a wingback

8 technique: A defender aligned head on a wingback

9 technique: A defender aligned on the outside half of a wingback

A gap: Gap between the center and guard

Backdoor: Technique of center or backside linemen on passes. They drop off the line and block rushers from the backside.

BC: Ballcarrier

Bench: A route against a two-deep secondary

B gap: Gap between the guard and tackle

Blocking surface: Shoulder, neck, and extended forearm used as a base for blocking

BS: Backside

BSLB'er: Backside linebacker

C gap: Gap between the tackle and end

Chair move: Lateral step by a back to run off a block followed by a vertical step straight upfield

Comeback: Outside route by a receiver who comes back to the line of scrimmage to meet the ball

Co-op: Technique of two blockers blocking a hard man and a backer

Crackback: Block by an interior lineman on a backer to the inside

Crossfield: Release by backside linemen to block downfield

Curl: Pass route by receiver who runs upfield and turns back to face the quarterback

Cutoff: Technique by a backside lineman to prevent a defender to his inside from pursuing a play away from him

DB: Defensive back

D gap: Gap outside the tight end

Double move: Used against man coverage. Receiver makes a false move before running his assigned route.

Fan: Block the defender to the outside

FB: Fullback

Fill: Protect an area vacated by a pulling guard

First level: Line of scrimmage

Flag: Pass route aimed at the flag in the corner of the end line or goal line

Flank: Area outside the wingback

FS: Frontside; the side the play is directed to

FSLB'er: Frontside linebacker

Hard man: A defender lined up within one foot of an offensive lineman

High-pressure control: Passive block using the hands from an upright position. Similar to a pass-protection block.

Hinge: Pass-protection technique when lineman is open. He steps to the frontside and hinges to backside rushers.

Horn: Technique by a guard to block a backer. Guard steps around the tackle while watching the backer. If the backer rushes, the guard blocks him.

Influence: Get the attention of a defender by pretending to block him

J block: Kickout block by a back in the halfback position

LOS: Line of scrimmage

Lead: Outside blocker in a double-team block

Level: Move by a safety man in a three-deep secondary that ends up in a two-deep coverage

LHB: Left halfback

Load: Block by a back on an interior lineman or end

Log: Block by a guard to seal a defender to the inside

Midline: Imaginary line running from the back tip of the ball between the feet of the quarterback and fullback

Open: Offensive lineman who is not covered by a hard man

Out-and-up: Pass route. Receiver fakes an out cut and then turns up the field and runs a deep streak.

Over the midline: Quarterback crossing the midline on his first step to the side of the play called

POA: Point of attack

Perimeter: Flank area

Pike: Move by a crossing receiver against man coverage. He drives upfield three to four steps and quickly continues crossing route.

Pitch phase: Position of quarterback and pitchback when a pitch is made by the quarterback

Post: Pass route aimed at the middle of the goal post

Principle blocking: Post if covered by a hard man; lead block inside, or influence and block out if open

PS: Playside

QB: Quarterback

Retain/release rule: Rule for backside blockers. If covered by a backer, block him; if not, release.

Retain: Technique of a blocker getting his body between a defender and the runner

RHB: Right halfback

Scoop: Backside tackle pulls to the center position, turns into the line, and scoops up any defender in his path.

Second level: Linebacker level

Skinny post: Pass route run between the safety and the corner

Stalk: Passive high block used downfield against secondary defenders

Takeoff: Pass route by a back that starts into the flat and turns upfield on a deep route

Third level: Secondary level

Trap: Inside-out block by an interior lineman

Uncovered: Offensive lineman with no defender aligned over him.

Under the midline: Quarterback's first step is to the backside of the play called. He does not cross the midline.

Wall off: Technique of using a high block to keep a defender from getting to the ballcarrier

Wham: Block by a back on an interior defensive lineman, usually from his halfback alignment

Zone: A pass defense where defenders are defending zones of the field rather than covering man-to-man

About the Author

Ron Carbone is the head football coach at Hamden Hall Country Day School in Hamden, Connecticut. Prior to accepting that position in 2007, he served 24 years as a head football coach at three Connecticut high schools: Derby, Ansonia, and Hamden. He compiled an aggregate record of 159 wins and 62 losses. Ron had 17 conference championships, an undefeated season, and two trips to the CIAC State Class LL championship game. Six of his former players went on to play professional football: five played in the NFL, and one played in Canada. Ron also worked as a college assistant at Yale University, and was the defensive coordinator at Southern Connecticut State University. He has received coach-of-the-year awards from the Gene Casey New Haven chapter of the National Football Foundation and College Hall of Fame, the District League, and the New Haven Gridiron Club, and has also been named the Ray Tellier Coach of the Year and the Connecticut High School Coaches' Coach of the Year. Ron received a gold ring from the New Haven Boys' Club for outstanding service to the community, and he was inducted into the Connecticut High School Football Coaches' Hall of Fame in November 2006. Ron resides with his wife, Rosemarie, in Hamden, Connecticut. He has five children and 10 grandchildren.